*Justice Was Her Calling*

# *Justice Was Her Calling*

THE FIERCE AND FASCINATING LIFE OF DOROTHY KENYON

*Jennifer L. Brinkley*

UNIVERSITY OF CALIFORNIA PRESS

University of California Press
Oakland, California



A portion of chapter 9 was previously published in "Dorothy Kenyon and Pauli Murray: Their Quest for Sex Equality in Jury Service," *Tennessee Journal of Race, Gender, and Social Justice* 12, no. 2 (2023): article 2, https://doi.org/10.70658/2693-3225.1227.

Library of Congress Cataloging-in-Publication Data

Names: Brinkley, Jennifer L., author
Title: Justice was her calling: the fierce and fascinating life of Dorothy Kenyon / Jennifer L. Brinkley.
Description: Oakland: University of California Press, 2026. | Includes bibliographical references and index.
Identifiers: LCCN 2026015923 (print) | LCCN 2026015924 (ebook) | ISBN 9780520432086 cloth | ISBN 9780520432093 ebook
Subjects: LCSH: Kenyon, Dorothy, 1888–1972 | Women lawyers—United States | Women judges—United States | American Civil Liberties Union—History | Women's rights—United States—History—20th century | LCGFT: Biographies
Classification: LCC KF373.K459 B75 2026 (print) | LCC KF373.K459 (ebook)
LC record available at https://lccn.loc.gov/2026015923
LC ebook record available at https://lccn.loc.gov/2026015924

Manufactured in the United States of America

GPSR Authorized Representative: Easy Access System Europe, Mustamäe tee 50, 10621 Tallinn, Estonia, gpsr.requests@easproject.com

35 34 33 32 31 30 29 28 27 26
10 9 8 7 6 5 4 3 2 1

publication supported by a grant from
**The Community Foundation for Greater New Haven**
as part of the *Urban Haven Project*

*For David, Gauge, and*
*my grandmother, Margaret*

The time calls for giants. And my subject is women.

DOROTHY KENYON

Dorothy Kenyon is a lady in a hurry. In fifty years at the Bar she has accomplished more in the name of civil liberties and common goodness than the rest of us could in a century.

ROBERT B. MCKAY,
*Dean, New York University School of Law (1967–75)*

Winning battles is the breath of life to her.

MILDRED ADAMS KENYON

CONTENTS

# PREFACE

Once I moved from law practice to academia, I created a course titled "Women and the Law." I wanted to explore the history of women lawyers and their treatment in, and by, the United States legal profession. Preparing curriculum about Ruth Bader Ginsburg brought me to Dorothy Kenyon. After reading about Kenyon's cases, I wanted to assign a book on her to my students, but none existed. In my opinion, Dorothy Kenyon laid the groundwork for Ginsburg's successful litigation strategies before the US Supreme Court in the 1970s. How could there not be a book about her life?

Gerda Lerner, a historian and leading scholar of women's history, believed that writing about women requires three levels of analysis. The first step is the compensatory history, which involves the identification of notable women who are "missing from the history."[1] The second step is examining that specific woman's contributions to history. How did she elevate her status? How did she elevate the status of others? The third and final step is studying how the woman is centered on her own terms within the annals of history. I wanted to use Lerner's framework to guide Kenyon's story. Why was Kenyon not better known? How did she overcome obstacles? In what ways did Kenyon advance women's rights and in what ways did she fail? How did her personal life intersect with her very busy professional and public one? I wanted to explore not just the impact of her life on others, but her own lived experience.

I threw myself into learning about Kenyon, starting with her archived papers. Following Kenyon's death in 1972 from cancer, Mildred Adams Kenyon, her sister-in-law, collected and moved Dorothy Kenyon's papers into her home. The voluminous collection eventually found its way to Smith College in Northampton, Massachusetts—Kenyon's undergraduate alma mater. This book relies heavily on her writings, speeches, and family records, shedding light on the personal relationships that molded the type of woman and lawyer she would become. Kenyon's own words, from decades of carbon copies of letters she sent to family, friends, and colleagues, reveal her beliefs, love of the law, and passion for civil liberties. Additionally, interviews with two of her grandnephews provide important contextual observations about her later years. Known as fiercely independent, Kenyon had moments of doubt, loneliness, and defeat, which balanced her many successes. The following chapters offer a comprehensive examination of the main events that wove together the fabric of her life.

# ABBREVIATIONS

| | |
|---|---|
| ACLU | American Civil Liberties Union |
| ALP | American Labor Party |
| CSW | Commission on the Status of Women |
| DOJ | Department of Justice |
| ERA | Equal Rights Amendment |
| FBI | Federal Bureau of Investigation |
| HUAC | House Un-American Activities Committee |
| NAACP | National Association for the Advancement of Colored People |
| NYU | New York University |
| UN | United Nations |
| UNESCO | United Nations Educational, Scientific, and Cultural Organization |

# TIMELINE OF IMPORTANT EVENTS

| | |
|---|---|
| 1888 | Born in New York City |
| 1904 | Starts at Smith College |
| 1905 | Minnie Kenyon, Dorothy Kenyon's mother, dies |
| 1908 | Graduates from Smith College |
| 1909 | Will Kenyon, Dorothy Kenyon's father, remarries |
| 1910 | Spends a year traveling in Mexico |
| 1914 | Attends NYU School of Law |
| 1917 | Becomes a lawyer |
| 1919 | Becomes a founding member of Barn House on Martha's Vineyard |
| 1924 | Moves out of Kenyon family home |
| 1930 | Establishes law office with Dorothy Straus (Straus & Kenyon) |
| 1931 | Joins ACLU national board of directors |
| 1936 | Named First Deputy Commissioner of Licenses in New York |
| 1937 | One of the first twelve women admitted to New York City Bar Association |
| 1938 | Appointed by League of Nations to sit on committee studying legal status of women |
| 1939 | Appointed Justice of Municipal Court, Third District, Borough of Manhattan by Mayor La Guardia; lost election to retain seat; sets up solo practice |
| 1946 | Appointed US delegate to United Nations Commission on the Status of Women |
| 1950 | First individual named by Senator Joseph McCarthy as an alleged communist |
| 1961 | Writes amicus brief in *Hoyt v. Florida* on behalf of ACLU |

1965 Sponsors Pauli Murray's appointment to ACLU national board; co-writes brief in *White v. Crook* with Murray

1966 Achieves victory in *White v. Crook*

1967 Undergoes ulcer surgery

1968 Helps open the West Side's Law Office for the Poor

1969 Barn House's fiftieth anniversary; diagnosed with stomach cancer

1972 Passes away; Pauli Murray delivers eulogy

# *Introduction*

She had a very strong ego, she considered herself to be brighter than most and she was intolerant of stupidity or ignorance. She didn't suffer fools.

EDWARD TIPTON KENYON,
*Dorothy Kenyon's nephew*

ON A CLEAR BUT COOL October evening in Midtown Manhattan, 1935, the Ambassador Theatre was abustle with activity. It was known as the triangle theater in the early stages of its build in 1920 because of its hexagonally shaped auditorium.[1] The building was the work of Herbert J. Krapp, who designed several theaters in Times Square before the Great Depression ended the building boom.[2] The walls, painted in shades of ivory and beige, were covered in neoclassical plasterwork stretching from the orchestra level to the boxes and mezzanine. Marble accents and crystal light fixtures enhanced the space, with the stage set behind a grand proscenium arch. Patrons filed into the theater, located their seats, and prepared themselves for a unique task: deliberating a murder case.

*Night of January 16th* had opened on September 16. It was a melodrama in three acts written by Ayn Rand, set in a New York courtroom. Twelve members of the audience were chosen to serve as jurors. Once selected, they left their purchased seats to sit onstage, becoming a part of the show. The play's producer insisted that the twelve jury members receive pay of three dollars for their participation, just as they would if serving on a real jury.[3] In New York at the time, women could not serve on juries. Because the management wanted to stick to a real-world scenario, only male audience members were selected to serve on the stage jury.

The defendant in the play, Karen Andre, was charged with murdering her lover, Bjorn Faulkner. A prosecutor and defense attorney, both male, called witnesses to present the evidence. After closing arguments, the jury was dismissed to deliberate while the character witnesses provided short highlights of their testimony, contradicting each other on important facts. Once the jury returned, a verdict was rendered. Every night a new jury was selected, and the verdict would be either guilty or not guilty. If found not guilty, the defendant would thank the jury. If found guilty, the defendant would let the jury know there would be no appeal as she would not be in the world to seek it. Then the curtain would fall.

On the evening of October 2, the crowd murmured, anxiously awaiting the beginning of the play. One audience member was particularly excited about the evening. Dorothy Kenyon, a lawyer and chair of the League of Women Voters, was itching for a fight. As she removed her coat, Kenyon prepared for a disruption.

The lights flickered, signaling that the show was soon to begin. When the curtain rose, the auditorium lights stayed on. The courtroom clerk onstage started selecting jurors. As the third juror was being summoned from the audience, Kenyon shouted, "Gentlemen!" She rose and addressed the hundreds in the theater, arguing that women should be permitted to serve on juries and predicting that New York would soon allow it based on what was happening in other states. She demanded that she should be "New York's first woman juror," exclaiming that she was "simply bursting with good citizenship!"[4] Unsure of how to proceed, the producer took an informal vote from the audience. There were no nays heard, so Kenyon's demand was granted. She took her place onstage.

At the end of the play, Kenyon voted with the stage jury, which issued a not guilty verdict and acquitted the female defendant. As a result of Kenyon's protest, the producer announced that in the future women jurors would be selected from the audience, but only at the matinee shows on Wednesdays and Saturdays.[5] Two years later, Kenyon's prediction came true: New York passed legislation allowing women to serve on juries. On the day of the law's enactment, Kenyon registered to serve.

This story is classic Kenyon. She used every opportunity she could to educate the public about the negative impacts of sex discrimination. She would not stop until the changes she wanted were made, even if it took decades. Kenyon's life spanned a critical swath of history, and she navigated the tumultuous times without losing focus on the end goal: equality for the marginalized. Without her, the landscape of women's rights, and equality in general, would look much different.

. . .

As a child, Dorothy Kenyon was skipping down a New York City sidewalk, hand in hand with her father, when she asked, "Can girls be lawyers?" He answered, "Why not, my dear?"[6] It was not an unthinkable career path in her family—her father, aunt, uncle, and brothers would all become attorneys. Because of her familial connection with the profession, she was not naïve about the obstacles that stood in her way because of her sex, but she thought the bumpy road would be fun. Kenyon enjoyed identifying the barriers to her progress—and then, knocking them down.

Kenyon became a lawyer in 1917, at a time when women were not accepted at all law schools. She went on to practice for over fifty years. Refusing to take a position at her father's patent law firm in New York City after graduating from New York University (NYU) School of Law, Kenyon forged her own path. A self-described fighter for the rights of the underdog, she volunteered with many organizations, including the American Civil Liberties Union (ACLU), of which she was a member of the national board of directors for over four decades. Kenyon lived her life on picket lines, in courtrooms, and in meeting spaces—fighting for the civil rights and liberties of women. She was described as a "gutsy fighter," a person who had the "odd talent for being able to confront an opponent with such wit that she would charm him at the same time that she was impaling him."[7]

As an adult, Kenyon stood five foot six inches tall and sported a 1920s bob; above her brown eyes sat heavy brunette bangs, "from under which she seemed to be peering out from a well-fortified position."[8] She loved to travel and never went anywhere without her bright red hatbox for her favorite hats. She adored animals, remarking that she liked "them better than people."[9] That said, she seemed to draw people to her, and her circle included many intellectuals and activists, including Pauli Murray, Eleanor Roosevelt, Roger Baldwin, and Constance Baker Motley.

Kenyon's relationship with her father, Will, was close. He fawned over her as a child with a pride that continued into her adulthood. Her mother, Minnie, passed away when Kenyon was a teenager. In a letter to Kenyon on her thirtieth birthday, Will told her that Minnie's life was one "of love and straightforwardness and consideration for the other fellow and never a thought for herself. May your life be as full of opportunities for service and of self-forgetfulness as hers was. Her love follows you. My love goes with you too."[10]

As her father had wished, Kenyon filled her life with service to others. She was a member of many local, state, and national organizations, including the Americans for Democratic Action national board, the Lower West Side Anti-Poverty Board, and the Consumers' League of New York.[11] Her service to the community, however, was not just as a volunteer. After several years in private legal practice, she made the transition to government. She served as first deputy commissioner of licenses in the Fiorello La Guardia administration and was eventually appointed a municipal court judge, making her one of the first female judges in New York City. She also was the only female member of a League of Nations committee assembled to study the legal status of women in other countries. After that, she was appointed the United States delegate to the United Nations Commission on the Status of Women (CSW). It seemed her star was rising when it came to receiving high-profile public appointments—until March 8, 1950.

In 1950, a Red Scare that was sweeping the country entangled Kenyon. Wisconsin junior senator Joseph McCarthy placed Kenyon first on his list of communists working in the State Department. Facing his accusations of promoting and participating in communist-front organizations, she did not shrink; rather, she was emboldened. Not known for biting her tongue, she called him an unmitigated liar, vermin, and a coward cloaked in congressional immunity, and demanded a Senate hearing.[12] A few days later, she appeared before the US Senate and successfully defended herself. Although she was ultimately cleared, the damage to her reputation had been done. Kenyon never received another public appointment, a fact that devastated her.

In her personal life, she seemed to have difficulty showing emotional vulnerability. Kenyon, who did not want to be placed in a box labeled "wife and mother," never married, nor did she have children. She derived great pride from being seen as independent. A friend and client, Dorothy Dunbar Bromley, was convinced Kenyon never married because "she couldn't bear the thought of yoking herself to a man—any man, whether or not he was a feminist who believed women were people. . . . She was not only a woman unafraid, she was the most fiercely independent woman I have ever known." Bromley retained Kenyon as her lawyer "because she could think rings around most other lawyers. . . . Dorothy was passionately committed to a client's interests—her combativeness served them well."[13]

A local paper spoke of what motivated Kenyon: "The ills, the injustices of the world arouse in her an exuberant indignation."[14] In fighting injustice, she could be argumentative, relentless, and cutting. A friend described her temper as something best avoided.[15] Kenyon loved a battle, rarely stopping to ask herself whether she was too fierce or entirely right. Frustration that she had to fight for the recognition people gave so willingly and easily to her brothers spurred her on. It constantly annoyed her to have to talk to men she considered her intellectual inferiors; even more vexing was when they refused to listen to her or, worse yet, took her ideas as their own. Slights, perceived and real, would fuel her rage throughout her career. In 1967 she wrote to Henry Schwarzchild, executive director of the ACLU's Lawyers Constitutional Defense Committee, calling him out for ignoring women: "[Y]ou don't even *see* us on the landscape. At least not as minds. And that is a chilling thought. . . . Can't you see that as craftsmen we are lawyers like you, not *women* lawyers! Are you *men* lawyers?"[16]

Starting in the 1920s, Kenyon advocated for women to serve on all state and federal juries. In the 1961 case of *Hoyt v. Florida*, Kenyon wrote an amicus brief on behalf of the ACLU—its first in a sex discrimination case—arguing to the US Supreme Court that seating an all-male jury in the Florida criminal trial of Gwendolyn Hoyt violated Hoyt's rights under the Fourteenth Amendment's Equal Protection Clause.[17] Although Kenyon's argument in *Hoyt* was unsuccessful, she was not dissuaded. Four years later Kenyon sponsored the addition of lawyer Pauli Murray to the ACLU board, and together they would use every resource at their disposal to obtain compulsory jury service for women in all states.

In 1965, Kenyon and Murray co-authored the ACLU's brief in the federal court case *White v. Crook*, successfully challenging an Alabama statute that restricted jury service only to white males. Their litigation strategy was to persuade the court to judicially reinterpret the Fourteenth Amendment's Equal Protection Clause, applying it to both race and sex discrimination. *White* successfully linked the civil rights and women's rights movements by providing evidence of the inferior status that both groups experienced.[18] Women and Black men were subsequently allowed to serve on Alabama juries because of Kenyon and Murray's efforts.

*White* was a remarkable victory for Kenyon, Murray, and the ACLU. The director of the US Department of Labor Women's Bureau, Mary Dublin Keyserling, wrote Kenyon with her congratulations, saying she believed women owed a debt to Kenyon for her insistence that the Fourteenth

Amendment should be applied to discriminatory statutes on the basis of sex.[19] Kenyon wrote a friend how happy she was to have succeeded. "You know, after you have beaten your heart out in a cause that everyone tells you is a goner, it's *fun* to have it come out your way."[20] She delightfully discovered that over the course of her decades of service to the ACLU she had slowly built the foundation necessary to give her preferred causes credibility.

Kenyon and Murray's strategies laid the groundwork for law professor Ruth Bader Ginsburg's success in sex discrimination cases before the US Supreme Court, starting with *Reed v. Reed*, a landmark case from 1971. The *Reed* decision marked the first time the Supreme Court applied the Equal Protection Clause of the Fourteenth Amendment to statutory sex-based differentials. It was an achievement Kenyon had been working toward for half a century. Ginsburg co-wrote her first sex equality brief in the case, and honored Kenyon and Murray by listing them as co-authors, giving them long overdue credit for their litigation strategy.[21] Kenyon's agreement to have her name appear on the brief was one of her last acts in litigating the cause of women. Years later, after joining the US Supreme Court, Associate Justice Ginsburg gave explicit credit to Kenyon and Murray, remarking that "[m]y generation owed them a great debt, for they bravely pressed arguments for equal justice in days when few would give ear to what they were saying."[22]

When Kenyon passed away from cancer a few days shy of her eighty-fourth birthday in 1972, Murray was asked to give the eulogy. A poet and prolific writer, Murray delivered a moving speech at St. Peter's Episcopal Church in Chelsea to the hundreds of mourners in the sanctuary. Murray spoke of Kenyon's importance to the ACLU and to the women's rights movement, and described Kenyon as the pulse beat of New York City. She went on to say, "At a time when we need renewal of our faith in the promise of liberty, equality and fellowship of men and women, white and [B]lack, rich and poor, the life of this remarkable woman reveals the essence of what is good in our society and what makes the struggle worthwhile."[23]

Kenyon deserves to be recognized for progressing and improving the status of women, on a local, state, national, and global scale. Yet her story also has a broader appeal and significance. Her life is a window through which to view important US historical developments. She was born during the Gilded Age, became a lawyer during the Progressive Era, worked during the New Deal years, and lived to see the second wave of feminism in the 1970s. By piecing together Kenyon's experiences, by critically examining the sacrifices that she personally made to improve judicial, legislative, and social institutions, we can learn about the obligations of citizenship, the importance of maintaining a democracy, and the persistence and patience required to make enduring change. Her efforts continue to benefit individuals, years after her death. This book places Kenyon firmly in the twentieth-century history of the United States—a distinction she rightfully deserves.

ONE

# *Do Right, Be Brave*

## A GILDED BEGINNING

Ambition took men and women to New York, and ambition shaped their lives once they were there.

CHRISTINE STANSELL,
*Historian*

RIVERSIDE PARK IN NEW YORK CITY abuts the Hudson River and is perhaps Manhattan's most spectacular waterfront park, providing a verdurous respite to the hustle and bustle of city life.[1] Its original construction included what is now known as Riverside Drive, a tree-lined street that curves along the edge of the park and waterfront. When Riverside Drive was built, the *New York Times* described it as "a perfect pleasure driveway, the costliest and the longest wholly within the confines of any city in the world."[2] In 1904 it stretched twenty miles, "passing through hundreds of thousands of acres of beautifully laid out park lands," with views rivaling those found in the English countryside. Mature trees dotted the landscape, and streetlamps and benches popped up throughout. The corner of Riverside Drive and 82nd Street is where Kenyon's family home would eventually be built, nestled in the safety and security of the Upper West Side.

Dorothy's parents, Maria (Minnie) Wellington Stanwood and William (Will) Houston Kenyon, married in Cincinnati, Ohio, on April 21, 1887.[3] They resided as newlyweds in a Manhattan apartment house, an older red brick building called "The Evelyn," located at 101 West 78th Street.[4] An elevated railroad ran near the apartment on Ninth Avenue, and shining sparks from the locomotive would rain down on the pavement in front of the building.[5]

Minnie was described as coming from "old Massachusetts stock."[6] Minnie's maternal grandfather was the principal physician in Arlington, Massachusetts, and her father was treasurer of a railroad before moving to Cincinnati, Ohio, so he could work at First National Bank.[7] Will was of Scottish ancestry; his father, a weaver, came from Scotland to Connecticut in the early nineteenth century.[8] Following graduation from Columbia Law, Will joined the firm of Browne, Witter & Kenyon, where he specialized in patent law.[9] He would go on to become a senior partner of the firm and the first president of the New York Patent Law Association.[10] A legend of the patent bar, he inspired the formation of the New York Intellectual Property Law Association in 1921.[11] He was involved with several important cases, including the patents for the telephone, the Edison electric incandescent lamp, and certain trolley car devices.

Dorothy's baby book, written by her father, is filled with thorough details about her beginnings as their first child. On Friday, February 17, 1888, the doctor and nurse were sent for at 3:30 a.m., and they arrived a few hours later. The doctor administered chloroform to Minnie, and at 8:40 a.m. Dorothy arrived, announcing her presence with healthy screams.[12] She weighed nine pounds, and her hair, the color of which some declared to be red, was soft and silky.

Will wrote his infant daughter a letter on March 1, 1888, from Cleveland, Ohio, congratulating her on her fourteenth day of life. He wanted her to know it was a happy world into which she was born, declaring: "I see all the way down the vista of your future ever widening and deepening circles of happiness proceeding from you. It is the desire of your Mamma's and your Papa's heart that every person you are ever thrown in with in this life may be the better and the happier for it, and that none may ever regret that you were born. . . . Do right. Be brave. Be loving. Be forgiving."[13]

On March 10, when Dorothy was less than one month old, the great blizzard of 1888 blew through New York City. Winds of one hundred miles per hour unleashed twenty-one inches of snow on the city streets. Four hundred lives in New York City were lost. In the aftermath of the storm, Will donated ten dollars to the Charity Organization Society of the City of New York in honor of his baby daughter. The organization sent a letter to Dorothy letting her know the good the money did for a widow and her three children, and wishing Dorothy a "happy babyhood, and a long and useful life."[14]

Dorothy was baptized on April 29, 1888, at the residence of Theodore Stanwood, Kenyon's maternal grandfather, in Cincinnati. By all accounts, she thrived as a baby. A June 17, 1888, note described her as having cheeks hanging down and multiple chins, and her "little legs are merely rolls of fat and flesh."[15] Though this may seem an uncomplimentary characterization, it was clearly written with awe and love. Her baby record meticulously details many experiences and milestones of her early life, ranging from the mundane—when she ate, slept, or went on an outing with her parents—to more singular events, such as receiving a new bathtub or crib, having a photograph taken, or attending a family gathering. Her mother was excited to discover Dorothy's first tooth (lower and left of center) on November 19, 1888, at the age of nine months and two days. In fact, it was such a cause for commotion that Minnie and Will sent a telegram about the tooth to family.

By eleven months, her vocabulary was not only growing but also indicating her intelligence. She would often say "Papa," but when asked to say "Mamma" she would pause, look at the person asking, then say "Papa," following this with a giggle as if she was telling a joke.[16] Her parents gave her endearing nicknames, including Dot, Dotty, and Dottsie. After turning one year old, Dorothy had her first illness—an attack of intestinal indigestion with a high fever. When the doctor came, he remarked, "What a pity she isn't a boy with that big brain."[17]

Dorothy would soon have siblings: Theodore, born in 1890, also known as TO, and Houston (pronounced Hoos-ton), born in 1899, also known as Houtie. Minnie gave birth to another boy between Theodore and Houston, Francis Wellington Kenyon, but he did not survive.[18] Although Dorothy had been clearly adored as the first child of Minnie and Will, once she was no longer an only child she had to fight for attention. This fighting spirit would stay with her for the remainder of her life. She later described herself as "a disagreeable little gal . . . very cocky."[19]

In 1894, Will built the house near Riverside Park, consisting of four floors and a basement. The family had the help of a housemaid and cook. Dorothy, Theodore, and Houston grew up comfortably in this upper-class environment, thanks to Will's law practice. Other New Yorkers did not fare as well. Following the Civil War, tenements were built as row houses on the Lower East Side, Lower West Side, and in the South Village. They were typically about four stories tall and housed up to twenty families.[20] Water and gas lines were rarely supplied in the buildings, and there was no fresh air due to lack of ventilation. The tenements were hotbeds for crime and contagion, eventually becoming slums in the next decades. The city enacted a law in 1901 requiring tenement owners to build additional ventilation, lighting, and indoor plumbing for public safety reasons.[21] Throughout her childhood, Dorothy's parents would shelter her from the poverty that characterized much of the city around her. Only in her adult years did Dorothy begin to notice how her privilege set her apart.

The New York elites held the Kenyon family in high esteem, and their lives reflected their social and economic status. Dorothy enjoyed riding horses and playing sports, including hockey, tennis, and ping-pong.[22] Will would awaken early, read the newspaper, and kiss Minnie goodbye, informing her that he would be home late. Dorothy later described her father dashing off each morning "in a whirl of papers, briefcases, and preoccupation. The world seemed to weigh on his shoulders and I have no doubt he thought it did. And it was late when he got back home. Sometimes he stayed at the office all evening, sometimes he brought work home with him. Saturdays and Sundays were almost as bad."[23] It was not until Dorothy was a practicing lawyer herself that she understood the kind of strain her father had been under.

The members of her family were erudite people. Dorothy shared with her father a love of reading, and she enjoyed curling up with a book and being oblivious to reality as she escaped in the pages. Dorothy and her best childhood friend spent many Friday afternoons making fudge and reading. She preferred the classics, like works written by Aeschylus and Euripides.[24] As a child, she read *Little Women*, then read the sequel, *Good Wives*, where Meg married and cooked. Dorothy exclaimed to her mother that Meg was doing her own work, clearly overcome by the idea that not everyone had maids.

Minnie, somewhat alarmed at the relative sophistication of Dorothy's literary choices, suggested to Will that perhaps Dorothy was not old enough to be reading certain books. Will responded by saying, "I don't care whatever books she reads, she's old enough to read and that's the way she's learning about life. She can read any old damn thing she wants."[25] Later, Dorothy wrote that her father was busy, tense, emotional, bookish, and shy, while her mother dominated the household and the children.[26]

Dorothy found enjoyment in writing, whether correspondence, stories, or poetry. Around age ten, she wrote a poem titled "My Father," expressing her pride in Will. An excerpt describes him as a hard worker:

My father is a patent lawyer,
He is like a great employer
There are many clerks in his office
He very seldom a case will miss.
He is the best lawyer in New York.
He once had a case about a form,
A case about an engine bumper
Also about a baby jumper.

He has a wife that no pencil or pen
Could fully describe, also two children
A boy and a girl whom he loves greatly.
His wife is sweet and very sedately.
He is fond of gold no wonder
For he seldom makes a blunder.
He plays in winter and summer
And seldom calls for the plumber.
He is very kind and good
And supplies us well with food.
He is six feet, some inches,
In work he never flinches.[27]

It seems that Dorothy preferred her father over her mother, and perhaps Will preferred Dorothy over his sons. He tended to spoil Dorothy, which she later believed was hard on Theodore. Will compared Theodore to Dorothy, once exasperatedly asking him, "Well, she gets A's and why can't you get A's?"[28]

The Kenyon family spent vacations in the Berkshires at their summer home, located on Main Street in Lakeville, Connecticut. Built early in the nineteenth century, the house was surrounded by large porches and wide lawns.[29] Dorothy later described how family meals at the house were punctuated by Will's antics at the dinner table, where he would pretend to misplace his glasses and help himself to food in wrong ways. To the delight of the children, and the annoyance of Minnie, Will would pour gravy on his salad or put jelly in his water glass, simulating the Mad Hatter from *Alice in Wonderland*.[30] Dorothy and her brothers adored their father's clowning at the table, and they would encourage the behavior as Minnie groaned.[31]

As Dorothy aged, tension increased within the household. She was a nervous and temperamental teenager who was often at odds with her parents. Dorothy and her mother had a particularly difficult relationship due to Dorothy's recalcitrant behavior. Minnie wanted Dorothy to find happiness in being a wife and mother. In Dorothy's mind, her mother's life was small and lacked the excitement that a career might bring. Dorothy wanted a crowded, expansive life—one where she did not have to make the same sacrifices as Minnie had made by choosing a life of domesticity.

Dorothy graduated with honors from the Horace Mann School, an innovative private high school, on May 31, 1904.[32] The school, founded in 1887 as a coeducational experimental unit of Columbia University, was named after the abolitionist, lawyer, congressman, and president of Antioch College.[33]

Mann believed that if only one sex could be educated, it should be the woman because of her influence as a mother.[34] The school educated many prominent individuals in the city, some of whom would later work with Dorothy at the ACLU, including Morris Ernst and Osmond Fraenkel, who would both serve as general counsel for the organization.[35]

Minnie believed it was important for Dorothy to leave home to obtain a college education, and she chose Smith College, an all-female school in Northampton, Massachusetts, as the right place for her daughter. Smith opened in 1875 as a Christian college, though it did not specify a particular religious denomination. Students were to be present at daily religious services and attend the churches designated by their guardians. A Smith education gave women "a broad and liberal culture" while developing and perfecting "the characteristics of a complete womanhood."[36] It was the first of the women's colleges to require the same entrance requirements as men's colleges.[37]

In the fall of 1904, Kenyon started at Smith as a sixteen-year-old pigtailed freshman living in Chapin House.[38] The red brick building, consisting of three residential floors, with tall white columns reaching to the second floor, had been built the year before, funded by John D. Rockefeller's donation of $100,000 to Smith, and is still in use today. Chapin House sits in the center of campus, boasting a wide lawn overlooking the gardens and playing fields.[39]

Sending Dorothy to college was a progressive choice. In that era, the higher education of women was very much a topic of debate, with many remaining convinced that women were not equipped for the physical and emotional rigor of the college classroom. By 1890, 60 percent of campuses across the United States were coeducational, but most elite universities remained open only to men.[40] Not everyone thought the experiment had merit, due to the dominant belief that women were intellectually inferior to men.

In 1873, a professor at Harvard Medical College, Edward H. Clarke, published a short book titled *Sex in Education; or, A Fair Chance for the Girls*. He wrote of pale girls ("girls of bloodless skins and intellectual faces") in college who, to fulfill course expectations, diverted blood and energy to their brain at the same time their reproductive organs were developing, resulting in harm to their bodies and to the future human race.[41] Women, Clarke wrote, should be trained and educated differently from men based on their "reproductive apparatus" and the obligation of maternity.[42] If men and women were educated similarly, he argued,

> there will be awakened within them a stimulus unknown before, and that separate study does not excite. The unconscious fires that have their seat deep down in the recesses of the sexual organization will flame up through every tissue, permeate every vessel, burn every nerve, flash from the eye, tingle in the brain, and work the whole machine at highest pressure.... Of course such strenuous labor will yield brilliant, though temporary results. The fire is kept alive by the waste of the system, and soon burns up its source. The first sex to suffer in this exhilarating and costly competition must be, as experience shows it is, the one that has the largest amount of force in readiness for immediate call; and this is the female sex. At the age of development, Nature mobilizes the forces of a girl's organization for the purpose of establishing a function that shall endure for a generation, and for constructing an apparatus that shall cradle and nurse a race.[43]

The first edition of Clarke's book sold out in just over a week, and incited numerous published rebuttals.[44] Many physicians agreed with Clarke's interpretation; the womb, they asserted, took over the mental and physical well-being of the woman, "producing a weak, submissive, uncreative, emotional, intuitive, and generally inferior personality."[45] Physical anthropologists at the time submitted that since women had smaller brains than men, their intelligence was less. Some concluded that because "women devoted so much energy to their reproductive organs" they had nothing left to use toward intellectual endeavors.[46] The study of subjects like mathematics, philosophy, and chemistry were seen by some as useless for women because their "deficient brain[s]" could not be expected to actually comprehend them.[47] Rather, such courses would make a woman "presumptuous and arrogant, and convert her into a person without grace, with an empty head and no heart."[48]

M. Carey Thomas, the first female dean in the United States and the first female president of Bryn Mawr College, wrote that women pioneers entering college "were haunted in those days by the clanging chains of that gloomy little specter, Dr. Edward H. Clarke's *Sex in Education*."[49] Administrators like Thomas had been frequently told that women's "brains were too light, their foreheads too small, their reasoning powers too defective, their emotions too easily worked upon, to make good students."[50] Thomas, however, argued that women's education should be identical to the education men received.

In the end, Clarke's theories about the pale intellectual girls were shown to be false. However, the burden of proof fell on women. As Eleanor Flexner writes in *Century of Struggle: The Woman's Rights Movement in the United States*, they had to demonstrate that "they would not sicken or die if they were exposed to logarithms—or to physical education. They had to combat, in addition to public prejudice, their own fears of being unladylike, of becoming unsexed creatures if they tried to persevere as physicians or politicians. . . . The battle had to be fought and won, not just once, but over and over again."[51]

. . .

Dorothy was excited for the opportunity to leave home and advance her education. Because of her father's encouragement, she did not lack any self-confidence in her ability to succeed at Smith. As a freshman, Dorothy expressed great interest in mathematics. Her professor saw her potential in the subject and wanted her to advance in it, but he had concerns about her sex, exclaiming, "But what could you, a woman, do if you did become an expert in higher mathematics? . . . There isn't anything really that women can do in that line."[52] Ultimately, Dorothy did not pursue mathematics, instead exploring other subjects, like Latin, psychology, and music, and finally majoring in economics and history.

At the end of Dorothy's first year at Smith, Minnie died of typhoid fever.[53] Losing Minnie was especially difficult for Dorothy's youngest brother, Houston, who was only six years old when his mother passed. Dorothy's aunt, Mary Kenyon, moved into the family home to help manage the household following Minnie's death. When Dorothy returned to Smith that fall, she tended to isolate herself from the other students, a condition that would persist throughout her time there. Perhaps it was because she was younger than many of her classmates, or maybe it was the start of her building walls around herself so as not to appear vulnerable. Much later, she indicated that she was exposed to something new while at college, namely "crushes"; describing them as "quite the rage," she said that the girls had them on each other and "definitely on faculty."[54] It is unclear if Dorothy experienced any crushes of her own while at Smith. However, this exposure could have laid the foundation for her experimentation with free love relationships in adulthood.

In her junior year at Smith, Dorothy was elected to Phi Beta Kappa, Chapter Theta of Massachusetts, an academic honor society established in 1776 at the College of William and Mary.[55] She asked her brother Theodore to come from Harvard to visit her, and as they were walking down a quiet path on campus shaded by elm trees, Dorothy broke the news to him about her election to the society. She was so emotional that Theodore later said he was not sure whether to congratulate her or commiserate with her.[56] It may seem odd that she was unhappy about the award, but at the time she did not want to be thought of as a scholar, a bookworm, or a bluestocking (a term used to describe an intellectual woman). Her reaction provides evidence that even despite Dorothy's independent spirit, she had moments of insecurity and self-doubt.

Dorothy later came to appreciate her intellectual nature and qualities. She joined the Smith Philosophical Society, serving on its executive committee, and was a member of Phi Kappa Psi Society, a literary society.[57] She also participated in physical activities at Smith. It was said she played tennis like a professional, and she was "a menace with a ping-pong bat in her hand."[58]

As Dorothy finished her four years at Smith, she prepared for several days of ceremonial celebration. The first event was Baccalaureate Sunday, with exercises held at First Congregational Church and Smith College president L. Clark Seelye giving the sermon.[59] The following day, June 15, 1908, Dorothy and her fellow graduates participated in Ivy Day, a tradition started by the class of 1884, in which, after chapel services, the students plant ivy on campus.[60] The next day, Charles Eliot, Harvard's president, was the featured speaker at convocation. A proponent of excluding women from attending liberal arts institutions, Eliot had earlier proposed that women's colleges should stop trying to emulate men's colleges and should become "schools of manners."[61] In his commencement speech at Smith, however, he apologized for his previous remarks that women were not worth educating in college. His thoughts on the subject were not completely egalitarian, however. Eliot stated that he now believed women should attend college, as they would "make splendid assistants to men."[62] When Dorothy heard him say this, she giggled out loud in the chapel.[63] She had no desire to assist any man, and later opined that this speech was responsible for her future unorthodox behavior.[64]

Following her graduation from Smith at age twenty, Dorothy returned to live at the family home in Manhattan. During this period she underwent a transformation from the loner she had been at Smith to a self-described social butterfly, flitting from activity to activity. It would take a few years for Dorothy to decide what she wanted to do with her degree. In the interim, she participated in leisure and civic activities. She spent time reading, playing tennis, and riding horseback, wintering in New York and summering in Connecticut. As she came from a prominent family, she was in no rush. Her options were wide open.

• • •

Dorothy's father would soon bring a new person into the home: his fiancée, Lestra Kinney. Some family members were thrilled to welcome Lestra, but Dorothy was not one of them. In a letter that nine-year-old Houston wrote Lestra, he declared that he was excited that his father was in love, and included a picture he had drawn of Will and Lestra kissing by the light of the moon, with Houston standing near them behind a tree, Theodore inside the house, and Dorothy far off behind a tree stump.[65] It is interesting that Houston depicted Dorothy being the farthest away from the newly engaged couple; perhaps he was able to pick up on the tension the relationship was causing in the family home.

Will and Lestra married on June 8, 1909. Seventy-five guests attended the wedding in a relative's home in Xenia, Ohio. The colors were green, white, and pink, with clusters of carnations and feathered asparagus ferns decorating the room. Houston was in the wedding; Dorothy and Theodore were not.[66] Dorothy, who had always been close with her father, was struggling. Although she behaved in a civil fashion, internally she was jealous and resentful of her stepmother. Even so, she remained in the family home with her father, Lestra, and her brother Houston.

In 1910, Dorothy traveled with Will and Lestra to Mexico. There they encountered a staggering level of poverty the likes of which Dorothy had never seen. Their year-long sojourn, however, included a string of luxurious activities. Lestra's sister, Clara Shields, visited them in Mexico City over the summer. In a letter home, Clara described Dorothy as a twenty-two-year-old beauty who had plenty of admirers.[67] They attended many balls, Clara said, with five or six private dances given for Dorothy. They enjoyed picnics, tennis tournaments, teas, dinners, and bridge parties. Yet despite all the fun they were having, Dorothy was beginning to experience a change in her values and beliefs.

Dorothy remarked later that she had not understood much about life until her trip to Mexico—not surprising, given her privileged and sheltered upbringing. In Mexico, she saw how wealthy British and American men exploited the oil and the labor force, making her acutely aware of society's class gradations.[68] She did not like what she saw, and it fanned a flame within her for dissent. She later said that it was during this year of travel that she acquired her "slant to the left."[69] The tennis-playing, carefree beauty from an elite family now became fiercely passionate about protecting those vulnerable to exploitation.

Dorothy's nephew Edward Kenyon, Theodore's son, later described the change in her personality following the trip. "She came back a different person.... She didn't hesitate to express her rage. She had a very sharp tongue... [s]he didn't hesitate to use it."[70] The transformation from socialite to reformer happened at an ideal time. Women were organizing to obtain the vote, to serve on juries, and to reform exploitative labor conditions. The child born in the Gilded Age of New York was now an adult during the Progressive Era, ready to fight for societal improvements.

Although she had plenty of money and no need to work, she remembered that her father told her she could be a lawyer. Dorothy was his firstborn, the child he had raised with Minnie, and now, as an adult, she set about following in his footsteps. Unlike her father, however, Dorothy did not have her pick of institutions. Law schools all over the country excluded women. One of her brothers would later be admitted to Harvard Law, the other to Columbia Law, but Dorothy could not attend either because of her sex.[71] She chose NYU School of Law, an east coast pioneer in legal coeducation, and the only law school in New York City at the time that admitted women.[72] It was also the school Dorothy's aunt had attended.[73]

If Dorothy's year in Mexico had lit a spark in her to be a change-maker, breaking into the legal profession as a woman would solidify her desire to provide service to others—a project that particularly benefitted the women lawyers coming up behind her.

TWO

# *Becoming a Portia*

## LADIES AT THE BAR

Law would be the instrument of their power.

JILL NORGREN,
*Political Scientist*

KENYON BEGAN HER EDUCATION at NYU School of Law in 1914. It was an energetic time for the field. Out of 606 women enrolled in all US law schools that year, 82 were at NYU.[1] The school was following the recent trend of requiring a three-year course of study, taught in both day and evening classes. During her first year of law school, with grades of A in Contracts, Quasi Contracts, and Personal Property, B in Property and in Criminal Law, and C in Torts, Kenyon received an honorable mention for her excellent work, ranking fifth in the honorable mention category.[2] Kenyon later said there were about seventy or eighty students who started in her law school class—only about ten, however, were women.[3] The NYU School of Law Alumni Directory shows that fifty-nine students graduated in the class of 1917—forty-seven were men and twelve were women, five of those being married women.[4]

Before women would earn the right to vote in 1920, NYU School of Law had graduated more than three hundred women.[5] Alumna Elinor Byrns, class of 1907, described herself and her classmates this way: "I am a restless woman. Almost all my chosen companions are restless women."[6] They were ready to use that restless energy to agitate for social reform. At NYU, Kenyon embraced the same spirit as the women in the classrooms before her.

After graduating, Kenyon refused an offer to join her father's law firm, as she did not have an interest in patent law. She thought she would be bored at her father's firm, plus she had concerns about some of their shared characteristics. Kenyon described her father as a prima donna and openly admitted that she had inherited the same trait. "I was perfectly certain that I would like to be a prima donna myself, and I was sure I never could be in a great big patent law office, so I would much prefer to go out on my own, be, you know, my own little frog croaking in my own little pond."[7] Kenyon wanted to stand on her own two feet and see if she could make it. Her brothers, however, were happy to join their father's firm, which later became known as Kenyon & Kenyon.

Kenyon's first job was as a law clerk at Gwinn & Deming, a small law firm that specialized in business matters.[8] While there, she made the acquaintance of Wolcott (Patsy) Pitkin. Pitkin had been a lawyer at Simpson, Thacher & Bartlett in New York City until his appointment in 1909 as assistant US attorney for the Southern District of New York. In 1912, he was named attorney general of Puerto Rico by President Taft.[9] Through his government work, Pitkin was connected to Colonel Edward House, a diplomat heading up a US government department working on peace relations.[10]

Expressing an interest in foreign relations, in November 1917 Kenyon wrote Pitkin asking how she could work with Colonel House. She described her interest in political science and law and said she would do clerical work if that was her only chance to contribute.[11] This letter marked a serendipitous moment in her life because of the personal relationship she would soon develop with Pitkin. He wrote back, responding that he could use her help with research and sending her a list of books he wanted her to read and summarize for him in an unpaid capacity.[12]

Pitkin connected Kenyon with some powerful individuals when she started working in Washington, DC, as a member of Colonel House's and Walter Lippmann's committee of scholars designing a document for world peace. Kenyon collected economic data for the Peace Conference of 1919 where twenty-one nations came together to develop strategies of peacekeeping.[13] She also helped Pitkin with a brief for the Kingdom of Siam that was presented to the Peace Conference.[14] While in DC she worked for the War Department as a clerk to the secretary of war, Newton D. Baker, from October 14 through December 4, 1918.[15] She then worked with the War Labor Policies Board, from December 5, 1918, through February 28, 1919, for a salary of seven dollars per day.[16] She worked under Felix Frankfurter in DC, the first Jewish law professor at Harvard, who would later serve on the US Supreme Court.[17]

This early work experience in Kenyon's life was certainly beneficial in helping establish a foundation for her career as well as helping her feel as if she was contributing to the war effort. Yet it did not help with her restlessness. She was working in a new town, in subservient positions to demanding men. She must have felt the desire to return to New York City where she had familial connections and could practice in the areas of law in which she was truly interested.

The early twentieth century was a difficult time for a woman to earn a living as an attorney, but Kenyon credited her courage and ability when it came to overcoming prejudice. Although she knew she was choosing a difficult path in refusing the offer to work with her family's firm, she was able to defy expectations because of her privileged upbringing, the support she received from her family, and her strong desire to pursue the law. But she also was able to practice law because women before her had demanded inclusion in the profession.

Pursuing a legal education and obtaining access to the bar were extraordinary accomplishments for women at this point in history, when they were simultaneously shedding ingrained Victorian principles. Women lawyers saw their profession as an opportunity to engage in intellectual pursuits, expand their limited economic opportunities, and reform archaic institutional norms regarding equality.[18] They did not receive a warm welcome into the male-dominated legal profession, however; indeed, many women had to seek legislative or judicial remedies simply to receive their diplomas or to become licensed to practice law. The history is a fascinating and frustrating one, yet it is largely unknown by lawyers in the twenty-first century.

. . .

It was not until the last part of the nineteenth century that law schools became the primary loci of legal training.[19] The first American law school to admit women was Washington University in St. Louis, Missouri, in 1869.[20] In that same year, Arabella Mansfield was admitted to the Iowa bar after apprenticing and passing the bar exam, becoming the first woman permitted to practice law in the United States.[21] In 1870, Union College of Law (which became Northwestern University) was the first law school to graduate a woman, Ada Kepley.[22] Belva Lockwood completed her law school education at National University in 1873; however, the school refused to provide her with a diploma. Months later, with the help of President Ulysses S. Grant, Lockwood received her law degree and was admitted to the bar of the District of Columbia. In 1876, she petitioned the US Supreme Court to be able to appear before it but was denied because of her sex.[23] Lockwood lobbied Congress for a change in the law, and in 1879 Congress passed legislation allowing women lawyers to practice before the US Supreme Court if they were a member of a bar in their state or territory, or of the Supreme Court in the District of Columbia.[24] As a result, Lockwood was the first woman to be admitted to practice before the US Supreme Court, as well as the first woman to argue before the Court. She also ran for the office of US president twice, in 1884 and 1888.[25] Late in her career Lockwood remarked, "I never stopped fighting. My cause was the cause of thousands of women."[26]

In most states, admission to the bar was set by statute, often using the masculine pronoun to define who could be an attorney. In Arabella Mansfield's case, the Iowa court interpreted the masculine pronoun to apply generally to all persons.[27] Other courts disagreed, stating that the legislators drafting the statute never contemplated women would practice law, so, using a strict statutory interpretation, women should be barred from practice. Myra Bradwell, a married woman, tried to gain admission to the Illinois bar after passing the state bar examination.[28] The Illinois Supreme Court refused to give her a license to practice law since she was a woman, a decision that was affirmed by the US Supreme Court on appeal. The Court said that because the right to practice law was not a right of citizenship, states could deny women entrance to the legal profession. In a separate concurrence to the Court's 1873 opinion in *Bradwell v. Illinois*, Justice Joseph Bradley explained why he believed women should not be permitted to practice law:

> Man is, or should be, woman's protector and defender. The natural and proper timidity and delicacy which belongs to the female sex evidently unfits it for many of the occupations of civil life. The constitution of the family organization, which is founded in the divine ordinance as well as in the nature of things, indicates the domestic sphere as that which properly belongs to the domain and functions of womanhood. The harmony, not to say identity, of interest and views which belong, or should belong, to the family institution is repugnant to the idea of a woman adopting a distinct and independent career from that of her husband. So firmly fixed was this sentiment in the founders of the common law that it became a maxim of that system of jurisprudence that a woman had no legal existence separate from her husband, who was regarded as her head and representative in the social state, and, notwithstanding some recent modifications of this civil status, many of the special rules of law flowing from and dependent upon this cardinal principle still exist in full force in most states. One of these is that a married woman is incapable, without her husband's consent, of making contracts which shall be binding on her or him. This very incapacity was one circumstance which the Supreme Court of Illinois deemed important in rendering a married woman incom-

petent fully to perform the duties and trusts that belong to the office of an attorney and counselor. . . . The paramount destiny and mission of woman are to fulfill the noble and benign offices of wife and mother. This is the law of the Creator.[29]

It is not surprising that Justice Bradley held those beliefs. At the time, Sir William Blackstone's *Commentaries on the Laws of England*, published in 1765, was a key textbook used in American law schools, influencing the lawyers and judges of the time.[30] Blackstone, a legal commentator who helped develop the doctrine of English common law in the eighteenth century, described marriage in terms of a new legal identity called coverture—where the married pair would become one person under the husband's protection.[31] Kenyon would remark on Blackstone in a speech to the American Association of University Women in Los Angeles, California, in June 1935, saying, "[H]e was read and worshipped throughout the length and breadth of this land. Every young lawyer read him by lamplight of an evening. He became our bible, our household word."[32] Kenyon quoted Blackstone as saying, "A mother is entitled to no power, only reverence."[33] Blackstone gave no room for women like Kenyon who wished to remain single or did not want to become mothers.

Kenyon was correct in that Blackstone's *Commentaries* infiltrated statutes across the country. This legislative acceptance created societal habits and customs that reinforced the idea of second-class citizenship for women, particularly around duties of motherhood. As Eleanor Flexner writes, "Habit and custom combined to make [woman] a creature believed to be capable of very little else."[34]

The US Supreme Court affirmed coverture in *Mackenzie v. Hare*, stating that "[t]he identity of husband and wife is an ancient principle of our jurisprudence. It was neither accidental nor arbitrary, and worked in many instances for her protection . . . to merge their identity, and give dominance to the husband."[35] Once she married, the wife's property, both real and personal, became the property of the husband to control. Women who married were returned to the rights of a child, becoming legally disabled, and the woman was regarded as less than a full citizen. Women could not vote, execute a will, enter into a contract, sit on juries, own and transfer property, or run businesses, for those activities were seen as actively harmful to women.[36] Audrey Wolfson Latourette explains: "This cult of domesticity or the cult of true womanhood, as the [separate spheres] movement was known, regarded women as morally superior beings whose social role mandated confinement to domestic duties, less [*sic*] they be contaminated by the realities of the brutal marketplace. Moreover, the law had established the framework within which women's rights could be constrained and separate spheres could be enforced."[37]

When women worked outside the home, the husband had the right to all wages of the wife. The marriage contract made her an inferior citizen, with few legal rights. Reva Siegel provides a detailed legislative history in her article "The Modernization of Marital Status Law: Adjudicating Wives' Rights to Earnings, 1860–1930."[38] As legislation was passed that improved the property rights of women, courts allowed wives to claim their earnings if their husbands were negligent in providing for them. Over time, as Siegel notes, courts viewed the wife's labor for third parties "as distinct from her marital duties" and permitted her to keep her wages.[39] While this provided a crumb of independence, a woman's right to pursue the career she wanted, especially those professions that were more lucrative, continued to be withheld in many places.

Unmarried women had an equally tough time, as they were thought of by some as lesser than married women. The unmarried woman was described in a 1909 article for the *New-York Tribune* as being "[l]ike the fringe of a shawl, belonging to it as an accompaniment, but not necessary."[40] It was argued that those who married had a fuller life and that if a woman was unmarried at age forty, it would be better to "take chances with a man whom she can respect and who is her equal in refinement and social position, and is congenial to her, than never to marry at all."[41]

. . .

As women gained admission to practice in some jurisdictions, bar associations often remained restricted to male lawyers. Networking with other women lawyers became very important, providing both emotional and professional support. The Equity Club was formed on October 6, 1886, by women lawyers and law students at the University of Michigan. With thirty-two members across the country, and with members in Europe, the women were able to build a coalition and find in each other a professional identity. Each member was required to write a yearly letter describing the daily battles faced by women in the legal profession, for distribution to the group as a whole.[42]

The club began at a time when the number of women lawyers in the United States had more than doubled. In 1880, the census reported that seventy-five women were lawyers. By the time of the next census in 1890, that number had grown to 208. In her book about the Equity Club, Virginia G. Drachman writes that the founders "were part of the first generation of women to enjoy the benefits of higher education. . . . [T]heir educational training set them apart from many young lawyers of their day—male or female—for former legal education was typically not a requirement for admission to practice law in the late nineteenth century."[43]

In 1881, Lelia Robinson became the first woman to graduate from Boston University Law School and, a year later, the first to be admitted to the bar in Massachusetts.[44] When she first applied for admission to the bar, she was denied on the basis of her sex.[45] She lobbied the legislature and it subsequently passed a bill, with unanimous support, allowing women to practice law in Massachusetts. She later wrote an article, "Women Lawyers in the United States," in which she listed women lawyers from across the nation, relying on the Equity Club for her research. The article provides a gripping history of the struggles faced by women law students and apprentices as they tried to access the profession. Robinson recognized that the acceptance of women into the legal profession depended on geography, as some locales were ready to welcome them, while others were not. "But in time," she wrote, "sooner or later, the lawyer everywhere who deserves success and can both work and wait to win it, is sure to achieve it, the woman no less than the man."[46] She also mentioned Charlotte E. Ray, the first Black woman lawyer in the United States. Ray graduated from Howard University in 1872, and practiced in Washington, DC, before moving to New York.[47]

In a letter to the Equity Club, Robinson drew a line in the sand about how women lawyers should present themselves. "*Do not take sex* into the practice," she wrote. "Don't be 'lady lawyers.' Simply be *lawyers*, and recognize no distinction—no existence of any distinction between yourselves and the other members of the bar."[48] Others disagreed. Ada Kepley, for one, urged members not to downplay their womanhood, thus ensuring "sweeter manners—purer laws."[49]

Drachman, in reviewing the letters of the Equity Club, found that "the question of the role of femininity in their professional lives" appeared constantly in the correspondence.[50] A common question involved the obligations of womanhood: how could they effectively be wives, mothers, *and* lawyers? A woman upon marriage would move to the sphere of domesticity with the expectation to produce children. Or she could remain single and have a productive career. It was not impossible to do both, but pressure would be exerted to leave the workplace so the family unit did not suffer. Some remained single in order to have a productive law practice. Others were married to husbands who were lawyers and would share the practice with them, in which case they became more of a legal assistant to the husband. Law was considered a masculine endeavor, and women who pursued it were considered peculiar.[51] Most in society believed that legal education was wasted on women because at some point they would choose to marry and not practice any longer.[52] Others believed that women should not be lawyers because they would "waste the court's time with endless argument off the point" or "would rely on feminine intuition rather than the law."[53]

Yet even in the face of opposition, women were choosing higher education and exhibiting a desire to enter the workplace. Many were choosing advanced degrees, like medicine or law. The idea of females becoming doctors was easier to comprehend because it was a natural extension of the woman's role as a nurturer. In 1910, there were approximately 9,000 women doctors in the United States but only 1,500 women lawyers.[54] Many who opposed the entry of women into the legal profession adopted a protectionist position, submitting that women should not have to "be sullied by the harsh and degrading aspects of legal practice."[55] Others had a more relaxed, but still protectionist, perspective, arguing that women could be admitted to practice because they were perfectly suited to represent *women* clients.

Dorothy Straus, a lawyer and activist who would later practice with Dorothy Kenyon, wrote the foreword for a 1920 book titled *Women in the Law: An Analysis Of Training, Practice, and Salaried Positions* on behalf of the Bureau of Vocational Information.[56] The purpose of the study described in the book was to provide a picture of what women faced in the legal profession. Straus had been practicing for nine years when she wrote her foreword. In it, she stated that "the law is still a field for pioneers." Straus said more women were becoming lawyers due to the "larger effort of women to become oriented in modern society, a society in which, whether praised or condemned, the profession of law plays one of the vital parts."[57]

*Women in the Law* noted that twenty-seven states did not prescribe a specific course of study for legal training.[58] Requirements for admission and instructional methods likewise varied among the states. The 1918–19 directory of law schools included 129 law schools overall, 102 of which admitted women students. Seven schools made the decision to admit women in 1918 alone, yet the state universities of Florida and Virginia remained closed to women.[59] As of 1920, 1,599 women had been admitted to practice across the country, and every state admitted women to the bar except Delaware.[60] That said, no women had yet been admitted in Wyoming, Virginia, or Rhode Island, as none had applied in those states.[61]

Even though women were widely permitted to practice law, many decided against it. Indeed, the study found that roughly one-third to one-half of women law graduates were not practicing. The reasons were varied: it was hard to get established, the work was lonely, other lawyers were uncooperative, and they encountered untoward prejudice.[62] Other reasons included the inability to afford the cost of a practice, lack of confidence, medical issues, and marriage. The women respondents divided into two camps regarding their feelings on marriage and the practice of law. One group thought of marriage as a vocation in and of itself, where a woman's primary responsibilities should be to her children and husband. The other group thought that society was recalibrating such that working as a lawyer and having a family were compatible goals. They believed a woman would be better at managing her family by also having a vocation because she could offer her children a greater understanding of the world.[63]

Popular opinion differed across the country regarding women in the legal profession. Many newspapers called women lawyers Portias, recalling William Shakespeare's *Merchant of Venice*, where Portia dresses like a man to impersonate a lawyer and eloquently defend Antonio from Shylock's demand for a pound of flesh.[64] Even though Portia was not an actual lawyer, popular culture employed the term to describe women assuming a role that traditionally belonged to men. Many women did not appreciate the use of Portia as they did not want "any distinction made for or against them because of sex."[65]

In 1911, a woman who practiced law in Boston gave an interview about the difficulties she faced, saying that she had to "fight against a prejudice that permeates the very atmosphere she breathes."[66] In 1919, a Louisville, Kentucky, newspaper supported women's efforts to become lawyers, describing them as assets to the legal profession and advocating that colleges open their doors so women could become lawyers.[67] However, a 1926 article in the *Lansing State Journal* opined that the days of Portia's views on mercy "went out along with the Victorian era" and warned that since women now had the right to vote (due to passage of the Nineteenth Amendment in 1920), the male's position in society was in peril. The author wrote, "Men were led to believe that when women came into their rights that all of us would be well protected, but it just isn't so. It still remains bad form for a man to hit a woman with a brick. Some day, if it is not already here, men will rue the day they allowed women to get into such a posture of boastfulness."[68] Similarly, a New Jersey newspaper criticized women who had attended college as holding a "delusional projection . . . to be a man" and asserted that higher education should be for men only.[69] In the newspaper's view, educated women emasculated men and resulted in a "deluge of mannish, bespectacled female lawyers, artists, [and] politicians."[70]

Black women lawyers faced discrimination based not only on their sex but also on their race. Because Black lawyers were excluded from the American Bar Association and most local bar associations, the National Bar Association was founded in 1925, providing a network for Black lawyers as well as an avenue to work to protect civil rights.[71] More than two-thirds of Black women lawyers belonged to the National Bar Association, but their representation still remained quite small. In 1941, one national count identified only fifty-seven Black women lawyers practicing in the United States.[72]

Despite opposition, women were finally admitted to Harvard Law School in 1950. When Erwin Griswold, dean of Harvard Law, announced that women would be permitted to enroll, he added a caveat: "Opportunities for women in the law still are limited, . . . and the [f]aculty is well aware that many able men are turned away from our doors every year. It is our expectation that we will admit only a small number of unusually qualified women students, for the present, at least."[73] Anger at the law school's decision to accept women extended beyond the Harvard campus in Cambridge. For example, a Florida newspaper printed the following:

> The latest victory of the powder-puff battalions is the decision of the Harvard Law School to admit women to its classes. Its breaching now by female bluestockings comes as a sour surprise, indeed, to many oldtimers. "Aren't there already enough women laying down the law to men?" they cry. They want to act like men and be treated like women. Naturally, the ordinary man thinks this is a little unfair of the fairer sex. He would like either to deal with a lady as a lady, or have the present code of ethics and etiquette modified to allow him to belt a presumptuous female with a baseball bat if she gets out of line. Right now he's confused. Should he take off his hat before hitting her?[74]

The twelve women who arrived at Harvard Law in September 1950 were very aware that they were under a microscope regarding their performance and conduct.[75] They also knew their opportunities upon graduation would be limited. Judges refused to interview women for clerkships, and prosecutors' offices refused to hire women on the assumption that they were "too soft" and could not "handle hardened criminal types."[76]

One person applauding Harvard Law's decision to admit women was Dorothy Kenyon. In an article for the *New York Times*, "Case (by One of Them) for Women Lawyers," she speculated how Charles Eliot—who had famously said, "Male and female minds are not alike and should not be treated the same educationally"—would feel about women being admitted to the law school. Kenyon described Eliot's Harvard as the "citadel of law, the most conservative, the most powerful of the professions, and the last refuge of the male." All that was about to change, now that women could be admitted as law students. She wondered if Eliot would have approved of the decision if he had seen the new sociological data suggesting that women excelled in the traits that made for a good lawyer. Because of these traits, Kenyon argued, which included strong inductive reasoning and the ability to persuade, the law could certainly be viewed as a woman's field. Even so, women still faced criticism in the law firm environment. She noted the sorts of questions and comments that young women lawyers heard in the law office: *What use can we possibly make of you? You'd make a fool of yourself and us in court. We can't work you late at night as we do the boys. What would the clients say? You may be a disturbing element, falling in love with people, and vice versa. We'll have to stick you in a law library, out of sight. In the unlikely contingency that you turn out to be good, you'll probably marry as soon as we've finished training you.* While recognizing such criticism, Kenyon speculated that Harvard Law would benefit from women's admittance, and one day critics would be proud of the women graduates.[77]

Brenda Feigen, who would go on to co-direct the ACLU's Women's Rights Project with Ruth Bader Ginsburg, was admitted to Harvard Law in 1966. There were 32 women in her class of 565 students. Feigen remembered professors who would ignore women in class except on what was called Ladies' Day—the one day a year when women were encouraged to engage in class discussion. Professors would enter the classroom each day saying, "Good morning, gentleman." She argued that "women were not getting the same education that the men were."[78] Law firms conducting on-campus interviews declined to hire women.[79] When women were interviewed by a prospective law firm, they would be asked if they planned on marrying and having children, and if so, how many.[80] Law firms feared that any female hires would inevitably marry and quit their position.

A survey conducted with women and men who had graduated from Harvard Law between 1953 and 1970 showed that women graduates were more than twice as likely as male graduates to say that, if they could choose all over again, they would have followed another career.[81] The survey also showed that women received less pay and received fewer job offers than their male colleagues.[82]

. . .

Throughout her adult life, Kenyon described lawyering as an inspiring occupation where an individual could study humanity and the rules that provide order in society.[83] In a 1935 WNYC radio interview, she recognized that women lawyers were still somewhat of a novelty, but that that was not necessarily detrimental. Because they were latecomers to the profession, they could view the law "as an outsider would, possibly more dispassionately, perhaps even with less illusions."[84] Kenyon believed that women had a valuable role to play in the use of law to resolve conflicts and that creative legal thought was critical in meeting the various social challenges presented both within and outside of the courtroom. In the radio broadcast, she added, "A lawyer will recognize that the law is a living fabric, growing and changing to fit human needs, and that it is his or her job to give it direction in the social interest."[85] She pointed out that although there were women lawyers, women plaintiffs and defendants, and women witnesses in the courts, women were still missing from the jury box. Kenyon urged New York's state assembly to pass a juror bill to allow women to exercise their full rights of citizenship.

Kenyon desired to make the law a more humane instrument for justice and social progress. She believed a lawyer was a social engineer with the ability to make the world a better place. She found the legal mind to be amazingly mechanical—so much so that she warned other lawyers to remember they were dealing with human beings as clients.[86] Her advice to young women entering the profession was especially pointed: she implored them not to allow others to call them "women lawyers," as she strongly believed this would segregate women. Kenyon also cautioned her female colleagues against impostor syndrome. She did not want anyone to believe they were not smart enough to make it. To her, it was the willingness to work hard that prepared a lawyer for a successful career. Fully aware that women encountered obstacles in the legal profession, and that many received a poor reception from their male colleagues, she declared that "it's a lucky and a nervy girl who can break through these barbed-wire entanglements."[87]

Educating women about, and encouraging them to pursue, a legal career would be a constant touchstone for Kenyon. In an article titled "Can Girls Be Lawyers?" she shared how her father encouraged her to become a lawyer. She wrote of the widespread notion—perpetuated, she claimed, by lawyers themselves—that the law was impossible to understand, which meant that lawyers had to be brilliant. To her consternation, she heard girls say they could not aspire to the profession because they were not smart enough. While she recognized that legal practice was often demanding and nerve-wracking, she insisted that most could be successful. All it required was talent and hard work.

> It is the excitement of controversy, of pitting your wits against somebody else's, of trying to prevail over somebody else. . . . If you like mental stimulus, if you like being on your toes and alert to what's happening around you . . . if you like to talk and debate, most of all if you like human beings and enjoy dealing with them, and if you like being in touch with what is going on in the world of affairs, then you *must* endeavor to be a lawyer. The law is not a fixed body of knowledge, it is in a continuous state of growth and development (like the human beings whose rules of conduct it is). Consequently lawyers must always be studying to keep up with it. They must not only know the law of the past, they must keep up with the law of the present, and, to a certain extent, they must help to create the future. . . . Every lawyer also has to do a lot of writing. . . . But a lawyer does not merely use his pen. He also uses his tongue. The art of public speaking, of marshalling facts and law into a persuasive argument, is one of the great arts of the lawyer. Many cases are won or lost on this score alone.[88]

Kenyon described her own tireless work ethic: "It's just that I've never learned to practice law and earn my living with any sense of relaxation or ease about it. I always work at fever pitch as though my life depended on it and as though *I* were the indispensable man in the case. Silly, of course, but I guess that's the way I'm made."[89]

Yet Kenyon did not work twenty-four hours a day; she also had a busy and complicated personal life involving family members, lovers, and friends that coexisted alongside the wins and losses she experienced in her work. She encountered both extreme highs and extreme lows in her adult life. She would fall in love, suffer heartbreak, be unwillingly thrust into a national political spotlight, and have a hand in creating progressive policy and litigation strategies that would change the legal status of women. And some of the complications in her life came from her own creation—a place called Barn House.

THREE

# *A Cooperative Association*

## FREE LOVE AND LOSS

There, where earth, sky and water meet, I drink in strength and beauty and am wholly recreated.

DOROTHY KENYON

HENRY BEETLE HOUGH, THE OWNER, editor, and publisher of the *Vineyard Gazette* on Martha's Vineyard, located off the coast of Massachusetts, described the island as a time for a "return to youth."[1] When lying on a hill or beach on a summer night, he wrote, one's problems would shrink. In 1918, Kenyon visited the Vineyard and fell in love—both with a co-worker and with the beauty of the Vineyard. One love would last her entire lifetime, while the other would result in deep loss.

In September 1918, Wolcott (Patsy) Pitkin invited Kenyon to a "mad party" at Chilmark, on the western end of Martha's Vineyard, for the Labor Day holiday.[2] One of the couples she met at the party was the Kings. Stanley King, one of Pitkin's Harvard Law classmates, served as the assistant to the secretary of war.[3] After leaving the federal government at the end of World War I, King returned to Boston, later becoming president of Amherst College.[4] King's wife, Gertrude Louisa Besse, was a poet who graduated from Vassar College and earned her master's degree at Radcliffe.[5]

As the party was breaking up, Stanley exclaimed that they should collectively buy a place on the Vineyard.[6] Over the winter, Kenyon followed up on this suggestion, persuading Pitkin and the Kings to form a cooperative with her so they could purchase property in Chilmark. Kenyon loved the sea—she was happy to live on an island (Manhattan) in the winter and wanted to live on another island (Martha's Vineyard) in the summer.

While waiting to purchase their summer playground, Pitkin established a law firm with Samuel Rosensohn in March 1919. He hired Kenyon full time for $25 a week, and she focused her practice on wage issues.[7] She served as president of the New York State Consumers' League, where she drafted the mandatory-minimum-wage bill for women and children in industry.[8] She also settled wage disputes in the ladies' garment industry in Cleveland, Ohio, helping to draft the Collective Bargaining Agreement of 1919 between the ladies' garment workers and manufacturers. Kenyon had a passion for working on labor and consumer issues, but she also enjoyed working with Pitkin.

The Kings found a property located on the rural west end of the Vineyard and purchased it on May 31, 1919. It was in a location called Mayhew Place and included a farm with a barn, chicken coops, and sheds, on about forty acres of land. In July, Gertrude bought more land south of the farm, known as the Vincent Cliffs.[9] On August 27, 1919, the group drew up a declaration of trust and established the Chilmark Associates, which allowed them and a few other individuals to collectively serve as trustees of the property through a cooperative enterprise.

One afternoon the associates met to choose a name for the property and adopted the name Stone Paddocks. After adjourning the meeting, they re-met at 10:30 that night for a vote to rescind the name and adopt The Barn instead. Later during the same week, The Barn was altered to Barn House.[10] The property was described as "a spartan adult summer camp with kids underfoot."[11] House rules for members and guests described Barn House as "the summer vacation place of an association of free and devoted members who share in the ownership of the property. It is in no sense a boarding house, and if considered or so treated it will bite."[12] The property was a rustic locale where intellectuals, lawyers, artists, and writers gathered frequently. At this "communal utopia" by the sea, members could leave the city behind, the laid-back atmosphere providing a welcome respite for free spirits.[13] Kenyon, referred to as the founding mother of Barn House, managed the cooperative and visited every summer from 1919 through 1971.

Barn House members paid an initiation fee and regular dues earmarked for community improvements and rehabilitation of structures.[14] Members and their guests visited the property each summer from the first of July through Labor Day, with guests paying a fee of $2.50 per day.[15] The members of the cooperative were expected to complete various chores to benefit the property. On one September 1925 list, the labor was divided among chores like preparing vegetables, washing dishes, setting the table, and taking out the garbage. Kenyon signed up for washing dishes and slicing vegetables. She also was the only member assigned to the last of the chores on the list: rabbit catching.[16] According to Kenyon's grandnephew John Fisher, all this activity also included a lot of singing.[17] Alcohol was locked in "a treasure chest," and a staff member recorded how much was consumed by each member for billing purposes.[18] Because there was no electricity in the barn, a large field-stone fireplace provided heat while candles served as the light source.[19] Meals were served promptly at 8 a.m., 1 p.m., and 7 p.m., with bells calling the members and guests to the table.[20] Children, not permitted inside the barn until they were teenagers, ate on the back porch.[21]

Because Barn House had no shoreline, a neighbor, Lucy Vincent, gave the members permission each year to access the shore through her property.[22] The chicken coops and sheds were renovated into rustic dormitories, with the barn serving as a meeting space. While some members stayed in the farmhouse, most stayed in the coops, or the original hen houses. Kenyon built a coop of her own, calling it the DK coop and choosing a pink floor.[23] Eventually there would be nine separate coops on the large property, some in eyeshot of each other, all spartan and meant only for sleeping. Barn House developed into a place that attracted individuals who enjoyed an old-fashioned ambiance with few of the comforts of modern life, such as electricity or indoor plumbing. Chamber pots were stored under the beds for use at night, as the communal bathhouse was a considerable distance away.

In 1926, Kenyon and Pitkin, together with their friend Elihu (Sec) Root Jr., jointly purchased a sloop yacht named the *Anchovy*. None of them knew how to sail, but they purchased books on the subject and hoped for the best. On the inaugural sail from New York City to the Vineyard, they discovered that practical experience, rather than the theoretical kind, was what they really needed. They did eventually reach Barn House but required the help of other individuals at sea to accomplish this.[24] The *Anchovy* was sold in 1928.[25]

In addition to novice sailor Sec Root, over the years members and guests included two founders of the ACLU, Roger Baldwin and Crystal Eastman (and her brother, Max, who was a writer, activist, and editor of *The Masses*, a publication for feminist expression, and the *Liberator*, a political publication), as well as Walter Lippmann (considered to be the father of modern American journalism, who founded the *New Republic* magazine), artist Warren Chappell, Felix Frankfurter (prior to becoming an associate Supreme Court justice), poet Padraic Colum, Secretary of Defense Robert McNamara, artist Boardman Robinson, biographer James MacGregor Burns, artist Thomas Hart Benton, and poet Sylvia Plath.[26]

The Barn House collective was described as a group that "fit in no category—and, of course, never did."[27] They went barefoot on the property and were known to put on shows and have costume parties.[28] Intellectual discussions and theatrical performances often extended into the early morning hours. As the years passed, the children would become the ones to put on theatrical performances on Saturday nights. Current member Jessica Ancker remembers the children going through the costumes and performing a production. Her mother, seated in the audience and watching their show, told Roger Baldwin, who was seated next to her, that she was having a difficult time following the plot. Baldwin responded encouragingly, "I can't either but I'm confident that it represents the triumph of good over evil."[29]

John Roche, a Barn House member who served as an aide to Presidents Kennedy and Johnson, recalled that the cooperative was a place to unwind: "We all enter into a conspiracy to avoid talking shop, anybody's shop. . . . To put it another way, this is a time to charge batteries."[30] Max Eastman described Barn House as a "colony of writing and painting and thinking folk."[31] He recalled an occasion when Stanley King stood on his head for five consecutive minutes on the beach, describing it as "an achievement never rivaled . . . by any other New England college president."[32]

Barn House shrouded itself in secrecy, fueling local residents' questions about the members. As one of their Chilmark neighbors speculated, "Who were these folks who formed a group, who lived together in crude sheds with no running water? They must be Communists, living promiscuously, holding wild beach parties."[33] The associates were considered radical, and it was gossiped that members and guests swam in the nude. It was not just gossip. A letter from Pitkin to Kenyon mentions that "everybody, including Natalie and Adam [Haskell], went in bathing 'as nature made 'em,' tho' the 'girls' wore their suits into the water and then took 'em off."[34] Their neighbor Lucy Vincent was aware of the nudity but paid it no mind. She was heard to say she did not check on the Barn House neighbors, and if she did not have to see them, she did not care what they did.[35]

Meanwhile, members were committed to their unconventional fun. In a letter to a fellow member labeled "Confidential (Obviously)," Kenyon discussed a script that was to be performed. "One idea I had was that the questions might come from the audience instead of from a written script and be unexpected and unrehearsed. This might put everybody on their mettle. For instance, 'How long were you a free love colony?' 'Where did you stand on naked bathing or dancing in the barn?'"[36] Barn House also inspired Kenyon's free-spirited fashion sense. In the early days, she wore purple sateen bloomers, which were quite daring for that time as women were expected to wear dresses or skirts.[37] She wore those same purple bloomers at Barn House for over twenty years, until one day they mysteriously disappeared. Kenyon viewed her friends as the likely culprits, but the mystery of the vanishing purple bloomers was never solved.

Writing about his first visit to Barn House, Roger Baldwin described Kenyon as a conversationalist who, "though she tended to make it one-sided," exhibited wit and a laugh that made "her everybody's friend."[38] He would get to know her better through her work with the ACLU, to which she was originally drawn through her relationship with Pitkin, who was general counsel of the organization in the early 1920s. Baldwin noted that Barn House members liked the simple life and rejected ideas of modernization. "I've heard some say it's the ultimate in snobbery to live this simple. Maybe it is. It can be attractive when you have the choice."[39] Baldwin, described by Samantha Barbas as "the guiding light of the civil liberties movement and one of the most influential figures of the postwar Left," dedicated his life to "working toward an ideal society."[40] It should be no surprise that he enjoyed the free lifestyle experienced at Barn House. Larry Hopkins, a classmate of Baldwin's at Harvard and a Barn House member, described Barn House as "the only successful communist society in the world."[41]

Kenyon invited a friend and client, Evelyn (Evie) Preston, to Barn House, and, although they both were married, Baldwin and Evie began a relationship. They divorced their respective spouses and Kenyon married the couple in 1936.[42] Baldwin remembered that Kenyon rented a studio apartment in Dell Brook, New Jersey, near the Baldwin home in Oakland, New Jersey, where she could see Evie on the weekends after driving out from the city. He wrote, "The studio was known for years as the Kenyon studio, and still out back of it I think are the graves of the cats Kenyon brought out from the city, little mounds with daffodils still blooming in the spring."[43] The Baldwins also owned a home in New York City and a summer home at Chilmark, Martha's Vineyard.[44] Their friendship flourished over the years.

As an aside, when Evie passed from cancer in 1962, Kenyon spoke at her memorial service. She said they discovered they had much in common when they met in the 1920s. Kenyon said it was a time where "[t]he social customs of decades were breaking up.... We knew our world was changing and we wanted to change too, we wanted to be useful and we wanted to use what we were quite sure we had lots of, namely brains. It was not so easy for girls to be brainy in those days." She described Evie as having a "longing to help the underdog," evidenced by her walking on picket lines and contributing funds to civil liberties groups. Kenyon also said Evie was a feminist, drawn to defending the rights of women to live their own lives and urging them to stretch their minds. She spoke about their time at Barn House, lying on the sand under the "hot summer sun" with "wave[s] curling now and then around our toes." The last time they spoke, by phone, Kenyon told Evie she would call once she returned from a trip. Evie told her not to forget, and Kenyon promised she wouldn't. Evie then said, "Good night. Sweet dreams." Evie passed away before Kenyon could call again. Recalling those days on the Chilmark cliffs and beach, "under blue sky and by bluer sea," she ended her tribute by saying, "I won't forget, Evie. Good night. Sweet dreams. Sweet friend."[45]

Kenyon often brought members of her family with her to Barn House in the summers. One of the members, Mary Hopkins, teased her about only coming to Chilmark if her family would be there.[46] Kenyon responded, "Don't you know by this time that I am blessed with a family that . . . insists upon eating out of my dish? All my life I have sought freedom and all my life in a short time I found my devoted family on the other side of my dish wagging all its tails and drinking as deeply as I. There must be some fatal charm about me."[47]

Kenyon's nephew, Stanwood, was one of the family members who would often stay at Barn House, eventually joining the group formally. Speaking of the anti-establishment environment there, he said, "We're all a little crazy here. At home, I'm a perfectly conventional fellow, but for some strange reason when I get here, something happens!"[48] The minutes of the annual meetings reflect the group's outlandishness. The associates once called a special meeting where it was unanimously agreed that if the unwashed continued to wash themselves on the Barn House beach, they would be shot on sight. To obtain support from the locals, Kenyon "was appointed a committee of one to make love to the islanders."[49]

But the associates could also be fractious. At the annual meeting in August 1939, Kenyon's brothers, Houston and Theodore, were appointed to a committee to consider the deed of trust and to make a report the next summer regarding whether inactive members had the authority to veto new members. When the brothers wrote to Kenyon in July 1940 to tell her about their appointment she was quite unhappy and said she believed that by failing to put her on the committee Stanley King intended to exclude her from deciding legal matters at Barn House. She wrote, "Stanley's only idea is to belittle and humiliate me as much as possible. . . . Stanley's specialty is turning families against themselves and we must outwit the old fox if we can."[50]

It appears King and Kenyon's relationship had broken down during the 1920s, and she minced no words in conveying her displeasure with him in her correspondence to her brothers. It is impossible to know, but one can speculate that her close relationship with Stanley's wife might have been to blame for the tension.

Theodore quickly wrote in response to this accusation, assuring her that "[y]ou and Chilmark mean so much to us, and Stanley King so little, that I am more than glad to accept any suggestion you have to make about the matter. . . . I would never want to see any change of this character made without your approval, as Chilmark will always seem to me to be a thing of yours and of your friends. I hope it may always remain so."[51] In her letter back, Kenyon pointed out that King had been trying to eliminate the Robinsons, who were original associates, from membership "and to act as though they no longer belonged."[52] There had been a disagreement between the Robinsons and King years before, and he refused to let it go. "My anger . . . was directed to the fact that Stanley put on the committee every lawyer except me—a direct affront of course and intended to be so."[53] King resigned as trustee, and from Chilmark Associates, in 1948.[54]

. . .

The summers continued to pass, and generations continued to congregate at Barn House, with children and grandchildren of the original associates regularly returning to the island. On August 9, 1969, Barn House's fiftieth anniversary was celebrated, starting at sunrise.[55] Kenyon attended the event in golden yellow, mingling "happily and zestfully" among the attendees.[56] Kenyon's love of Barn House was a critical part of who she was. The summers in Chilmark brought her friendship, love, and family, as well as heartbreak. Yet she never seemed to regret the time spent there. For more than fifty years, Kenyon entered the property near the blue mailbox and walked the sand, stones, and dunes of the Vineyard. She was deeply protective of Barn House.

In 1970, Kenyon led a fight to reclaim a tract of Martha's Vineyard called Noman's Land, an unoccupied small island just off the beach.[57] Noman's Land had originally been leased to the Navy for explosive ordnance target practice. The federal government bought the land in 1953 and the testing switched from explosives to smoke-emitting projectiles.[58] Periodically, visitors to Barn House would hear booms in the distance, the auditory result of Navy planes dropping bombs on Noman's Land.[59] Migratory birds, including ospreys, eagles, and peregrine falcons, were also observed stopping there, and Kenyon wanted to make it a bird sanctuary.[60] Deciding to stage a protest, she secured a small boat. At eighty-two years old, wearing a dress and hat, she had someone take her in the boat to the island, where she stood on the beach trying to wave off the planes as they came in. Eventually the land was returned to the birds as, beginning in 1970, parcels of the island came under partial management of the US Fish and Wildlife Service. The Navy transferred full ownership of Noman's Land to the service in 1998, and it is now a national wildlife refuge. However, it remains closed to the public due to the potential safety risks associated with unexploded ordnance devices.[61]

In a *Vineyard Gazette* article published in 1970, the Barn House collective was described as having begun as a commune, with approximately twenty-two families in its membership—all of whom were expected to work for a few hours each day and to eat together at joint meals. One guest described the associates as "the original hippies."[62] That same year, a party was held to celebrate Kenyon's fifty-second summer at the Vineyard. She was described as a liberating force in the women's movement, as well as someone who played a "fabulous game" of ping-pong. Kenyon was also labeled the "Mother Protectress of Barn [H]ouse."[63] A guest who had worked with Kenyon when she chaired the New York Americans for Democratic Action, known as a "liberal anti-Communist group," said Kenyon had ruled Barn House with an iron fist, while also describing her as having "great qualities of openness and wit. Phoniness cannot remain in the same room with her."[64]

One of the last letters Kenyon wrote about Martha's Vineyard was in August 1971. She was having breakfast on her terrace in Chelsea, watching ships like the *La Belle France* sail up the Hudson River and longing for the Vineyard and her old sailing boat, the *Anchovy*. That said, she still held New York City close to her heart, writing that it has "compensations even for Vineyard Islanders and I find it possible to love both my islands."[65] Whenever Kenyon spent time on Martha's Vineyard, she enjoyed walking the dunes and staring at the water. She thought that fall was the loveliest time of year on the island.[66] Kenyon proclaimed that she would have gone to the island throughout the year, if not for all the time she had to spend "grubbing in New York" for her living.[67]

Today, members still gather in the summer at Barn House, from June through Labor Day. Families flock back to stay in the coops, though the property is less primitive than it was in the early years. What started as a type of intellectual commune in 1919 has continued to hold a place in the lives of those who explored the land as children. Members and guests still help with the chores, mowing, painting, repairing stone walls, path clearing, and cleaning. Each summer a cook is hired. Meals are still eaten together in the barn, with the bells summoning members to the table. Children are now permitted into the barn to share meals with the adults. The coops, named after original members, are still standing, extending the legacies of those who established Barn House.

Member David Owen is the archivist of the Barn House group. He put together a centennial book about the first one hundred years of the collective. Flipping through its pages is like taking a walk through the twentieth century. Photos turn from black and white to color, and clothing and hairstyles change. Yet one thing remains consistent: the joy of the members and guests that leaps from the pages. The reader can sense the stress slipping away from the individuals in the photos, and almost hear their sighs of relief as they went about enjoying nature and each other's company. It is a unique place with a rich history, where salt air, blue sky, and acres of green grass continue to beckon members back, summer after summer. Kenyon and her cohorts would be proud of the continuation of Barn House. They created a collective that persisted.

. . .

Henry Beetle Hough described the waves breaking and crashing on the shores of Martha's Vineyard this way: "It is the past living in the present, a final assertiveness before the advent of sleep and peace."[68] It is an apt description as well for the relationship Kenyon shared with Wolcott (Patsy) Pitkin. Theirs was a passionate affair, rising to a breaking point, a high crescendo, before disastrously crashing. It would leave Kenyon haunted for years, her past desires for what could have been clinging tightly, like a lingering ghost.

Kenyon had started working for Pitkin after writing to him in November 1917 requesting employment advice. He had connected her with Colonel House and also employed her as a research assistant. In May 1918, he wrote to tell her that he had recommended her for a job in Washington, DC.[69] By that point, their relationship had advanced beyond a purely professional one, and this letter also suggested that, if she were to be in New York the next week, perhaps they could renew their "sporting arrangements."[70]

During the summer of 1918, Kenyon invited Pitkin to her Lakeville, Connecticut, home several times. Her father, Will, recorded his impressions after meeting Pitkin as follows: "He seems to be a man of gentle birth and pleasant manners, widely travelled and widely read, and modest and yet interesting in every way. He was easy to entertain and unpretentious. He seems to be quite unconventional, and indeed, I should say from all I can observe that the unconventional is perhaps his hobby."[71]

After the "mad" house party weekend at Martha's Vineyard, Pitkin wrote Kenyon saying how happy he was that she had liked the party, and that his friend Gertrude, Stanley King's wife, liked her. Pitkin told Kenyon that he had taken great pleasure in the fact that they had gotten along so well, as it provided a "widening, more valid background in friendship. Something like the pleasure in finding that we both enjoyed getting wet in the rain."[72]

Pitkin's mentioning of Gertrude Besse King in his letter to Kenyon was no accident. In fact, correspondence from this time indicates that Kenyon, Gertrude, and Pitkin were involved in a love triangle, or as they called it, a cooperative association. As Leigh Ann Wheeler writes in her book *How Sex Became a Civil Liberty*, "[I]n the spirit of honesty and openness popular among free love proponents of the day, Pitkin informed the women about the nature of his relationship with each of them" and hoped jealousy would not interfere with their ability to be in this cooperative relationship.[73] He did not need to worry, at least as far as Gertrude was concerned. Astonishingly, Gertrude would write letters to Kenyon that gave advice on how to be in a relationship with Pitkin while she was involved with him as well.

The triangle would prove difficult for both Pitkin and Kenyon, especially as it appears that Kenyon's feelings for Pitkin may have been stronger than his for her. His letters to her display behavior that is now described as gaslighting. In one letter, Pitkin wrote about his cycle of running away from Kenyon: "If I did love you, as you do me, it might be easier in some ways."[74] In a later letter, he complained that Kenyon wanted more of him than he could give "without doing violence to my own needs." He accused her of asking for too much, which, he claimed, prevented him from giving her anything. In particular, he told Kenyon that her neediness robbed him "of all sense of freedom and spontaneity."[75] He wrote that Kenyon would tell him one day that he did wonderful things for her, but the next day would say he was killing her: "You do that in office hours—*which* I've tried every way I know to tell you *I won't stand!*" He felt she was using her job at his law firm to keep tabs on him and "cramp" his sense of freedom and warned her that she hurt him deeply when she, as he characterized it, forced him to be impolite. Through the years, letters to Kenyon from both Pitkin and Gertrude discussed Pitkin's need, or demand, for freedom.

In a letter dated December 22, 1918, Pitkin wrote that he was glad Kenyon was finding Gertrude to be "gentle and unterrifying," and that he believed that "she is probably as much in need of you as you are of her." In this same letter, he speculated that their friendship may have been predestined. He also told Kenyon that she should no longer dodge Stanley King, and that she should have a "clean conscience" when it came to him, indicating that King was aware of the triangle forming between Pitkin, Gertrude, and Kenyon.[76] It is unclear, however, how much he did know and when. A search of King's archived papers did not provide any substantiating evidence.

The first summer at Barn House, Kenyon seemed to be suffering because of her feelings toward Pitkin. Natalie Haskell, one of the original Chilmark Associates, later revealed she had been aware that something was going on between the two of them. Natalie's spouse, Adam, must have also had a clue. Mystified, he asked his wife at one point why women were so attracted to Pitkin.[77] Because the close proximity of the coops made concealment impossible, Gertrude, Pitkin, and Kenyon seemed to make a deliberate choice to engage openly in this relationship, with friends, and Stanley King, having full knowledge.

Later that summer, Kenyon had a run-in with King, though it is unclear exactly why. Natalie recalled that "Stanley took it upon himself to have a confidential talk with [Kenyon, telling her,] 'Pull yourself together, make yourself agreeable or take the next boat out.'"[78] Natalie felt he had no business behaving like that, since they were all equal members of the collective.

In a 1920 letter to Kenyon, Gertrude mentioned that her husband had remarked on her feelings toward Kenyon, saying, "Seems to me, you and Dorothy are getting very chummy." Clearly, his observation was not off the mark, as Gertrude signed this letter: "[I]f thanks weren't so inadequate, I'd want to 'thank' you for letting me love you."[79] In another letter, Gertrude asked Kenyon to continue to be patient with her, saying that her love for Kenyon and her faith in a life for them ran deep. "Beyond and below and through the things that are in conflict between us, I reach out to you, and that you have let me find you is a blessedness that makes even the pain something that I wouldn't ask to have taken away. To think that you could bring me joy! You do."[80] Pitkin, meanwhile, had also been observing and contemplating the dynamic between the two women; "[Y]ou may find that you have no reason at all to be jealous of Gertrude," he wrote to Kenyon, "or that you've more reason than you thought."[81]

While Gertrude was writing affectionate correspondence to Kenyon, she was also coaching her about how to be more cooperative regarding their mutual feelings for Pitkin. In one letter, for example, Gertrude wrote that she loved Pitkin "the same way that I do my own soul."[82] Despite her own feelings for Pitkin, however, Gertrude let Kenyon know she was happy to be involved in their relationship. "That it is you instead of someone else is the sweetness, the unbelievable miracle of us, the continuing gentleness that is one of the great assets of my daily living."[83]

There is no mistaking that Gertrude and Kenyon had strong feelings for each other. Historian Susan Ware writes that this type of "intense female friendship" was socially acceptable at this period in history as a way for women to fulfill their personal life "without the constraints of marriage and heterosexual convention."[84] In a later letter to Kenyon, Gertrude wrote how it was "wonderful you've ever wanted me at all" and that she "honestly, consistently, uninterruptedly loved and guarded" Kenyon.[85] Their correspondence talked of them meeting in New York, at Kenyon's Lakeville home, and at Barn House. Gertrude expressed difficulty in dodging family commitments to get away to see Kenyon, but in one letter she discussed taking the midnight train to visit her, confessing that she had "a craving to see [Kenyon] and to know (or perhaps to feel) the richness and sweetness of—I suppose—just being with you."[86] In another letter, Gertrude settled for written correspondence as a substitute "for my arms and eyes and talk—just being there and willing to curse and laugh and fight and love with you."[87]

In an August 1920 letter, Gertrude described their situation as exquisite, patient, beautiful, and inspiring.[88] The next month, Gertrude cautioned Kenyon against pushing too hard with Pitkin, as this might cause him to cut off the relationship. Gertrude urged her to adapt to Pitkin's "wants and peace, his point of view" and to "live along as though you had what you wanted!"[89] In October 1920, Gertrude wrote of her own experience and the balance she had to strike to be in the relationship with Pitkin and Kenyon. "I play fair with you. If it involves taking care of your interest to the best of my ability with him, it has been my most punctilious concern." In this same letter, Gertrude assured her that their primary interests were not in conflict if, in fact, they both wanted Pitkin to have "maximum freedom and health and poised strength . . . the basis of our cooperation." She went on to speculate that their secondary interests probably clashed—referring specifically to the idea that one would win out over the other with Pitkin. Gertrude wanted the status quo to remain, and for the three of them to share each other, but observed that Kenyon clearly wanted that to change. "If the 'Lord' isn't in the status quo, let all the winds of Heaven blow it away. (This is not indifference, it is a worship of freedom, even *my own* freedom not to hold.) . . . There's no sense in fighting for what can't be won by weapons, can't be given away, or taken."[90] Later that October, Gertrude acknowledged that Kenyon was a "very all-or-nothing" type of person and warned her that such an attitude would end their cooperative relationship.[91] Gertrude observed that Kenyon was giving Pitkin the "impression of misunderstanding him. I don't think this would be necessary if you waited for *his* pace!"[92] She warned Kenyon not to force things with him, or ask him to analyze the relationship, as that was likely to irritate him, suggesting instead that Kenyon be patient so she could enjoy the richness of their situation.

The correspondence between Gertrude and Kenyon extended into 1921. In April of that year, one of Gertrude's letters had a reflective quality. Gertrude wrote that she had the same sense "that I had two years ago, that I will die without your ever having known how near I was. . . . What I do care about is that you should catch now and then, something of how much store I put by you, of how warm and sweet and precious you are to me. I love the you that I have struggled to reach. And time and again I retreat to the oasis of you and drink and drink."[93]

Meanwhile, Pitkin continued to feel pressured by his relationship with Kenyon. In August 1921, Pitkin wrote to her saying he needed a "rest from problems," and that he did not want her to come to Chilmark because he wanted a "breathing spell" to determine two things: what they had in common and if their relationship, such as it was, could be saved and built upon.[94] He wrote again on that same date, telling her that they each had lives to lead and needed freedom to know that nothing they did from moment to moment would make any difference in their relationship.[95] A few days later, he wrote again, saying he thought they wanted the same thing out of their association, even though he felt that, earlier in the summer, he had been constantly hurting her, which "didn't leave room for any freedom."[96] He characterized their liaison as having been "energy sapping and time wasting."[97]

This theme in their correspondence continued into the fall. In October 1921, Pitkin wrote to Kenyon stating once again that he was frustrated with her behavior. He said she made him feel like a failure, and that she seemed dissatisfied with their relationship. He wanted a sense of real freedom from Kenyon.[98] In response, in a rare letter kept by Kenyon in her records that she wrote, she told Pitkin that her problem with the relationship seemed to be a case of hope deferred, yet she kept returning to it with "fresh courage."[99]

Later, she wrote him again to tell him how much she wanted to have things the way he liked them, because that was the key to their relationship. This letter included her observation that, when he was happy, "everything gets radiant around me, and I want to shout and dance."[100] While acknowledging that she tended to be "too eager," she told him that "sometimes encouraging words from you keep me going for days and days," and closed the letter by telling him that "my arms are around you. They can't help it." She understood their relationship needed "no particular pressure of time and no sense of it being an occasion." She wrote she was just "bursting" to "laugh and play and let out all the happiness you fill me with."[101] It is unclear if she ever sent or showed these letters to Pitkin.

Although their association continued, Gertrude also began to express frustration, specifically with Kenyon's behavior toward Pitkin. In February 1922, Gertrude wrote Kenyon to say that she had seen Pitkin in New York and had given him what he wanted, "up to every spare minute he had."[102] At that point, she expressed her wish to stay out of Kenyon and Pitkin's relationship, while at the same time recognizing that she had helped them indirectly in the past. "You and I, my dear, are in our funny relation, able to weather a good deal, pretty deeply founded, and you have me, even when other things may seem to be slipping . . . You do lovely things, and I *want* to give you all sorts of leeway anyhow."[103] However, Gertrude's desire to distance herself from Kenyon and Pitkin's problems did not last, and she assumed a mediator role again in a later letter, including a warning that Pitkin was tired of Kenyon's problem with their triangular relationship.[104]

When Barn House opened for the 1922 summer, Gertrude urged Kenyon to stay away until she was ready "for this sort of life."[105] Pitkin also asked Kenyon to back off that summer. In August 1922, Pitkin wrote Kenyon wanting a return of their relationship to a lighter and less intense state, saying that he was incapable of anything else.[106] In a letter to Pitkin dated September 1922, Kenyon wrote that she tried to do things the way he liked, but confessed that "you're so much *me* that it's hard, it's *awfully* hard to keep steady and not act like a fool and bother you."[107] She begged him to give her "a little bit of an answer" about how he felt, assuring that if he did, he would never hear another word about all her letters that went unanswered. She also pleaded with him to tell her he was not too discouraged by her.[108] Again, it is unclear if she ever sent this letter to Pitkin.

Pitkin and Kenyon took a break from their relationship sometime during the fall of 1922. That November, Gertrude wrote a letter to Kenyon that mentioned this break, and that Pitkin seemed set on it. Gertrude still wanted to see Kenyon, writing that she loved Kenyon "brimmingly" and, as Gertrude put it, they both had "seen the same wonder and beauty."[109]

Pitkin also mentioned their break, calling it both "inevitable" and "constructive."[110] In another letter, he wrote that Kenyon's emotions were underfed and "when they have reached the point of *near*-starvation, they leap up and react upon anything in reach."[111] He also mentioned that he had talked to his law firm partner and they had decided that they needed to cut their finances, which meant they would not be able to keep Kenyon busy and could not afford to raise her salary. Accordingly, he recommended ending the "business experiment" on January 1, 1923. Kenyon had offered to stay on at Pitkin's firm without being paid, and Pitkin responded that, while he appreciated her offer, that would be impossible. He felt the end of the business relationship would "be a blessing" for them personally. "[T]here is a strain involved in a business relation between us as long as your emotions are starving that—I think—would prevent the business relation from ever being wholly satisfactory as a thing in itself."[112] He explained that he felt this would allow their relationship to expand in the long run.

Not only was Kenyon losing her lover, but she was also losing her job.

By the time January rolled around, Pitkin was again sending letters to Kenyon in which he discussed working on their relationship. In one, Pitkin explained that he knew she loved him, and that he wanted to give her what she wanted; however, what he could give, and what she had first loved about him, was something "very light."[113] Pitkin suggested, because he wanted her to give him "a chance to take the initiative," that she run away from him for a while. It is not clear if Kenyon got the message that Pitkin was sending with this letter, as only a month later she finalized her will, naming Pitkin the sole executor of her estate and devising all her property to him.[114]

In February 1923, Gertrude wrote Kenyon, telling her that in Kenyon she had found "a miracle" and that there was never "a red rose you ever sent that has failed to reach my heart."[115] As it turned out, this was the last letter Kenyon would receive from Gertrude. In April 1923, tragedy struck the King family. On April 7, Stanley King wrote a letter to Kenyon to give her the news that his six-year-old daughter, Margaret, had died the night before from appendicitis.[116] King told Kenyon that Gertrude did not know about Margaret's death, as she was seriously sick and in the hospital. Then, on April 11, King sent a telegram to Kenyon with four words: "Gertrude died last night."[117] It was assumed Gertrude passed from a brain tumor.[118] Gertrude and Margaret were buried together in a cemetery in Springfield, Massachusetts.[119]

Pitkin was distraught over Gertrude's death. In a letter to Kenyon, he wrote about how happy he had been to have been free with Gertrude, and that he wished he could have prolonged her life. He questioned whether Kenyon was able to behave like Gertrude had and "play freely and gaily with *all* the things dearest to us," and accused Kenyon of being too "detailed and microscopic."[120] Although correspondence between the two continued for several years, their relationship cooled over time.

In 1924, King published a posthumous volume of Gertrude's writings, *Alliances for the Mind*. Walter Lippmann wrote the foreword for the book, explaining that the essays published in it were written "in the midst of a busy life which seemed to her friends peculiarly gallant. [Gertrude] had, as one of them said, a cavalry temperament which made her wish to go fast and take a chance, to swim too far out in bad weather and drive too quickly on slippery roads, which made her in controversy a distressingly incisive and ironical adversary."[121] Two years later, King privately published a volume of Gertrude's poetry, *To My Dreams*.[122]

An undated note from Kenyon, written to herself, goes through the timeline of her relationship with Pitkin. She mentioned the beginning of feelings for him in 1918 and how she had become involved physically with him. She wrote about wanting "something active *from* him."[123] She wrote that the physical side must go, and she did not want to see him alone. She expressly indicated that she wanted to keep in touch with his mother, who was someone she had visited and written to throughout the years. Further, she wondered whether and how she could consult Pitkin about work and indicated that she would still like to see him if other people were around. She then wrote about a relationship with Elihu (Sec) Root Jr., writing, "Will it matter to him if Sec is my lover?"[124]

In the 1920s, Kenyon began a friendship with Sec Root, a lawyer whose father, Elihu Root, received the Nobel Peace Prize in 1912 and was also a former senator, secretary of state, and secretary of war.[125] Sec was a friend of Pitkin's who came to Chilmark as a guest.[126] Kenyon and Sec passed letters back and forth for several years. Their letters were not as passionate as those between Kenyon and Pitkin, the likely reason being that Sec was not single. He had married Alida Stryker on December 7, 1907.[127]

Their correspondence, which began in 1923, was both warm and intellectually stimulating. That December, they attended the Swedish ballet together, where they were seen by his "disapproving cousin and her mother."[128] In spite of this potential awkwardness, Sec said he had, nevertheless, enjoyed their time together. Their Chilmark friends appeared to have noticed some kind of relationship between them; as one explained it, "Dorothy wanted to experience everything, and Sec was glad to accommodate her."[129]

Sec was an artist, and he frequently sent sketches and drawings to Kenyon. In an August 1924 letter, Sec wrote about his feelings toward Kenyon.

> There are things, lots of things in the world that grow dull or ugly as one gets to know them well. . . . But there are other things, sometimes quite hard and perilous and forbidding things, that grow happy and beautiful as you grow to know them closely. You are one of those things, dear, honest, prickly friend. I think you try on purpose to show on the surface everything that is rough and terrifying about you and to keep deep in ambush what is generous and gentle and dear. I don't mean that the roughness is not part of the beauty of you. It is. If you weren't hard enough to tell and to be told the truth, if you were less independent, less ready to stand hard work and poverty for the sake of freedom and the right to tell whomsoever you please to go to the Devil, something would be gone from the beauty and clarity of that gentler side of you. I have known you a long time, Dorothy. I have argued law with you, quarreled with you, bootlegged with you, sailed with you. . . . The better I have grown to know you, the more I have found in you to admire and to love. . . . I think that you are, day by day, quietly, practically, by free choice and without conceit or dramatization a crusader in a great and very hard and lonely cause.[130]

Most of their correspondence was not so serious, however, and sometimes they engaged in joking and sarcasm. In an October 29, 1924, letter, Sec wrote: "Dear Dorothy, you are as good a friend as I ever had . . . you are many noble and endearing and admirable things but *sometimes* you talk like a bloody idiot."[131] Occasionally, Sec would write to Kenyon about his depressive spells, and in one letter told her about how he was "low in mind" and wished he could sit by a big fire with Kenyon and Pitkin.[132] Because Sec was often ill, letters sometimes included discussions of his medical issues. Kenyon seemed to welcome the fact that Sec saw her as a true confidante. She wrote him in December 1924 telling him the telephone was right by her bed in her apartment so they could chat any time he felt like it.[133]

Their correspondence continued into 1927, when Kenyon invited Sec up to her apartment when he was in town.[134] During this time, they wrote to each other about their mutual friends, including Stanley King, who had decided to remarry. Sec declared that he was glad King would be able to have a fresh start: "I believe in that. Life is a good deal like a campaign in the field, particularly as people get older. Casualties begin to mount up and the survivors ought to close their ranks and go on together."[135] In 1929, Kenyon wrote Sec asking if he wanted to come see the "lovely moon on the river."[136] He wrote back saying he wanted to come see her, regardless of whether they would be able to enjoy the view, as it would be good for his morale.[137] In a 1930 letter, Sec, Kenyon, and Pitkin made plans to celebrate Sec's birthday together.[138] As the decade went on, however, the letters and visits between these three friends became less frequent.

Although Kenyon saw less of Pitkin through the years, they continued to write to each other. He spent a lot of time in Europe, and she kept busy with her civic activities and legal practice. It was her Chilmark friends Valentine and Ethel Pulsifer who came to visit Kenyon in Chelsea to break the news that Pitkin had married Félicie M. Riehl, his mistress in Paris, on November 26, 1932. Even after all the years that had passed, this news shattered her. Kenyon went pale and broke down, weeping. Ethel expressed surprise at Kenyon's response, saying she had never seen someone cry the way Kenyon did that day. She understood that Kenyon had had strong feelings for Pitkin but she assumed Kenyon had moved on by that time. Given the amount of tears Kenyon shed, and her inability to stop crying, it was clear her feelings for Pitkin had remained close to the surface.[139] Natalie Haskell remembered when Pitkin returned from Paris with his French wife. She was in New York staying with Kenyon, and they went to make a call on Pitkin, who had been ill. "His wife received us politely, her gold tooth gleaming in the foreground . . . I never saw either of them again, he made it clear that he did not expect his old friends to include her in the future."[140] In June 1937 Kenyon revoked her prior will that specified Pitkin would be the sole beneficiary and drafted a new one that named Sec the executor of her estate and devised all her property to him.[141]

Kenyon was private about her romantic relationships, leading members of her family to speculate about them. Her nephew Edward Kenyon reported that Kenyon had a romance, if not a serious extramarital affair, with Sec, and that he wanted her to marry him but she turned him down. Edward clarified that Kenyon's reason for rejecting Sec was not that she did not like him, but "because she thought that . . . she would just be a wife and mother, and never have the career that she wanted if she married him. So she didn't. . . . From what I understand from Houston, that relationship went on for quite a while. She decided not to marry him although he wanted to marry her."[142]

Edward opined that Kenyon's sexual inclination was a heterosexual one, as she had several relationships with men during her life, and that the relationship with Sec was probably thought by her family to be her most serious.[143] When Sec passed away in 1967, Kenyon wrote to a member of Sec's family expressing her condolences. She said that she "was happy that when he came to die, he died at once and in the midst of all the things he loved to do most—except perhaps for sailing little boats. Maybe he had given up holding the tiller, although that is the way I like to remember him best."[144]

Kenyon's relationships with Pitkin and Sec suggest that she was attracted to unavailable men. Gertrude, too, was unavailable. Though Kenyon would go on to have other relationships, no one seemed to compare to Pitkin, and none of her later beaus made her want to commit to marriage. Pitkin remained an undercurrent throughout Kenyon's adulthood. In Pitkin she found a mentor, a lover, and a facilitator. He gave her career opportunities, though his motivations appear self-serving. Pitkin connected her with powerful people and introduced her to the ACLU. He held a major place in Kenyon's life, both personally and professionally. To a woman like Kenyon, who was wired to win, Pitkin's refusal to choose her must have been a crushing defeat.

FOUR

# *A Maverick and Public Servant*

## LAWYER AND JUDGE

> I don't like politics. I always pick the losing cause. I guess I'm crazy about the underdog. But I think I'm helping women by leading my kind of life.
>
> DOROTHY KENYON

BY 1924, AT AGE THIRTY-SIX, Kenyon had moved out of the family home and into an apartment on Beekman Place.[1] By the end of 1930 she had moved to 433 West 21st Street, in New York City's Chelsea neighborhood, where she would remain for the rest of her life. It was a one-bedroom apartment with a living room, dining room, kitchen, and den. Natural light streamed through tall windows, highlighting a fireplace. The apartment, which was often cluttered with papers and books, had a terrace with a view of the Hudson River. The building was newly built when she moved in, containing sixty-nine units and standing thirteen stories high.[2] Luckily, there was an elevator to take her the eleven floors up to her doorstep. Behind the building was a private courtyard for residents, and the front of the building faced a tree-lined street.

She established a law firm with Dorothy Straus in 1930, known as Straus & Kenyon, at 475 Fifth Avenue in New York City. It was a general practice firm, with a focus on tax matters, consumer causes, and labor issues. Straus, a Democratic activist, was chair of the New York League of Women Voters municipal affairs committee, and was an active member of several local and state committees advocating for the advancement of women.[3] They were known familiarly as the two Dorothys.[4] Straus and Kenyon started their law firm during the Great Depression, which began with the stock market crash in 1929 and continued through several banking crises in the 1930s. The banks struggled so much during this period that for a week in March 1933 all banking transactions were suspended due to a presidential proclamation to curb banking failures and stabilize the country's financial system. Millions of

Americans were unemployed, with nearly one-quarter of the workforce out of work. Families lost their homes and capitalism was in crisis. However, the law firm persevered during this time of financial upheaval, with several men working for the two Dorothys.[5]

While in private practice, Kenyon devoted significant effort to organizing cooperative leagues. Together with attorney Walter Frank she incorporated the Consumers Cooperative Services, starting with small cafeterias and grocery stores. The goal of cooperatives was to "bring about a more equitable distribution of wealth and a higher standard of living by decreasing the cost of consumer goods without impairing the buying power of labor."[6] In addition to being one of the original incorporators of the Consumers Cooperative Society, Kenyon was an officer on several cooperative boards, a legal advisor to many New York City cooperative housing projects, a delegate to the Cooperative Planning Committee for Metropolitan New York, counsel for the Cooperative League of the United States of America, and a member of the committee to draft model state laws on consumer cooperatives. Proud of her work on cooperatives, she made the following statement during World War II:

> When I found myself last month under the gruesome shadow of Hitler and fascism in Europe, I realized more poignantly than I ever had realized before the old truism that if we want to keep our freedom, and to enjoy the peace and plenty that everybody wants in this world, we must work harder than ever to cement the bonds that make for that peace and freedom, one of the most important of which is our own democratic cooperative technique. Not idealism alone, but hard-headed thinking should force us into great expansion of cooperative activity in this country and into close association with the cooperative movement abroad. Only thus can democracy survive. I am therefore prouder than ever to call myself one of the builders, in a small way, in this creative field.[7]

Kenyon believed cooperative housing provided protection for its members against speculative practices. Cooperative housing projects allowed the people who lived there to participate in the planning of the project, own shares in it, control its cost, and receive annual refunds after expenses.[8] In her neighborhood of Chelsea, Kenyon helped organize twenty-eight hundred families into cooperative living.[9] In fact, Kenyon's own apartment building was a cooperative enterprise, in which tenant-owners signed thirty-year leases.[10] This was a way for a tenant to put roots down in a place and establish ownership in their community, which was sometimes difficult to do in New York

City. Because cooperatives represented a relatively new area of law, it gave Kenyon an opportunity to help craft new rules. She was building a strong resume in this area of the law.

Kenyon found great satisfaction in her work, even if it was far from lucrative. Although Kenyon asserted her fierce independence, she relied on her family for financial support. Her father, Will, gave her an annual allowance well into her adulthood. Records show that she received $600 from him in 1906, and this amount increased over the years. By 1923, she was receiving $3,000 per year.[11] She would never be a wealthy woman, describing herself later in life as "practically penniless."[12] She was frugal, and most of her furniture was shabby and inherited. Her nephew Edward Kenyon described her as never caring about money, speculating that "most of her clients were non-paying clients."[13]

Will's death in 1933 forced Kenyon to reflect on how much he had supported her over the years. She was forty-five years of age, yet she felt untethered. Ultimately, his death reinforced her belief that being independent was the best way to survive.

> Suddenly I felt the world change. I was in another generation, not a little girl anymore, but a grown-up person at last. And it made me feel utterly different.... Suddenly you have to stand on your own two feet. Babyhood is over. Existentialism came into my life then and has never left me. Husband, children, friends, one can really never depend on anybody else but oneself in the long run. Even they are dependent on *you*.[14]

When Houston wrote to Kenyon about the disbursement of Will's estate, he told her that he wanted to subsidize her to, as he put it, equalize the "inequality of opportunity which you will no doubt ascribe to my wearing pants." This was in spite of the fact that her father had wanted to divide the estate's assets equally between his three children, after providing for his wife, Lestra. However, the size of the estate had decreased drastically because of the Great Depression, and Theodore and Houston received a larger inheritance than Kenyon because they were partners in the law firm that Will had established. As such, Houston wanted to send monthly payments to Kenyon to try to "effectuate Father's original purpose."[15] The monthly payments would continue through the rest of her life.

The money the brothers gave to Kenyon would come to be known as the "DK Trust." Edward Kenyon, a lawyer at Bourne & Noll in Summit, New Jersey, and one of Theodore's sons, eventually became the trustee of the DK

Trust and, in this capacity, sent monthly payments to Kenyon.[16] There were also payments made to her outside the trust; for example, Houston sent Kenyon money for her cook and carfare.[17] Edward spoke of how much Kenyon relied on her brothers to support her, particularly in her later years. "I doubt Dorothy ever bought anything. Houston and my father subsidized her a lot . . . and she lived kind of hand to mouth. . . . I think she had some tough years when there wasn't enough money to pay the bills. And my father and uncle made sure that Dorothy stayed above water."[18]

Her familial support, educational opportunities, and connection to high-ranking officials in her personal and professional networks provided her with access few individuals enjoyed. She was making strong networking connections in both the private and public sectors. Her wit, coupled with her intelligence, made her an attractive candidate for government appointments.

• • •

Fiorello H. La Guardia served in the US House of Representatives before winning election as New York City's mayor in 1934.[19] He served as mayor for three terms.[20] Though the mayor supported women's careers and appointed women to positions in city government, he failed to prioritize appointing women to top positions in his administration.[21] Even so, it was still progress for women and they supported him at the ballot box for his efforts.

In 1936, Kenyon was named first deputy commissioner of licenses in New York by Mayor La Guardia. Her friends believed she was appointed because of her "record as a valiant worker for so many progressive causes."[22] The only lawyer among the deputy commissioners, she earned $7,000 a year in the position.[23] As someone who had always been interested in the intersection of economics and government, she found the work suited her perfectly. Kenyon believed strongly in her position as deputy commissioner, writing that the Department of Licenses "touches intimately the lives of hundreds of thousands of citizens" in making sure businesses were operating to benefit the public interest.[24]

In her role, she helped regulate pool halls, pawn shops, employment agencies, laundry facilities, and theaters, inspected businesses to ensure their compliance with licensure requirements, and took care of the health and welfare of the city. Not only did she feel a deep responsibility to the area where she was born and raised, but participating in good government gave her the opportunity to give back and develop creative solutions. For an article in the *Smith College Alumnae Quarterly* in February 1937, Kenyon wrote about the process of affecting change: "It is so easy to damn with free and easy damnation when one is completely irresponsible. It is not so easy when one must take responsibility for the consequences. . . . Our Department, the entire city government, is experimenting; it is feeling its way cautiously after all the years of graft and indifference, using its power sparingly, but prepared to use it wherever it can be used for good."[25]

Kenyon became an in-demand public speaker, supported by the mayor who encouraged her to go out and make friends for him. She would go anywhere she was invited to speak—universities, women's associations, union meetings. In fact, she accepted speaking engagements all over the country and soon required speaking fees. In Kenyon's mind an educated public was a critical part of democracy. Through her speeches, she wanted to expand the arc of democracy as well as encourage others to take action to improve the status of women.

As deputy commissioner, she fought to have prostitutes treated through social rehabilitation rather than incarceration. Kenyon never deviated from her belief that prostitutes did not conduct their business in a vacuum. To punish the woman and not the male paying client was incongruous to her and she thought prostitution should be decriminalized.[26] Decades later, she wrote a letter to the editor of the *New York Times* reminding readers that prostitution was not a one-way street: "Without men, bless their warm little hearts . . . prostitution couldn't exist."[27]

Many progressives at the time disagreed on how government should respond to prostitution. Some thought it could be abolished if prostitutes were provided alternate economic means of survival, while others thought abolition was impossible and prostitution should be confined to specific locales. Lawyer Anna Moscowitz Kross, believing that prostitution was a social problem and not a criminal one, suggested prostitutes be diverted from criminal court to medical professionals who could provide treatment for venereal disease. Instead of a criminal sentence, a physician, psychiatrist, and lawyer would review the case and provide a treatment plan that would focus on rehabilitation.[28]

While deputy commissioner Kenyon headed up a committee to study how courts should handle the prosecution of prostitution. The committee recommended the opening of clinics where prostitutes could anonymously receive medical treatment for venereal disease. Kenyon recognized that prostitutes experienced educational, emotional, and economic hardships. "Instead of being tried and sentenced for a penal offense," she said, prostitutes "should be offered shelter, food, guidance and vocational training, and in this fashion be led to a better way of life."[29] However, Mayor La Guardia had campaigned as the man to clean up New York City. He wanted to restore good American morals to the community. Decriminalization of prostitution and the services Kenyon recommended directly contradicted his political platform.

Kenyon and the mayor disagreed on another matter as well. At the time, burlesque was a type of variety theater that used sexual innuendo. Once considered entertainment for the working-class population, burlesque had been embraced by a new group—middle-class New Yorkers.[30] Burlesque replaced the expensive Broadway shows, taking advantage of darkened theaters that could not draw audience members because of the financial strain from the Great Depression. As burlesque expanded to more theaters, opponents started putting pressure on the licensing commissioners to deny renewal licenses. This was a new strategy as opposed to license revocation. The courts had previously said licensing commissioners could only revoke or suspend a theater's licensing "if municipal officials had first obtained a conviction on obscenity charges."[31] Thus, without a criminal prosecution, the licensing commissioner could only suspend the licenses at the end of the licensing term.

As Mayor La Guardia launched his reelection campaign in 1937, an anti-burlesque campaign by religious organizations, including the Catholic church, was pressuring him to end burlesque altogether.[32] The mayor abhorred the theaters, calling burlesque "commercialized filth," and blamed burlesque for a rise in sex crimes. He asked Kenyon to investigate the city's burlesque establishments with the intention that she recommend their closure. She went to the theaters, taking with her a male companion.

In her report to the mayor, she described the shows as vaudeville with a comedian, skits, chorus girls, and strip-act girls. She wrote that a few of the girls were "quite surprisingly lovely," though most were not. As the evening progressed, "the skits get rougher and the strip-act girls better looking and more seductive." She wrote that the Department of Licenses rule about covering the breasts "was almost universally ignored," but the rule for torso covering was somewhat observed by the dancing girls using a piece of satin fabric that called more attention to the groin area than had they been completely naked. Kenyon found this to be a "lesson in the futility of rules which can be obeyed with literal exactness and yet achieve almost exactly the opposite results from the one intended."[33]

Kenyon was interested in the motivations of the audience members, describing them like so:

> There in those hot dirty theatres, in that stale smoke filled air, all around me were crowds of old men, young men, boys in their teens, gaping, snickering, guffawing, racing down the aisles to grab a front seat the instant anybody got up out of one, all of them personally participating in the show to an extent that you never see in the "legitimate" theatre, the whole thing a horrible commentary on our civilization and the way it starves people of beauty and decent sex expression. As I looked around at the audience it seemed to me it was full of my licensees. There were the ice-men, the truck-drivers, the laundry agents, the pool parlor and pawn shop operators, the automobile salesmen, the stand keepers that I licensed in the daytime. Here was where they went nights. All the little people of the city, drab men with drab wives at home, here they came for the kind of release from drab lives that a fairy story or a moving picture of Hollywood life is supposed to give. . . . I only know that the burlesque is not beautiful, it cheapens sex, and it seems on that account a real source of danger to the adolescents who flock to it.[34]

Kenyon's major worry was not with the welfare of the performers or the adults who came to the shows, but with the teenage boys in attendance. She hoped they would "grow up into a better civilization than ours."[35] Concerned that the law allowed boys ages sixteen and up to attend the shows, she recommended raising the age of entry to eighteen. Kenyon also recommended a rule change that did not allow women to be on stage with "breasts or the lower part of the torso uncovered, or so thinly covered or draped as to appear uncovered." She pointed out that their department could not revoke a license until a conviction for obscenity was obtained, so they had to wait for law enforcement to act. She wrote of the danger of censorship and that it was not wise to allow one individual to define obscenity, as they could use that power in a discriminatory, arbitrary, or even corrupt fashion. Instead of the department issuing more rules that would not be followed, Kenyon recommended letting law enforcement lead the way by filing charges of obscenity for individual theaters. If convicted, the license commissioner after a hearing could determine what to do with the theater's licenses. She believed that was the best way to ensure fair play and due process. Kenyon recommended that New York's burlesque theaters remain open, later characterizing them as "the only form of beauty in the lives of ice-men and messenger boys."[36] After Kenyon submitted her report, the mayor ignored her recommendations.

Facing threats of shutdowns, burlesque theaters continued to hold shows, with a total of fourteen theaters in operation. City officials were able to convict two employees of Harlem's New Gotham Theatre on obscenity charges, allowing the license commissioner to revoke its license.[37] Other theater licenses were slated for renewal on May 1, 1937, and they were denied. Additionally, Mayor La Guardia banned the use of the term "burlesque" in any theatrical advertising.[38] All fourteen theaters, which combined had once attracted three hundred thousand patrons each week, were closed.[39]

Kenyon was a founding member of the National Council on Freedom from Censorship, so she had strong reservations about the mayor's actions in restricting the burlesque theaters' expression. As a result, she felt she could not remain in La Guardia's administration. Her anti-censorship stance was not uncommon for women coming of age during the Progressive Era. Liberal activists believed government censorship was repressive and ineffective. The Women's City Club, of which Kenyon was a member, railed against censorship, denouncing book bans, condemning the revocation of burlesque licenses, and demanding the repeal of state movie censorship.[40] Although she was not surprised by the mayor's order to abolish the burlesque theaters, it spurred Kenyon to submit her resignation.

Mayor La Guardia had a reputation for being colorful and aggressive. Biographer Alyn Brodsky described him as "a man to whom being disagreed with was an alien concept; a man who could devastate verbally (and at times threaten physically) a foe."[41] Even so, Mayor La Guardia did not hold a grudge against Kenyon. He enjoyed their easy banter, and they seemed to have a good relationship. Remarking near the end of her life on her resignation, Kenyon remembered the conversation she had with the mayor on the subject. "Mayor La Guardia said, 'Oh, Dorothy, everybody in the telephone book wants the job and here you are walking out on me.' And I said, 'Fiorello, you know, the truth is I love you, and I just have an idea you're a pretty tough boss and I think . . . I'm gonna keep on loving you a little longer if I don't work for you.'"[42] After resigning as deputy commissioner, she returned to practice at Straus & Kenyon with the goal of balancing her law firm obligations and her desire for public service.

• • •

Though every state bar was open to women lawyers by 1920, many local bar associations excluded women from membership. One of the arguments against allowing women into the New York City Bar Association was that there were not enough toilets in the association's headquarters, so additional plumbing facilities would have to be built.[43] Another cited obstacle was that the organization's constitution used the pronoun "he" regarding membership.[44] Women lawyers missed out on some key benefits due to their exclusion. For example, the association's clubhouse had one of the best law libraries in the city, but it was only open to women one day a year.[45]

In the early 1930s, the association, comprising more than one hundred male lawyers, considered lifting the ban against women members but ultimately decided against it. In response, Kenyon commented: "We can only regard the stand of the die-hards in their last refuge of the male as ridiculous. The fight has only begun."[46] As with most things in her life, Kenyon would not give up on what she wanted. Call it stubbornness, resilience, or incredible patience—she was going to keep fighting to be in the room with the ones making the important decisions in her profession. Kenyon would go on to say the record of the association's exclusion of women was "almost too painful to describe."[47]

Kenyon and Straus found an early champion in Charles Culp (C. C.) Burlingham, a past president of the association, who wanted them to be among the first group of women members of the New York City Bar Association.[48] Burlingham and Sec Root drafted a petition that included both Dorothys' names for admission to the association. Their names, placed at the top of the list, remained on a blackboard at the association for an entire year, indicating how slowly the association was making progress on the issue. Finally in 1937, the ban on women as members, in force for sixty-eight years, was lifted thanks to a new interpretation of the organization's constitution. Specifically, it was deemed that the word "he" could also mean "she." Twelve women, including Kenyon and Straus, were in the first group to be admitted, which also included Susan Brandeis, daughter of Associate Supreme Court Justice Louis D. Brandeis.[49] Another prominent lawyer in the twelve was Florence Perlow Shientag, who began her career as a law secretary for Mayor La Guardia and who would be the first woman appointed as a federal prosecutor in New York.[50]

Kenyon subsequently obtained admission to practice before other courts as well. Her law partner, Dorothy Straus, was one of those who petitioned for Kenyon's admission to practice before the US Supreme Court in an application dated January 14, 1938. The other was Sec Root. Both practiced in the State of New York, were themselves members of the bar of the US Supreme

Court and moved for Kenyon's admission due to her upstanding personal and professional character.[51] Her reputation in the legal community was stellar. In an article published in the *New York Times* on January 29, 1938, Kenyon was described as one of the "best known women lawyers in the country."[52]

Because of her legal acumen and her post–World War I work experience, Kenyon was appointed by the League of Nations to sit on a committee tasked with studying the legal status of women in other countries.[53] The committee's purpose was fact finding. Because Kenyon believed that discrimination was such an important social issue, she was especially eager to examine the civil rights of women across the globe.

Kenyon was excited about the group's task, but she was troubled by the fact that she was the only woman on the committee. She said it was "incredible that only one woman should be named on a body concerned primarily with matters of interest to women throughout the world. It is like going back to the dark ages and feudalism, when women were considered as chattels—something I thought we had gotten away from."[54] She thought it critical for women to gain admission to professional careers, stating that professional women had "to be twice as good as a man to achieve the slightest recognition.... They are relegated to the most menial of positions, are given the lowest of salaries, and pull the wage scales down. That is true here; it is true abroad."[55] Although the committee was beginning to make strides in the areas of public law and voting rights, it was unfortunately derailed by events leading up to World War II.

Meanwhile, the fact that she had resigned from Mayor La Guardia's administration did not mean he ceased to hold Kenyon in high esteem. On January 21, 1939, he appointed her to serve as a justice of the Municipal Court, Third District, Borough of Manhattan. The seat had been vacated as the previous judge, Benedict F. Dineen, had been elected to the New York Supreme Court.[56] Kenyon thus became one of the first female judges to serve on the bench of the New York City courts.[57] At the time of her appointment, she was the only woman judge in Manhattan.[58] As a judge, she received an annual salary of $10,840.[59]

Initially, the mayor had offered her positions in the Magistrate and Domestic Relations courts, but she rejected both—the Magistrate judgeship because she viewed it as the court of lost hopes, dealing as it did with petty criminal offenses, and the Domestic Relations Court judgeship because "it smelled of women and children, and that was social work."[60] Kenyon's comment indicates internalized misogyny, which is sometimes found in her body of writings. She tended to use this strategy to curry favor with men in male-dominated organizations. She also struggled with the label of "feminist" while espousing the very ideals of feminism.

Even though Kenyon did not desire a Domestic Relations judicial position, she believed in that court's benefit to the community, stating that it provided a "magnificent opportunity for creative thinking on the part of socially minded lawyers" in developing solutions for families in crisis.[61] Mayor La Guardia would soon make news filling the position she had declined. On July 22, 1939, he appointed Jane Bolin to the Domestic Relations Court, which itself was a recent initiative, having been established in 1933.[62] Bolin had attended Yale Law School, the only Black person in her class and one of only three women students. Classmates, unhappy that she was there, allowed doors to hit her in the face as she entered or left classrooms. Some faculty refused to acknowledge her presence. Despite this discrimination, Bolin was the first Black woman to graduate from Yale Law School, in 1931. Her appointment to the Domestic Relations Court made her the first Black woman to sit on the bench in the United States.[63] She served in that position for almost four decades, being reappointed by three mayors.

Kenyon's court was known as the "Poor Man's Court," as the cases heard in it generally involved less than $1,000 in damages.[64] The smallest lawsuit she considered was when a woman sued for a lost bundle of laundry calculated to be worth three dollars. Kenyon did not find the smaller claims frivolous, however, saying "those little claims often represent everything the litigant has."[65] While other courts might have been more prestigious, she believed her court was every bit as important. Not only did the Municipal Court touch the lives of citizens in a more intimate way than other courts, but it was also one of the busiest courts in New York City, trying three times as many cases annually as the trial court did.

> [T]he real reason we're important is because the cases mean so much to the people who come before us. Take the case of the WPA worker who, when everything he possessed was stolen out of his hall bedroom, sued his landlady for the enormous sum of $20. That $20, mind you, was the value of everything he possessed in the world. Or take the case of the young boy who paddled out in a rented canoe into the middle of Jamaica Bay to play his new $10.00 portable radio and the canoe was swamped and the radio ruined by the wash from a careless speedboat. That boy brought his radio into court and played it to me, and wept when he listened to its squeaky sound. Now those seem like small

> cases perhaps, but if you were the WPA worker who had lost everything he possessed, or the boy whose radio, the pride of his life, was ruined, you would think it was worth bothering about.[66]

Kenyon spoke about the importance of women being in the courtroom. New York had passed its law permitting women to sit on juries in 1937, so the juries in her courtroom now included women.[67] Kenyon encouraged housewives to look beyond their immediate families, encouraging them to "interest themselves in public affairs, in legislation that affects their homes. By doing so they can exert an effective influence on the forces that make our society what it is. We women have power nowadays. Let's use it."[68] As a judge, she married couples, yet she modified the vows to omit the word "obey" in the ceremony, saying she did not want to ask that of the bride.[69]

She believed women needed to awaken to the role they could and should play in maintaining democracy. At a dinner held in her honor in 1939, she remarked, "The emancipation of women is linked up to democracy."[70] To a local paper, Kenyon explained her belief that "women are natural democrats. As they acquire a world viewpoint, they will see that democracy is the only hope for preserving their homes and the lives of their loved ones. Women should be leaders in the fight for democracy, and as they pull together, they will be."[71] She insisted that women must use their right to vote, saying, "We as women have the power of the vote to unlock the door to freedom, and apathy is the greatest barrier that exists. If we are not participating in government, it is our own fault. The door is open, and we can, if we wish, cross the threshold."[72]

In a 1944 article titled "Women as Citizens," Kenyon reminded women of their responsibility to vote. At the state level, she encouraged women to support reforms addressing education, child labor, equal pay for men and women, and proper care for children of working mothers.[73] As World War II continued to rage, she also advocated for the inclusion of women in military registration. She proposed the addition of at least one woman on every local draft board throughout the United States and advocated for the appointment of women to high posts in the departments of State and Defense.[74] Kenyon knew, of course, that the proposition of women replacing men in the workplace was a heavy lift. Giving the right to vote to women was one thing, but direct competition with men for employment was another thing entirely.

Kenyon would encourage women to participate in democracy throughout her life. Even in her later years she wanted to see more women in legislative office, telling them, "Run for office. You have nothing to lose but your chains (and a bit of cash)."[75] In a 1968 letter to the editor of the *New York Times*, she advocated for more women on the bench, at all levels of courts: "We know that women can be crackerjack lawyers (there are many to prove the point) and are equally capable of making splendid judges, certainly in terms of ability and temperament if not in experience due to lack of opportunities."[76] To her, it made sense for the judiciary to represent the diversity of the citizenry. Kenyon said it was essential to put "a flock of women on the Supreme Court to educate it a little."[77] Unfortunately, a woman justice would not make it onto the US Supreme Court in Kenyon's lifetime.

In the fall of 1939, in order to keep her appointed seat on the Municipal Court, Kenyon had to run for election, and she did so on the American Labor Party (ALP) ticket.[78] The ALP consisted of varied interests, including Socialists, trade activists, and union supporters.[79] Formally launched on July 16, 1936, the party was relatively new to the political scene.[80] In New York City at that time, the only real opposition to the ALP was the Democratic Party, "dominated by the Society of Tammany, a private fraternal society."[81] Kenyon's was one of the toughest Tammany districts in the city, which meant that she would "be battling old-line Democrats."[82] Yet when people expressed doubt to Mayor La Guardia about Kenyon's ability to win, he admonished them not to worry, that she could take care of herself. Kenyon campaigned vigorously on the fact that she was a child of the West Side and had spent her life trying to improve her community. C.C. Burlingham announced the formation of a nonpartisan city-wide lawyers committee to help elect Kenyon to the Municipal Court. Dorothy Straus, her former law partner, served on the committee, along with Sec Root.[83]

Although Kenyon worked hard campaigning, she was defeated handily by her opponent, George M. Carney, receiving 9,031 votes to Carney's 21,189. Democratic candidates swept the other Municipal Court vacancies as well.[84] Kenyon would later write that the turnout for her was larger than she expected thanks to her friends and supporters.[85]

Kenyon's brother Theodore wrote to his son Stanwood about the defeat. "Poor Dottsie got up at 5 a.m. and made the rounds of the 87 polling places during the day."[86] Theodore and his wife brought Kenyon supper at her apartment later that evening, but she was too tired and nervous to eat or even enjoy a cocktail—a true oddity. They took her to campaign headquarters for the election returns. At around 10 p.m. Kenyon conceded, wiring a message of congratulations to her opponent, and returned home exhausted and bitter, trying to maintain her dignity. Kenyon still had to finish the last few weeks of her judicial work and then find a new job. That said, the loss appeared not to have soured her on politics altogether, for that November she told a newspaper reporter that she was thinking of running for Congress.[87]

In later years, reflecting on her time as a judge, she acknowledged she had not been the most popular member of the judiciary, describing herself as "a varmint."[88] If a political leader tried to talk to her about an upcoming case, she would report the communication to the district attorney to avoid the appearance of impropriety. She upheld ethical boundaries, which those who wanted to exercise undue influence over the court did not take kindly. At that time, the city courts were riddled with corruption. A 1930 state investigation listed various instances of perjury and bribery, as well as incidents of police officers framing defendants.[89] Kenyon stayed above the fray, refusing any attempts to influence her judicial decision-making.

Interestingly, in November 1939, for an assignment in his freshman English class at Harvard, Stanwood wrote a short story about Kenyon's experience on election night. It is fascinating to read because, even though it is fictional (a note at the end states that it was based on facts), it contains many references to Kenyon's life and reveals how her family felt about her. The Municipal Court judge in the story is named Dorothy Frazier, described as a woman wearing red, with thick pageboy bangs framing a "tired forehead and stubborn brown eyes." The fictional Frazier was a prominent lawyer known for her interest in social reform, who lived in a simple apartment on West 21st Street. Stanwood wrote that Frazier had been among the first female jurors in New York, and she was "practical in her attitude towards women's rights and opposed vigorously those women who were urging an amendment to the Constitution which would put women on legal equality with men in all respects. She had worked long and hard for laws like the New York State Minimum Wage Law for Women and knew that any such amendment as was proposed would undo all the gains that had been made for women."[90]

Stanwood's father, Theodore, was depicted in the story as Fred, a successful patent attorney, who at one point looks around Frazier's apartment and thinks how sad it is that "poor Dot" never made the place a home. Both Fred and Dorothy had "inherited their father's individuality and reserve" and "their mother's sense of humor and deep interest in people." Fred was greatly devoted to his sister and acknowledged that as "a woman in a man's profession" she had a more difficult path than he did. The fictional Fred recognizes that her participation and leadership in causes that benefited the underdog were more important than taking the time to make a comfortable home. In the story's discussion of the election and Frazier's defeat, the words Theodore had written in his letter to Stanwood about the events appeared verbatim, including the observation that Frazier was "stubbornly disgusted with 'the whole filthy mess'" and wondered how "could the voters be so blind and stupid!"[91]

• • •

In 1940, with her service as a judge behind her, Kenyon set up a solo practice at 50 Broadway in New York City, overlooking Battery Park. She primarily handled estates, cooperatives, corporations, and constitutional matters. Due to her public speeches and writings, she became nationally known as an advocate for the causes she championed, including minimum wage laws, unemployment laws, legal protections for juveniles, housing improvements, and other social welfare interests. In a 1944 publication, Kenyon continued to encourage women to participate in civic activities. Acknowledging the importance of voting for national candidates, Kenyon cautioned women against neglecting state and local elections. "Take as much interest in it as in the broader question of world policy. For, after all, the world begins at home."[92] Kenyon encouraged voters to research where candidates stood on issues, and to support those who would vote in the best interests of all New York citizens.

Kenyon would only have to wait a few years for another high-profile public appointment. She was appointed by President Harry S. Truman on November 8, 1946, as the US delegate to the UN Commission on the Status of Women (CSW).[93] She was confirmed by the Senate on January 18, 1947.[94] The UN was brand new at this point, having been established in October 1945. Its charter advocated for fundamental freedoms for all, without distinction as to race, sex, language, or religion.[95] The CSW was one of nine commissions operating under the UN's Economic and Social Council.[96] Kenyon hoped to help shape the international community's approach to improving the rights of women.

The State Department's advisor to the CSW, John D. Tomlinson, referred to Kenyon as a lively addition to the commission, saying she tended to be cheerful and humorous. Her colleagues listened closely to her when she spoke, which led Tomlinson to believe she was the body's most respected member.[97] Her friend Roger Baldwin, a founder of the ACLU and consultant to the UN on human rights, described Kenyon as playing a critical part at the UN, in a way that "sparked the international expansion of women's rights."[98] On April 12, 1948, in appreciation for her efforts, Kenyon was named Woman of the Year by the Women's Trade Union League, an organization that included working-class women and elite women in its membership.[99] Its priorities were "democratic trade unionism and legislative reform."[100] The league advocated for eight-hour days for working women and the minimum wage, both foreign concepts at the time.[101]

During her three-year CSW term, Kenyon fought for greater female participation within the UN and led the effort for an international treaty that would establish equal rights for women. The CSW worked toward equal pay for equal work, educational opportunities, and the eradication of domestic violence across the globe.[102] In May 1949, she was pleased to report that the focus on voting rights for women had been successful in Chile and Belgium, where women had won the vote the year prior.[103] Additionally, the UN Educational, Scientific, and Cultural Organization (UNESCO) had appointed a woman to its staff to investigate educational opportunities for women, and the CSW would be studying discrimination in cooperation with it. Kenyon said one of the greatest truths the CSW had discovered was that women basically desired the same things across the globe regarding equality.

Kenyon noted that women all over the world received less pay for doing the same amount of work as men. She saw no rationale for this, other than that historically women had been denied financial compensation for their labor. As delegate, she brought a resolution asking for equal pay for equal work, the first of its kind to be introduced at the UN.[104] It received unanimous support from the countries serving on the commission. Kenyon also supported protective labor legislation for women, and she was opposed to the Equal Rights Amendment (ERA), believing the removal of protective laws would lead to exploitation of women workers.[105] Originally introduced in 1923, the ERA was, according to Kenyon, a clumsy device that would "wipe out the good laws as well as the unwise ones."[106]

As a result, the New Jersey Federation of Business and Professional Women adopted a resolution protesting Kenyon's position as UN delegate, saying she clearly opposed equal rights for women if she opposed the ERA.[107] Kenyon's advisor at the UN, Rachel Nason, addressed the attacks, denying any allegations that Kenyon opposed equality or had been inconsistent in her views.[108] Kenyon responded that anyone who could read English would be able to see from her record how passionately she had fought for sex equality. She cited many of her past activities, including encouraging the CSW to champion an Equal Nationality Treaty; driving the CSW's engagement with issues of equal pay, married women's property rights, and equal educational opportunities; and requesting that the UN and UNESCO conduct a study on discrimination. Ultimately, she was not removed from her position.

Though some progress had been made, Kenyon believed that some higher-ups saw the CSW as unimportant, and as a result it was provided insufficient resources. There were individuals in the State Department who wanted the CSW to fail, and Kenyon described in correspondence with friends her battles with those who did not appreciate the CSW's successes.[109] She saw the work as important and constructive and did not hide her feeling that it was being treated discourteously.[110]

At the conclusion of her term, Kenyon desperately wanted to be reappointed to the CSW. She called on her many contacts for support, including former first lady Eleanor Roosevelt, who wrote a letter to President Truman advocating on Kenyon's behalf. The American Association of University Women and the Committee on Women in World Affairs also wrote to President Truman and Secretary of State Dean Acheson endorsing Kenyon's continued service on the CSW.[111] Kenyon tried to have US Supreme Court Associate Justice Felix Frankfurter personally deliver a letter to Secretary Acheson requesting that she serve another term. She chose that back channel on the advice of her friend Molly Dewson, a political activist. Dewson had worked on the suffrage campaign before becoming research director for the National Consumers' League. Described by Susan Ware as "America's first female political boss," Dewson served as director of the Women's Division of the Democratic National Committee in 1936, which placed her in control of eighty thousand women and made her responsible for revitalizing the Democratic Party during that decade.[112] As it turned out, Dewson had a reason for suggesting that Kenyon attempt this means of self-advocacy: Dewson had used the same route successfully for herself. Justice Frankfurter had received many requests to pass letters to Secretary Acheson, and the only exception he ever made was for Dewson.

In declining to deliver a letter on behalf of Kenyon, Frankfurter said it would imply some sort of importance merely because it came from him. What he had done for Dewson, he told Kenyon, "merely shows what a weak character I have and that Molly has power to browbeat me."[113] He hoped she would understand, but he had to adhere to certain standards.

Kenyon wrote him back, saying she understood his position and that she had only asked based on Dewson's recommendation, calling him, somewhat condescendingly, "oh perfect judge."[114] In reality, Kenyon was angry at Justice Frankfurter for failing to deliver the letter, and her anger would only grow through the years, ultimately culminating in her calling Justice Frankfurter "the most blindly deluded male chauvinist of them all."[115] Eventually Kenyon sent a letter to Secretary Acheson herself, outlining the good she had done as a delegate. She highlighted a CSW meeting in Beirut, where the objective was to become acquainted with the problems of the Arab world firsthand and to develop plans for improving educational, political, and economic policies. "Human rights," she wrote,

> are one of my passionate preoccupations and, as a woman pioneer in the fields of law and the judiciary, I am keenly aware of the fact that women are human beings too and that the battle of women for equality and freedom is only a part of the larger battle for human rights generally. I am also deeply concerned in the building up of the United Nations and in its conversion into the strong instrument for peace, security and freedom that the world so desperately needs.[116]

While Kenyon was trying to stay on the committee, rounding up as much support as she could, others were lobbying against her. Florence L. C. Kitchelt, chair of the Connecticut Committee for the ERA, had previously aired her grievances against Kenyon in a *Washington Post* letter to the editor, protesting Kenyon's service on the CSW.[117] Kitchelt wrote President Truman and Secretary Acheson in strong opposition of Kenyon's reappointment as well, citing Kenyon's opposition to the ERA.[118] In her letter to Secretary Acheson, she alleged that Kenyon had been inconsistent during her time as delegate and flip-flopped in her beliefs about democracy and equality. She also cited a UN consultant's description of Kenyon as a "menace" to other commission members.

Ultimately, Kenyon and her friends were unsuccessful in lobbying for her reappointment. India Edwards, director of women's activities for the Democratic National Committee, carried major influence in political appointments of women. When asked by a newspaper reporter how she selected women for positions, Edwards said, "They are qualified—beyond argument." The reporter then offered a second qualifying factor: "they are 'good' Democrats, worth rewarding."[119] Kenyon, unfortunately, did not find herself in the latter camp. Instead, the appointment went to Olive Remington Goldman, Democratic candidate for Congress from her district in Illinois in both 1946 and 1948.[120] In response, Kenyon said she was not altogether surprised that President Truman appointed "a good little Democratic lame duck" as her replacement.[121] In a June 30, 1976, letter to Mildred Adams Kenyon, Kenyon's sister-in-law, India Edwards wrote that Kenyon served only one term because it was the policy of the Truman administration to rotate such appointments.[122]

In January 1950, President Truman wrote Kenyon a letter of appreciation for her service. He noted that her earlier service as an expert member of the League of Nations Committee on the Legal Status of Women had been an asset to their work. He also indicated that he was aware she had carried the work of the CSW at a sacrifice to her heavy law practice. He hoped they could continue to call on her for consultation "on the numerous technical problems which arise in working to achieve equality for women in all countries," and concluded by signing the letter: "Very sincerely yours, Harry Truman."[123] Kenyon wrote the briefest possible note in response: "Thank you very much for your kind letter of January 10. I am always happy to serve my country and the United Nations. Very sincerely yours, Dorothy Kenyon."[124]

Kenyon's disappointment at not being reappointed to the CSW was great. She hoped another public service opportunity would present itself, as she felt she had more to offer regarding the advancement of women. A junior senator from Wisconsin, however, had no intention of letting that happen.

FIVE

# *Named First*

## ACCUSED BY MCCARTHY

It is hard to have a witch-hunt without witches.

ELLEN SCHRECKER,
*Historian*

KENYON WAS IN HER LAW OFFICE on March 8, 1950. A few days before, she had given a rousing speech to the Youngstown chapter of the American Association of University Women in her role as its second vice president. In her remarks, she drew upon her work with the Commission on the Status of Women, asserting, "A nation without emancipated women doesn't have real democracy. . . . Show me a nation where women are treated as second-rate citizens and I'll show you a low type of civilization in that nation. When women are in the background, the nation is, too."[1] She was now back in her office, hard at work for her clients. The bells of Trinity Church were chiming in the distance.

Over two hundred miles away, in the crowded Senate caucus room in Washington, DC, Chairman Millard Tydings opened a hearing of the subcommittee of the Committee on Foreign Relations. The purpose of the Tydings subcommittee was to investigate charges of disloyalty within the State Department made by Senator Joseph R. McCarthy.

As the chimes rang in Chelsea, so did Kenyon's telephone. Her assistant answered, then interrupted Kenyon: "A reporter from Washington wants to speak to you. Says it's urgent."

"Tell him I'm in conference."

"He says it's a matter of life and death."

"Tell him my conference is too." As her meeting wrapped up, Kenyon picked up the phone. The reporter relayed that Senator McCarthy had begun reading lists of card-carrying Communist Party members in the State Department, and that Kenyon's name had been the first on the list. The reporter asked if she would like to comment.

"Of course. Who the heck is Senator McCarthy?"

"He's that new freshman senator from Wisconsin. Any comment?"

"Never heard of him. Tell him he's an unmitigated liar."[2]

The phone rang again after she hung up with the reporter. On the line was Kenyon's senator, Herbert Lehman. He apologized for not reaching her before the reporter. He said he was on the way to the Senate floor to refute the charges and advised her to demand a hearing. "Send a telegram to Senator Tydings, who will arrange a date right away. It's most important."[3] Kenyon hung up the phone, stunned into silence. However, the phone continued ringing. It would keep ringing until one in the morning.[4] She had suddenly been thrust into a club she did not want to join—those whom Senator Joseph McCarthy, to build his national visibility and career, identified as "reds."

• • •

Socialism, the idea of a utopian society where all property and land is collectively owned and there are no social classes, began in the nineteenth century as a response to rapid industrialization and the vast wealth differences between workers and industrialists.[5] The Bolshevik revolution of 1917, a violent overthrow resulting in the establishment of the Soviet Union and the rise of communism, led to the first Red Scare. In response, the Immigration Act of October 1918 allowed the government to deport people if they belonged to a revolutionary organization. Thousands of people were arrested across the United States, with some being beaten and held without due process.[6]

Communism continued to spread, however, and its popularity increased during the 1930s. It changed its image from a radical organization to one that formed partnerships with progressive groups to encourage social reform.[7] As the Communist Party made its way into labor union organizing, it became a substantial force on the left, recruiting working-class people along with intellectuals who desired an end to capitalism. However, an anti-communism wave was spreading, with politicians labeling some progressive groups "as agents of the Soviet Union."[8] This wave was so chilling that many individuals withdrew from any type of political activity.[9]

In 1938, the House Un-American Activities Committee (HUAC) was created. It was initially proposed by Martin Dies Jr., a Texas Democrat, to investigate "the extent, character, and object of un-American propaganda activities in the United States."[10] Hearings were held in which testimony entered the public record without support or verification. The HUAC declared 640 organizations, 438 newspapers, and 280 labor groups as potential communist fronts.[11] The ACLU was accused of having an affiliation with the Communist Party multiple times during the Dies hearings.

Historian and journalist Fred J. Cook describes this period in history as "a time of national paranoia in which the greatest power on earth expended its energies hunting for communists under every bed; in which millions of average Americans looked fearfully over their shoulders, wondering whether *they* would be tapped next to explain themselves before the grand inquisitors."[12] There was an "us versus them" mentality deepening across the nation, with politicians concerned that "aliens absorbed scarce jobs and relief funds."[13] Between 1939 and 1940, Congress considered over forty alien and sedition bills.[14] The Roosevelt administration modified policies to identify disloyal federal employees. It was established that fitness for government employment required the employee to be loyal in both acts and thoughts. In 1941, the Federal Bureau of Investigation (FBI) was tasked with investigating complaints of disloyal federal employees, an activity that intensified during the Truman administration.

During World War II, emergency federal agencies had been established to meet necessary requirements for the war effort, and some employees had not been properly screened because of exigent circumstances created by the war. Federal agencies soon merged and employees were transferred to the State Department. In 1945, a committee was formed to screen State Department employees and ensure their loyalty. Almost four thousand cases were reviewed over two years.[15] Americans at the time had become somewhat obsessed with domestic communism, which resulted in serious threats to individual civil liberties. The bottom line was that fear was spreading throughout the country that the communist influence would infiltrate and take over the government.

Following the war, the Senate Foreign Relations Committee observed that it had become "increasingly apparent that the Soviet Union did not contemplate a cooperative and friendly relation with democratic peoples."[16] The United States was dealing with increased hostility from the Soviet Union, as well as a pending war in Korea and the rise of communism in China.[17] The McCarran rider to the Department of State Appropriations Act of 1947, enacted by Congress on July 5, 1946, authorized the secretary of state to "terminate the employment of any officer or employee of the Department of State or of the Foreign Service of the United States" when necessary to secure the interests of the country.[18] On March 21, 1947, President Truman, via Executive Order 9835, established a loyalty program in which federal agencies could investigate and issue loyalty-related findings regarding employees of any department or agency of the executive branch.[19] President Truman's rationale for the executive order was "to protect the security of the Government and to safeguard the rights of its employees."[20] The order specified that the Civil Service Commission would facilitate the investigations; within a matter of months, however, the FBI had taken over those investigations.[21] President Truman authorized the attorney general to create a list of totalitarian, fascist, communist, subversive, and other organizations that advocated acts of force or violence. In 1947, the attorney general sent a list of ninety-three organizations to the loyalty review board, with names continuing to be added over subsequent years. As of November 1950, 197 organizations were on the attorney general's list.[22]

Within the State Department, the Division of Security administered its loyalty program, which included sending biographies and fingerprints of employees to the FBI. If the FBI had information on someone that indicated disloyalty, it conducted a full field investigation and reported its findings back to the State Department, whose loyalty board would review the reports and decide loyalty. If the individual's loyalty was doubted, they would be terminated, though the individual could appeal the decision.[23] From October 1, 1947, to March 1, 1950, the State Department loyalty board disposed of 246 loyalty cases, holding a total of thirty hearings.[24] The board found two employees to be security risks, and five employees resigned before their charges could be resolved. Those accused of being disloyal had a difficult time defending themselves, as the source of the information was usually not disclosed.[25]

The Republican Party leadership accused the Truman administration of knowingly allowing communists to be employed in important government positions and not preventing government secrets from falling into the hands of "alien agents and persons of questionable loyalty."[26] It was clear that the political climate of recent years, coupled with international events, had created space for propaganda and disinformation to be readily accepted. Americans were anxious about the Cold War, and many citizens supported attacks on the Truman administration as "vicarious revenge upon an 'Establishment' that had long kept them in their place."[27] Senator Joseph McCarthy identified this undercurrent and used it as an opening to enter the national stage. The little-known senator from Wisconsin would soon become a household name.

On February 9, 1950, McCarthy delivered a speech to the Ohio County Republican Women's Club at a Lincoln Day dinner in Wheeling, West Virginia. As he spoke, he held a piece of paper that he said contained a list of active members of the Communist Party who were working in the State Department. This assertion exploded across both the national and local media. If his charge was true, then the State Department was employing individuals who were spying on the federal government. At the time, the State Department had over fifteen thousand employees. It demanded that McCarthy produce the names so it could investigate.[28]

It is unclear today how many names were actually on McCarthy's list. Some reports said he used this phrase: "I have here in my hand a list of 205 that were known to the Secretary of State as being members of the Communist Party and who, nevertheless, are still working and shaping policy in the State Department."[29] James K. Whitaker, news editor of the local radio station in Wheeling, swore before a notary that he recorded and transcribed the speech, and McCarthy had used that exact number, 205.[30] McCarthy himself, however, told a radio station interviewer the next day that he had stated in his speech that he had fifty-seven names of "card-carrying members of the Communist Party"—a dramatic decrease overnight.[31] McCarthy inserted a version of his Wheeling speech into the *Congressional Record* on February 20, 1950, and that version indicates he had fifty-seven names.[32] His story continued to change, varying from individuals who were card-carrying communists to loyalty risks to being simply connected to communists.

Later, a reporter for the *Wheeling Intelligencer* said "there can be no doubt that Senator McCarthy did use the figure '205' in referring to his list of men in the State Department" who were members of the Communist Party.[33] However, when McCarthy was asked by another journalist about what was written on the paper he held in Wheeling, McCarthy replied with a grin, "An old laundry list."[34] No one seemed to know just what he had said, including McCarthy. A friend of his, journalist Frederick Woltman, recalled that McCarthy and his staff would often "wrack their brains for some lead as to what he said in that Wheeling speech."[35] Regardless of what was in fact written on that paper, the idea of it being the type of list McCarthy claimed it was created fear in the American people.

Secretary of State Dean Acheson would later write a book about his career at the State Department. He described McCarthy's Wheeling speech as the "rambling, ill-prepared result of his slovenly, lazy, and undisciplined habits with which we were soon to become familiar."[36] Acheson recognized the harm McCarthy was causing—and would continue to cause—in his crusade against communists in government. McCarthy, in turn, criticized Acheson's masculinity, saying the secretary's way of condemning communism was "with a lace handkerchief, a silk glove, and with a Harvard accent." McCarthy advocated for using force to combat communists, not "kid gloves or powder puffs."[37]

On February 20, 1950, McCarthy gave a speech on the Senate floor reiterating that he had fifty-seven names of individuals who were "either card-carrying members or certainly loyal to the Communist Party."[38] He also claimed that there were eighty-one employees at the State Department who were disloyal. Believing this was a partisan attack on the Truman administration, on February 22, 1950, the Democratic-controlled Senate adopted Resolution 231 authorizing a subcommittee to investigate McCarthy's claims.

Senator Millard Tydings, a Democrat who was known as "the conscience of the Senate," headed up the subcommittee, which included fellow Democrats Brian McMahon and Theodore F. Green and Republicans Henry Cabot Lodge Jr. and Bourke Hickenlooper.[39] The choice of Senator Tydings as chairman was meant to convey the seriousness of the investigation, as he had a reputation of honesty and efficiency.

Senator McCarthy would serve as the subcommittee's first witness. He had been under intense pressure since his speech in Wheeling to disclose the names in a public hearing. He was finally ready to comply with that request.

• • •

On the morning of March 8, 1950, McCarthy walked down the marble hallway toward the Senate caucus room where a public hearing was being held, the first of many to come before the Tydings subcommittee.[40] He had slept the night away in his office while his staff typed up his dictation and prepared his exhibits for the hearing.

McCarthy wrote that he carried "the picture of treason" in his briefcase from his office to the red-carpeted caucus room, hoping to alert Americans about the danger of communism and the failed foreign policy of the current administration.[41] The subcommittee members were seated behind a long table at the end of the room as McCarthy took his place at the microphone on the table facing them. Tydings, stock-still in a hand-tailored three-piece suit, faced McCarthy, who appeared rumpled. Press tables surrounded

McCarthy with recording devices and Klieg lights. McCarthy's testimony demonstrated the tactic he would employ throughout his time in the limelight: guilt by association. If someone was a member of a board or committee of which there might be one or more communist members, known or unknown, McCarthy would brand that person a communist through their association with that organization. The burden of proof would then fall on the individual accused to show that they were neither a Communist Party member nor a member of a subversive organization. If an individual had signed a petition or joined what they thought was a reputable group years before, no matter how weak those ties might have been or become, they were now at risk for being labeled a communist.

As the cameras rolled, McCarthy named Kenyon first, accusing her of belonging to twenty-eight communist-front organizations and stating that nine of the twenty-eight had been identified by the attorney general as subversive groups.[42] McCarthy's goal was to use Kenyon to embarrass the State Department, which, he further testified, had paid her $12,000 per year.[43] Kenyon was not employed by the State Department at that time or ever, although it had paid her a stipend when she was working with the UN Commission on the Status of Women.[44] McCarthy's identification of Kenyon was further flawed in that it failed to show how Kenyon had influenced policy during her service as a delegate. Kenyon's appointment to the CSW was honorific—which meant that she had not been granted access to foreign policy secrets. Both Kenyon and the State Department later acknowledged that she had never gone through the loyalty screening investigatory process due to the honorific nature of her appointment.[45]

When McCarthy first identified her, he asserted Kenyon had sponsored organizations that had been found to be subversive, like the Conference on Pan-American Democracy.[46] He presented a paid political advertisement that had run in the *New York Times* on October 9, 1944, as evidence of Kenyon's "deep-rooted" red activities. The advertisement was an open letter to New York governor Thomas E. Dewey asking the governor to issue a pardon for Morris Schappes, a faculty member at City College who was investigated for subversive activities and eventually fired along with other communist-leaning employees.[47] The ad had been signed by judges, state representatives, academics, artists, lawyers, and other professionals—including Kenyon, whose name stood alongside almost three hundred others; five hundred additional signatories went unnamed due to space constraints.[48] McCarthy used this ad to suggest Kenyon's guilt by association, saying, "The test of a real red Fascist or fellow traveler is a constant adherence to the rapidly shifting Communist Party line over a long period of years. Here again we have our prominent State Department official, Dorothy Kenyon, crying aloud in her anguish for a fellow red."[49]

An ironic sidenote is that Kenyon's name appears that day a second time on the same page of the *New York Times*, in an advertisement titled "Two Apologies." In it, the Women's Division of the New York National Citizens Political Action Committee discussed a luncheon honoring Eleanor Roosevelt, offering apologies to the thousands of women who could not attend due to space limitations at the Commodore Hotel ballroom. Kenyon was listed as a member of the committee in this advertisement, which also reminded readers to register to vote and to "[r]ing doorbells for democracy!"[50]

McCarthy, meanwhile, accused Kenyon of supporting "nefarious purposes" and participating in "un-American" work, and provided seventeen exhibits as evidence of her subversive activities.[51] Each time McCarthy cited an organization of which Kenyon was accused of being a member, Tydings insisted the dates of association should be compared to the dates when the organization was labeled subversive. It was later shown that several of the groups McCarthy alleged to be affiliated with communism were never declared subversive.[52]

In his testimony, McCarthy described the Communist Party as seeking "the aid of fellow Communists, fellow travelers, suckers and just plain dopes."[53] McCarthy went on to accuse US Ambassador at Large Philip C. Jessup as having an affinity for communism. He also testified that the wife of the secretary of state, Alice Stanley Acheson, was listed in the HUAC records as a sponsor of the Congress of American Women, which had been branded a subversive organization by the attorney general. He did not directly allege she was a communist, but he implied she had been duped into providing her support.[54]

His testimony was soon splashed across newspapers throughout the country. The *New York Post* wrote that McCarthy's attack on Kenyon showed he was neither a scholar nor a gentleman, as her record was "crowded with evidence of her devotion for the democratic cause."[55] Indeed, McCarthy failed to point out that while Kenyon was at the United Nations, she was acclaimed for her vocal opposition to the Soviet point of view.[56] It was not a secret that she had feuded with the Soviet delegate, Madame Popova. In a January 14, 1948, UN memo, it was noted that although Kenyon and Popova's relationship had improved, there was still friction.[57] Later that year, the bad blood between the two seemed to intensify. Kenyon criticized Popova's assertion that women in their country experienced equality with men, pointing out that they were poorly represented in government positions. She noted that women in the United States could at least run for office, while women in the Soviet Union had to be handpicked by the Communist Party. "Paper participation in government is too flimsy a foundation to advance the principles of democracy or of women's rights," she remarked.[58]

When the UN CSW traveled to Beirut in March 1949 for a meeting, a pool of reporters accompanied them to document the occasion. There, Kenyon criticized the Soviet Union's refusal to permit Soviet wives married to foreigners to live abroad with their spouses, describing the policy as "an outrageous limitation on the rights of women."[59] More than three hundred wives of US citizens, as well as sixty-five husbands, could not leave the Soviet Union, she stated. Madame Popova lashed out, saying that the United States discriminated against women too—just look at the fifteen states that prohibited interracial marriage.

Kenyon argued that the best way to defeat the Soviet Union was to support Europe economically while also promoting democracy.[60] One journalist wrote that Kenyon clearly defended the American way of life, often engaging in exchanges with the Soviet delegate about the importance of democracy.[61] Kenyon, writing later about the trip, explained that "where women are degraded, without freedom or a sense of civic responsibility, there everybody is degraded. Where women are free and equal, that is a free land."[62]

Benjamin Mandel, an HUAC staffer since 1939, was an ex-communist who helped design congressional investigations into individuals named by McCarthy. He had been recruited to the HUAC by J. B. Matthews, an ex-socialist and self-described communist fellow traveler. Matthews became an informant to the HUAC, and compiled a collection of left-wing letterheads and other documentation.[63] Mandel and Matthews worked together for years, doing research for the HUAC. The night before McCarthy named Kenyon, he and Matthews had stayed up until two in the morning preparing the remarks. They compiled a three-page list of organizations Kenyon had sponsored, boards of which she had been a member, and petitions she had signed. In the J. B. Matthews papers housed today at Duke University, attached to McCarthy's statement about Kenyon is a confidential page that clearly notes Kenyon's anti-communist viewpoint. "In 1949," it reads, "Dorothy Kenyon . . . signed a Workers Defense League (radical, anti-communist defense organization) statement to the United Nations protesting Soviet Union slave labor." Moreover, "[i]n the Congressional Record of May 23, 1947, pp. 2599–2600 is a statement by 87 American Liberals describing a true liberal, and an attack is made on the Communist Party of the United States as being controlled by a foreign power. Dorothy Kenyon is one of the 87."[64]

Kenyon was a poor first target, her anti-communist viewpoint being well documented both in her own correspondence and in media reports. The day after McCarthy named Kenyon, Mandel wrote to New York writer Benjamin Stolberg expressing frustration with McCarthy's first choice, writing that Kenyon had a clear history of fighting against communism. However, as first noted by Landon R. Y. Storrs, Mandel did not speak up on Kenyon's behalf as the charges continued.[65]

The State Department issued a statement that Kenyon was not an employee and that her UN appointment had terminated months earlier. On March 9, 1950, McCarthy responded with a supplementary statement, which was entered into the record:"Even though this individual may no longer be with the department, the case, in my opinion, is still extremely important in that it will shed considerable light on the workings of our loyalty program."[66]

McCarthy, of course, had reasons for naming Kenyon first. He wanted to draw attention to what he believed was an incompetent screening process at the State Department. Supporters of McCarthy argued that he made a sufficient case for "doubting the adequacy of the State Department's loyalty-security program," since it had not explored Kenyon's background.[67] However, as his opponents argued, given that her appointment was merely honorific and not employment per se, there was no reason for such an examination to have occurred.

Kenyon sent a telegram to Chairman Tydings on March 9 requesting an opportunity to appear before the Senate to "attack Senator McCarthy's outrageous and maliciously false charges."[68] Senator Tydings read her telegram before the subcommittee upon its receipt.[69] In a closed meeting, the subcommittee decided Kenyon would give her own testimony the following Tuesday, March 14, 1950, in the Senate caucus room.

Of course, Kenyon had been passionately speaking up in support of democracy for many years. In a 1939 letter to the state secretary of the American Labor Party she declared, "I am not a Communist or anything even remotely resembling one. I am just an old-fashioned believer in democracy who gets awfully weary sometimes of all its ructions but would never, never give it up."[70] When it came to fighting McCarthy's accusations, it was up to Kenyon to build her defense, and her past writings and speeches would help a great deal.

While serving as deputy commissioner of licenses in New York City she had given public speeches to many organizations, including some segments of the population with which she had not associated before. Regarding those speeches, Kenyon remembered that "there was terrible poverty and terrific unemployment everywhere. In these groups there were a great many poor immigrants and many of them were Communists." She had also appeared as a speaker for organizations, or supported advertisements, without fully vetting them. "I was probably reckless in lending my name," she later admitted. "We weren't taking the Communists very seriously in those days." In her law office, Kenyon and her supporters worked on reconstructing her records related to organizations she had joined or those to which she had lent her name in support. Described as "trying to gather up the forgotten strands of a lifetime," they were tasked with writing the most important speech of her life.[71]

Kenyon found an advantage in being first on McCarthy's list. Though she described herself as "running scared," as the first of the accused to respond she could set the direction for what would happen.[72] She counted herself lucky because she had a documented history that she could turn to, including copious files related to her public activities. Additionally, Senator Lehman, who had initially reached out to her to tell her the news, was a friend and she felt he had her back. Her brothers, sparing no expense, hired an attorney to represent her, Theodore Kiendl of Davis Polk Wardwell Sunderland & Kiendl. Kenyon would later describe him as her "fine Republican Wall Street lawyer."[73]

Organizations in which she had served sprung to her defense. The American Association of University Women issued a press release touting Kenyon's "devotion to democratic ideals. . . . In word and in deed, [Kenyon] has been a life-long champion of human rights and individual freedom—-a philosophy which is the direct antithesis of communism."[74] Kenyon had been a member of the ACLU national board since 1931, and that organization immediately came to her defense as well.[75] Roger Baldwin, executive director of the ACLU from 1920 to 1950, knew that Kenyon felt "kindly to any force on the left" and that she had been one of the few members who had opposed a ban on communist members of the ACLU board.

Because the ACLU had been accused of being a communist front during the Dies committee hearings, there was strong concern that the public would associate the organization with communism. An HUAC hearing was later held where Dies backed off his allegations, saying there was no evidence the ACLU had communist ties. Yet the ACLU was rattled and wanted to purge the board of any communist members. On March 4, 1940, the ACLU had asked Elizabeth Gurley Flynn to resign, a charter member who had served on the national board since 1920 and who joined the Communist Party in 1937. She refused, which led to her expulsion vote by the board.[76] Flynn called the incident an "unseemly farce," and her ouster caused long-lasting division among the board members.[77] Kenyon had opposed the dismissal of Flynn, later writing, "In a time of overwhelming tension and fear we set up a sort of loyalty oath test for ourselves."[78] Kenyon described the ACLU as succumbing to "a state of hysteria" and said that Flynn had always been forthcoming about her "Communist connections and convictions." Kenyon advocated for rescinding the resolution that expelled Flynn. In 1976, the ACLU board formally reversed the 1940 decision to expel Flynn, saying "it signaled one of the worst periods of the ACLU" and that the expulsion "contradicts our basic opposition to guilt by association."[79]

Although Roger Baldwin knew Kenyon had sympathies for those on the left, he never heard Kenyon commit herself to communism. Nor was she ever purged from the ACLU due to communist affiliation.[80] Rather, the ACLU joined Kenyon in urging McCarthy to repeat his charges against her outside of Congress, where he was not protected by congressional immunity and could face legal action. He did not accept that challenge. In the few days following his allegations, Kenyon made it clear that she was "unalterably opposed to the vicious disease of Communism and all its fronts."[81] She also called McCarthy a "lowdown worm," declaring that she was "mad enough to say he's a liar and can go to hell."[82]

Before the hearing, Kenyon wrote a letter to her family:

> I'm going on trial for my life before a Senate Sub-Committee on Tuesday. May I, therefore, leave this testament with you as my dying gasp? Subject—guilt by association. 1. I was born in a Republican family and have associated with them all my life. I am therefore a Republican. Guilty. 2. As soon as I got sense I began to associate with the Democrats. I am therefore a Democrat. Guilty. 3. I've always been awfully fond of Norman Thomas, even when I didn't agree with him (which was practically always). I am therefore a Socialist. Guilty. 4. I've heard Paul Robeson sing once at a concert (the nearest I ever got to the man). I am therefore a communist. Guilty. 5. I spent a month once with the Arabs and came home indoctrinated with the refugee's sufferings. I am

therefore anti-Israel. Guilty. 6. I have consorted all my life with Jews, who (next to the Scotch—me) are among our smartest people. I am therefore pro-Israel. Guilty. 7. I see a lot of women. I see even more men (every chance I get). I am therefore a woman or a man. Guilty. 8. I consort with the Girl Scouts (bless their hearts), along with such well-known communists as Helen Hayes and Mrs. Irving Berlin. I am therefore a scout or a girl. Guilty. 9. I care passionately for animals, have cats, am a member of the A.S.P.C.A., am troubled by the tortured little donkeys of North Africa and the whales of the North Atlantic (to whom the Norwegians et al. are less than kind). I am therefore an animal (not a bad idea). Guilty. 10. I am about to start a society for the restoration of sanity to certain Senators. I am therefore a Senator (not such a good idea). Guilty.[83]

On March 14, 1950, Kenyon, wearing a black dress and black-feathered hat, arrived in Washington, DC, her brothers by her side. She opened her remarks in the Senate caucus room by describing how she had felt when she was accused the week prior. Kenyon admitted to making some "impulsive remarks in unparliamentary language" when she first heard the allegations; however, she also expressed deep resentment at the "outrageous charges" that had been "broadcast over the entire nation without any notice or warning."[84] Kenyon vehemently denied being a communist, instead describing herself as an "independent, liberal democrat, devoted to and actively working for such causes as the improvement of the living and working conditions of labor and the preservation of civil liberties." According to the *Washington Daily News*, when Kenyon stated that "there wasn't a Communist bone in her body" the ladies in the Senate caucus room responded with loud applause that overtook the banging of the gavel.[85] Another account described Kenyon as "peppery," with a "clear voice that often rose in anger."[86]

Kenyon went through each of the allegations, testifying that once it became clear that she was affiliated with a subversive organization, she withdrew her support. For example, she had been active in the American Labor Party in New York, a third-party political movement dedicated to labor rights that began with liberal support. Kenyon fought against the ALP's increasingly communist-oriented leadership, but once she realized her efforts were failing, she quit the party.[87]

She introduced a letter she had written on June 15, 1949, to the National Council of American-Soviet Friendship, in which she asked that her name be removed as a sponsor because they were using it without her permission. In the letter she said that she had become a sponsor in 1943 or 1944, "when the Germans were at the gates of Stalingrad and the United States was deep in admiration of the great courage of the Russian people"; however, since that time she had observed the council become mere apologists for the Soviet government and she no longer supported the organization.[88] She further testified about her tense relationship with Madame Popova and how she had criticized Soviet slave labor camps in various writings, speeches, and meetings.[89] Based on this criticism, Maria Sharikova, assistant chair of the Moscow Soviet on the Rights of Women, was reported to have declared that Kenyon had slandered the Soviet people.[90]

As Kenyon concluded her prepared remarks, she reiterated her intolerance of dictatorship, cruelty, oppression, or slavery of any kind. "I submit that the record proves without question that I am a lover of democracy, of individual freedom and of human rights for everybody, a battler, perhaps a little bit too much of a battler sometimes, for the rights of the little fellow, the underdog, the fellow who gets forgotten or frightened or shunned because of unpopular views, but who is a human being just the same and entitled to be treated like one."[91] She testified that her faith in people, coupled with her impulse to fight, was her religion and lamented the fact that the false allegations had jeopardized, if not destroyed, her reputation. "The truth may never catch up with the lie but insofar as I can, I desire to regain as much of what I have lost as possible and I have faith that this subcommittee will see that justice is done."[92]

Senator Hickenlooper, the only Republican present on the panel that day, then questioned Kenyon, eventually informing her that he did not have "the least evidence, nor do I have any belief, that you are subversive in any way . . . [o]r disloyal."[93] He asked her whether any State Department official had questioned her about her membership with subversive organizations, to which she offered an emphatic "never."[94] His cross-examination was "prolonged but level in tone."[95] He told Kenyon that McCarthy had only meant to "suggest that your membership in organizations at least later termed subversive was a matter for concern so far as security risks go in the State Department." Kenyon responded that she was "trying to keep her temper," but McCarthy had charged her with "a great deal more than that."[96] She skillfully answered questions and clearly denied the allegations. Her three hours of testimony were later described as "blistering," as she disproved each charge McCarthy threw at her.[97]

At the closing of the questioning, Kenyon's counsel read into the record a letter signed by several prominent New York attorneys, among them a former secretary of war and a one-time presidential candidate, endorsing her loyalty and character. Kenyon's friend C. C. Burlingham circulated the letter to the press. McCarthy's charges were called "so fantastically false that here in New York where we all know Miss Kenyon they might well be ignored."[98] The letter writers described Kenyon as an "able and experienced lawyer" who had served New York City with distinction, earning her "a high reputation for her ability and her character." They closed by saying, "No citizen of New York is a more loyal American."[99]

And with that, the hearing ended. Kenyon took the 6 p.m. train back to New York, and for the next twelve hours she described herself as "dead to the world."[100]

McCarthy said he did not appear at Kenyon's hearing because he had no interest in questioning her. The subcommittee, however, had previously decided McCarthy would not be free to question her.[101] This clearly bothered him. He repeatedly sent requests to the Tydings committee members for permission to examine the witnesses that were giving testimony, but he was denied.[102] In a response to McCarthy on April 5, 1950, Chairman Tydings said: "You will recall that none of the persons charged with this very serious offense, has had opportunity to cross-examine you when you appeared as a witness against them. . . . Now that the accused persons have been denied the privilege of cross-examining you when you testified against them, it seems only fair that the same procedure be followed when they are testifying in their own behalf."[103]

• • •

The information in Kenyon's FBI file was declassified on October 10, 2000. The portion of the file about Kenyon's testimony, prepared by a special agent from the Washington field office, notes that Kenyon categorically denied all of McCarthy's allegations; did not know that some of the organizations of which she was a member were subversive, and had withdrawn from them upon finding out; and was a registered Democrat. It states that at the end of her testimony before the Senate "she was greeted by loud and spontaneous applause."[104]

The file indicates that the FBI had been investigating Kenyon prior to 1950. In May 1942, the War Department compiled a short report on Kenyon's history. Citing a reliable source, the report said that Kenyon was connected to the ACLU and had protested the speech of the mayor-elect of New York City, provided financial aid to "political prisoners, radical agitators, and workers in distress," and been involved in a Kentucky coal mine strike in 1932.[105] According to the file, the case was originated by the New York FBI office, which conducted a neighborhood investigation to determine "the subject's feelings at the present time toward the international situation, and her true feelings toward the Communistic cause." The agents were also tasked with developing a confidential informant so Kenyon's connections to the Communist Party could be determined. The report notes that Kenyon was "closely associated with movements for advancement of women in all fields of endeavor—labor, social, professional, etc.—along with Mrs. Carrie Chapman Catt, Fanny Hurst, and other prominent women crusaders." The report also references Confidential Informant N, who had reported that Kenyon was a member of a group "organized to aid the followers of Trotsky. This would indicate that subject is not a supporter of the Communist Party."[106] The American Committee for the Defense of Trotsky had been formed in 1937 to try to clear Leon Trotsky of charges made against him at the Moscow trials, a series of trials in the Soviet Union in 1936–38 alleging treasonous activities by Trotsky (in absentia: he had been exiled from the Soviet Union in 1929) and other defendants.[107] Kenyon and other prominent liberals had joined together to "safeguard Trotsky's right to asylum" and to also consider a libel suit against communist publications that were defaming him.[108]

The FBI security investigation on Kenyon was closed on April 3, 1944, concluding that it had failed to produce specific evidence that she was an active member of the Communist Party and that no further investigation was warranted.[109] This would not be the end of its investigatory reach into Kenyon's life, however.

In 1947, an office memorandum was sent to FBI director J. Edgar Hoover from Special Agent D. M. Ladd. Congressman Karl Mundt, a Republican and member of the HUAC, had called the FBI asking about Kenyon and whether the FBI had investigated her when she was appointed to the UN Commission on the Status of Women. Agent Ladd informed Mundt that the FBI had not received an inquiry from the State Department to conduct such an investigation and in any case did not investigate UN appointments. The agent further stated that Kenyon was associated "with various organizations and by reason thereof, [Ladd] would not have 'given her a clean bill of health.'"[110]

Because her position on the UN CSW was an honorific appointment, she did not have to undergo an initial loyalty investigation. But in the summer of 1948 Kenyon was required to complete a government loyalty form, which she did on July 14. The State Department loyalty board cleared Kenyon, allowing her to continue her work on that commission.[111] Although the State Department was satisfied with Kenyon's loyalty, the FBI would soon start another investigation into her activities.

In a letter dated March 21, 1949, the New York Field Division of the FBI was directed to conduct a full field loyalty investigation into Kenyon.[112] Bureau files indicated she had been connected with various organizations that were deemed un-American by the attorney general, including but not limited to the Washington Committee for Democratic Action, the American Committee for the Protection of the Foreign Born, and the American League for Peace and Democracy. According to the information collected and added to her FBI file, Kenyon was alleged to have been affiliated with thirteen organizations listed as either controlled or influenced by communists. There were also several reports showing that Kenyon had lent her name to statements or advertisements in support of individuals or organizations the FBI deemed subversive.

Correspondence was sent to Director Hoover with the findings of the field office's loyalty investigation, in which Kenyon was described as "probably one of the most active 'joiners' who has come to the attention of this office."[113] The investigation had turned up evidence that she had been a member of, or associated with, sixty-three organizations, eleven of which were cited as subversive by the attorney general, and twenty-three that were regarded as front organizations.[114] One of the latter organization types, for example, was the ALP, the political party Kenyon was affiliated with in 1937–1939 and in 1943–1946.[115] All that said, the file noted that neighbors, fellow employees, and associates reported that she was a joiner, but that they considered her loyal.

Once the full field investigation was completed, a summary dated February 15, 1950, was sent to Director Hoover. He also received a letter from the US Civil Service Commission stating that Kenyon had separated from federal service prior to a decision on loyalty, so they could not offer any help in the FBI investigation.[116]

An FBI office memorandum dated August 22, 1950, indicated that an informant, Steve A. Cardullo, a business agent for Seafarers International Union, claimed that Kenyon had spoken at a Workers Alliance event in New York. The Workers Alliance of America was a group of merged socialist and communist organizations. Cardullo told the FBI that Kenyon wore a red dress during the event and in her speech stated that "she was not wearing a red dress for nothing."[117] To him, that was proof she was a communist.

The FBI security investigation continued into 1951. A report states that Informant T-1, Louis F. Budenz, advised that Jack Stachel, a leader of the American Communist Party, had told Budenz that Kenyon was a communist.[118] However, the report states that six other informants, with their identities redacted, had advised that Kenyon was not a known member. Budenz had been one of the top members of the Communist Party and editor of the *Communist Daily Worker.* He ultimately renounced his membership and became a government informant. Budenz was a frequent witness during the Senate investigations and hearings. In the years after leaving the Communist Party, Budenz, by his own estimation, spent over three thousand hours helping the FBI.[119]

In 1952, Kenyon was the subject of a perjury investigation, which arose from her Senate testimony that she did not know Alger Hiss.[120] Hiss was a Harvard-educated lawyer who had studied under Felix Frankfurter and clerked for Justice Oliver Wendell Holmes Jr.[121] In 1944, he joined the State Department and personally delivered the UN charter to President Truman upon its creation. Hiss, however, was ultimately accused of being a communist, an accusation he denied. The FBI investigated him, which eventually led to his being charged with perjury. He was convicted in 1950 and served almost four years in federal prison at Lewisburg Penitentiary.[122] An FBI informant claimed to have been introduced to Hiss by Kenyon.[123] The government ultimately declined to prosecute Kenyon because there was no additional corroboration that Kenyon did, in fact, know Hiss.[124] Although Kenyon avoided prosecution, the impacts of the Senate hearing, as discussed in the next chapter, rippled throughout her life for years to come.

SIX

# *The Aftermath*

## MCCARTHYISM HASN'T LEFT US YET

> I prefer, if you must knock me down, to be on my feet—not my knees. It is a more natural posture for me.
>
> DOROTHY KENYON

REDBAITING, OR THE ATTACK on someone as a communist, benefited from a widespread rumor that feminism disguised communist ideology while also advocating for the destruction of the family unit. Attacks were coordinated to target individuals espousing feminist viewpoints.[1] As women organized for social reform, they found themselves under increasing attack. Loyalty investigators targeted prominent women in the 1940s and 1950s, including international affairs expert Esther Brunauer, economist Mary Dublin Keyserling, New Deal activist Caroline Ware, labor activist Esther Peterson, and lawyer Pauli Murray. Landon R. Y. Storrs writes in her book *The Second Red Scare and the Unmasking of the New Deal Left* that loyalty charges against women in government positions had antifeminist sources, and that "leftist" women were overrepresented among those facing federal employee loyalty cases. "Because the Communist Party theoretically supported women's equality," Storrs explains, investigators reasoned that feminists might well be Communists."[2] Although Kenyon was outspoken against communism, particularly involving the Soviet Union, she had also pushed vigorously for women's equality while on the UN Commission on the Status of Women. This painted a target on her back. Additionally, it was widely believed the Communist Party lured in wealthy women because they were prone to idealism and had "been exposed to college professors."[3]

Emotionally, Kenyon did not recover quickly from McCarthy's allegations, saying that the experience had been quite a shock to her system. Houston's wife, Mildred Adams Kenyon, was one of many who wrote to encourage Kenyon, urging her not to let McCarthy's attack have a lasting effect:

> Of course the attack was irritating, frightening and disgusting.... It would seem to me a serious tactical error, free from every point of view, to admit that McCarthy has inflicted any lasting injury at all. You can lambaste him up and down the country—or you can deny him even the solace of advertising him by mentioning him.... But to admit even to yourself that he inflicted any lasting hurt seems to me a confession of weakness which is not warranted. It would mean giving away part of the victory which you have won.... [D]on't let McCarthy have the satisfaction of knowing that he inflicted even a pin prick.[4]

Kenyon continued to write about the impact of the McCarthy episode years later. "Whether I realized it then or not, my whole life had changed in those few hours. And so would that of countless other innocent people soon to be caught in McCarthy's cruel sadistic game of hunting communists. Everyone caught up in it got smeared a bright red."[5]

After the Senate hearing, Kenyon wrote to her brother Houston with thanks for the family's support, acknowledging that it had been impossible to offer her appreciation at the time and it was still difficult to do so. "Things like that are too deep for words." She called it "a master stroke" for them to have hired Theodore Kiendl. "[I]t was awfully good for me. I even took their advice, which astonished Kiendl." She gave credit to Houston for making her remarks better, referencing a disagreement the two of them had had while preparing them. "You have to forgive me if, when I'm in the throes of composition, I'm not quite human. That statement was my life blood. It *had* to get out of my system, said by me in my own words, that Sunday morning—or I would have blown up. I'm sure you understand."[6]

An article in the *Chicago Sun-Times* declared it unlucky that McCarthy chose Kenyon for his opening case, as she had spent her life "battling for the rights of women and for social justice." According to the article, Kenyon was not afraid to "join like-minded persons to promote social and economic justice in the best American tradition," and the article noted that her valiant testimony would encourage others to "fight back with equal vigor and courage."[7] *Life* magazine described McCarthy as "blundering" in presenting his evidence against Kenyon, and judged that his case had backfired.[8]

McCarthy spoke of Kenyon before the Senate again on March 30, 1950, explaining why he had presented her case first: "[I]t was presented, not because Judge Kenyon herself was important but... to show just what being 'cleared by the loyalty board' meant.... Unfortunately, it happened to be the case of a lady." McCarthy specifically said he had not accused Kenyon of being a traitor, but merely pointed out that the loyalty board should have found out why she joined the suspect organizations "before giving her a clean bill of health."[9]

Kenyon had many supporters. Former First Lady Eleanor Roosevelt penned a newspaper column defending Kenyon, saying that any woman who had ever served on a committee with her would dismiss the accusation with a smile. "The only possible criticism of Dorothy Kenyon I can think of," wrote Mrs. Roosevelt, "would be that she hoped at times to accomplish more good things than I believe can be achieved all at one stroke."[10]

Another defender was Herbert Block, a cartoonist for the *Washington Post* who signed his work as Herblock. In March 1950, Block published a cartoon that showed senators pushing a Republican elephant toward a rickety tower of tar barrels; the top barrel was labeled "McCarthyism," and thus he unintentionally coined the term.[11] Block focused many cartoons on the HUAC through the years, including one for Kenyon's hearing. In it, McCarthy is crouched on the floor, hiding underneath coats in the Senate cloakroom. A man walks in reading a newspaper with the headline "Dorothy Kenyon Answers McCarthy Charges." McCarthy whispers to the man holding the newspaper, "Pst—is she gone yet?"[12] Kenyon hung the cartoon on her office wall, calling it "the greatest trophy" of her life.[13]

Decades later, Block wrote of the disregard given by congressional committees to the reputations of individuals they were accusing. "The end," he said, "justified the means. The purpose was not only to defeat but to destroy. And many reputable people in and out of government were ruined." Block went on: "But it was McCarthy, with his animal cunning and his instinct for publicity unfettered by any sense of morality or honesty, who personified the intellectual terrorism of the time." According to Block, McCarthy could not bring an end to communism abroad, so decided to "scapegoat and destroy people at home," finding in the process a lot of support from citizens who were angry about their lots in life and needed someone to blame.[14] Kenyon later wrote about the helplessness she felt, stating that "hundreds upon hundreds of innocent persons (famous or otherwise, quite indiscriminately, and mainly otherwise) were ruined, sometimes totally destroyed, body and soul, by the evil genius of this strange and immensely evil man."[15]

Letters of support poured into Kenyon's law office and home. Senator Lehman's letter applauded her for the "fine impression you made and how completely you answered the charges against you."[16] Attorney Stanley Kreutzer, of the law firm Kreutzer, Heller & Selman in New York City, noted, to his delight, that the McCarthy smear had "turned out to be a boomerang . . . to make prominent your decency, loyalty and integrity."[17]

Kenyon was not the only one who received letters about the affair. One of Kenyon's friends wrote to McCarthy on her behalf, saying she had known Kenyon to be a loyal citizen all her life. She reprimanded McCarthy for the accusations, noting the irreversible consequences of such an attack.[18] Anna Lord Strauss, president of the League of Women Voters, wrote to Senator Brian McMahon in support of Kenyon. In his response, he described Kenyon's testimony before the subcommittee as "a devastating reply to those who attempted to destroy her reputation and her character. Seldom in my experience in the Senate have I heard a more effective witness before a Congressional inquiry."[19]

Not all members of the league were supportive, however. A member of the New York City chapter withdrew her membership in an angry letter to the league's secretary, criticizing the organization for allowing someone so disloyal to America to be a member.[20] The president of the chapter replied via letter the same day, expressing her shock that anyone would believe the allegations against Kenyon, especially considering how well documented it was that Kenyon had fought against communistic ideas while serving on the UN CSW. She wrote that Kenyon had provided financial and moral support since the earliest years of the organization and was considered a valued member.[21]

Kenyon also received hate mail. A letter from California declared that McCarthy was justified in his charges against Kenyon, telling her to "go ahead and hang your head in shame, or better still hang that head by a rope. We hate people like you."[22] A correspondent from New Jersey wrote that, although they did not think she was a communist after the Senate hearing, they did conclude that she was foolish.[23] A letter from New York called Kenyon a traitor, a sellout, and declared she "should be hung for it."[24]

Not all press coverage was positive, either. A reporter who attended the Senate hearing described Kenyon as "a plump little lady . . . subdued in a slightly shrill way" and questioned what influence associating with communists might have had on her thinking. "If Miss Kenyon hasn't a communist bone in her body, as she protests," the reporter declared, "it would nevertheless have been better if she had remembered that a man, or a woman, is known by the company they keep."[25] Another reporter wrote that when "a person appears on a large number of Communist or Communist-front activities, the assumption must be that that person has made a voluntary choice to associate with such people."[26]

Meanwhile, Kenyon had surveillance concerns. For example, she received a confidential letter from Rachel Nason, her aide while Kenyon worked with the UN, warning her of telephone wiretaps. Nason also mentioned that she had collected many of Kenyon's past files from when she was with the CSW and had written analyses to show Kenyon's repeated views against communism.[27] Kenyon forwarded Nason's letter to her lawyer, Theodore Kiendl. He had previously advised her that the phones were probably tapped; this seemed to confirm the hunch. She also included her own note thanking him for his help and saying he was exactly what she needed. "Had you not been there I doubt whether I could have kept myself under control."[28] She told him not to spare any expense on his bill to her, and to not accept any payment from her brothers for the fees, as she would pay it.

Kiendl wrote back saying he was delighted to represent her in "a matter of such unusual interest," though someone remarked to him that "no one needed a lawyer less" than Kenyon did. Speaking on behalf of his partners at the law firm, he said they had decided that they did not want to charge Kenyon any legal fees. He said, however, if she insisted on paying as an "independent liberal Rooseveltian democrat," then the sum would be $500. They would not accept a penny more and would prefer to offer their representation free of charge. Kiendl seemed to have enjoyed his role in representing Kenyon, writing that he had never had a "more interesting assignment or a client more willing to accept my advice and counsel under the most trying conditions."[29]

. . .

In a letter to a friend, Kenyon said that she was considering filing a slander suit against McCarthy. Upon reflection, however, Kenyon had decided that she wanted a second opinion. "Libel and slander suits are not an adequate remedy, you know," Kenyon wrote. "The final result in the innocent person's favor is often wholly overlooked, whereas the charges themselves get a much wider spread than they would otherwise have." She went on: "There are times in one's life when obviously one must bring a libel suit. I do not believe, however, that this is the time in my life. Do you agree?"[30] Her friend agreed with the assessment not to file.[31] It was better to move on.

Though her friends and family encouraged her to put the allegations behind her, Kenyon found it difficult to leave the experience in the past. She made a critical error on April 7, 1950, by appearing on Lawrence Spivak's radio broadcast, *Meet the Press*. Kenyon's segment lasted just over twenty-seven minutes. For the duration of the broadcast, four panelists (William White from the *New York Times*, Lawrence Spivak from the *American Mercury*, Frank Waldrop from the *Washington Times*, and May Craig from the *Portland Press Herald*) bombarded Kenyon with questions regarding her loyalty. She responded in a feisty tone to many of the questions. At one point she was told to relax, to which she responded, "You think I can? Well, I distrust you more than ever after saying that."[32]

The moderator, Ernest Lindley, opened the show by describing Kenyon as "an active, aggressive figure in the civic affairs and politics of New York City . . . a joiner, a member of almost countless organizations, and a generous backer of many causes that bore a welfare label." He described her appearance before the Senate as a "counter attack [that] overwhelmed the mere men of the senate investigating committee." She was questioned about a statement she had made that Alger Hiss was a sacrifice to the hysteria created by the HUAC. She didn't recall using the word "sacrifice" but admitted that it was her opinion that "the Alger Hiss case was a product of the hysteria." Spivak asked if Kenyon believed her name and reputation had been used and exploited by the communists. She said she was perfectly certain of it. When asked why she would have been picked on, she responded it was because she "was a liberal in New York City. I had, was known as a person who was in support of civil liberties." Waldrop asked why she associated with communists. Kenyon adamantly responded,

> I do not, sir. What's the matter with you? Come over here and I will tell you how I answer a thing like that. I do not associate with the communists, but you perhaps are not aware of the civil liberties position, which is to the effect that everyone is entitled to the liberties guaranteed under the Constitution, even those whose ideas we abhor, therefore I believe in civil liberties for communists and I think a great deal of confusion in this matter has arisen from the fact that those who believe in civil liberties defend the civil liberties of communists but do not defend communists.

She went on to state that the communists wanted to turn Americans on one another and to confuse the liberals with the communists. They began joining "honest liberal organizations" and then "hung on to the names of the people who were liberals, who were outspoken, who, like me, defended the civil liberties of communists as well as of Ku Klux Klanners and so on. And they have continued to make use of our names every chance they got with the hope that they could create confusion and thereby help to win the ideological battle."[33]

The moderator asked if she was considering the possibility of legal action against Senator McCarthy. She responded that she was if he would make a statement outside of Congress. Even though she had been falsely accused, she believed that congressional immunity should continue. As she put it, "[C]ongressional immunity is absolutely essential for congressmen. They simply must have it. The proper way of handling that situation, as I understand it, is not to take away their congressional immunity, which is invaluable. It is to make them impose upon themselves certain rules in respect to their investigations." Craig asked what Kenyon's exact complaint against McCarthy was and Kenyon responded that he had stated she belonged to twenty-eight communist-front organizations, which was a lie, "both in regard to the innuendo of disloyalty and also in regard to my belonging to twenty-eight or anywhere near that number of communist-front organizations." To conclude her segment, Kenyon reiterated that the communists had used the liberals and that it was not common knowledge in the 1930s that they needed to be more careful about lending their names to organizations. The moderator concluded: "Someone has said that the fury of a woman's scorn is exceeded only by the fury of a woman who believes she has been falsely accused. As to the merits of the current controversy, we leave it to our listeners to render judgement."[34]

A reporter for the *Times-Herald* in Washington, DC, described the episode as a tearing apart of Kenyon, saying that she "swirled and fished and wove" but could not answer the tough questions.[35] Her supporters believed she was harassed while on the show, but McCarthy's supporters believed she only backed up his claims while making an "ASS" of herself, as one listener wrote in a letter to Kenyon after the show aired.[36] Another letter writer called Kenyon a "poor fool" and accused her of having lied when she said she was not a communist.[37] A third explained how she wanted to "get to the bottom of your affinity to pro Communist causes" and asserted that "a woman who has become a judge is not stupid." She accused Kenyon of being an active worker on behalf of organizations to further the communist agenda.[38]

Kenyon struggled to come to terms with the negative perception of being a joiner in service organizations. To her, community service was an obligation of good citizenship. She described herself as having "great energy, curiosity, enormous interest in ideas and in people, above all great faith in the power of ideas."[39] She did not want to be disillusioned by the difficulty of effecting change; instead, she wanted to be an optimistic part of making change happen.

Lawrence Spivak wrote to Kenyon after the show, letting her know that he had heard from listeners who described the program as stimulating. At the same time, he admonished her for being careless in joining organizations she had not checked out, telling her that someone of her importance should ensure that their name was not exploited. He wrote that she had been sure not to engage with fascist organizations but, like other liberals, had failed to be as careful with the perceived acceptance of communist ideals.[40]

Spivak's letter angered Kenyon, and she fired off a response on April 13, 1950. She accused him of promoting the show as "spontaneous and unrehearsed," yet in reality he had "been boning up for days in advance, framing loaded questions, dripping with wrong assumptions and wronger innuendos." At least the Romans had been honest, calling their show a circus when they threw "poor little Christians to the lions. . . . You, however, dress it up."[41] Kenyon also attacked his journalistic integrity, writing that truth was not his objective, that he only wanted to peddle controversy to listeners, and she warned him that the American public would suffer from this. She had accepted the invitation to appear, she complained, because she thought there would be real discussion, but instead she had found the deck stacked against her.

In several letters to friends and family following the broadcast, Kenyon admitted it was a mistake to go on the show: "Once more I am afraid I committed a folly by jumping into something without knowing as much as I should have about its nature. I did very badly on it."[42] A friend wrote to Kenyon, chastising her for going on the program. She strongly encouraged Kenyon to move on and leave the allegations in the past.[43]

At the behest of mutual friends, Houston's wife, Mildred, wrote Kenyon to ask her why she was still talking about McCarthy in public. Mildred had not listened to the *Meet the Press* broadcast but heard that Kenyon had been given a rough time on the show. "[I]f that is true," Mildred explained, "it was a feather for McCarthy which he will make good use of. For all these reasons and a lot more I do think you'd be wiser to turn off the Klieg lights and refuse to let people exploit you any further. . . . The sadistic appetite of the American public is a terrible thing and I hate to have you sacrificed to it."[44]

• • •

After its first public hearing on March 8, 1950, the subcommittee held public or executive hearings on thirty-one subsequent days, ending on July 7, 1950.[45]

Although the White House at first refused to turn over loyalty files, the president later agreed to make them available for the subcommittee's viewing. According to the files, out of a total of eighty-one alleged State Department employees, only forty were employed by the State Department at the time of the review.[46] Seven had never been employed by the State Department, and thirty-three had left their employment there.

Upon receiving the State Department files from the White House, Senator Hickenlooper remarked, "I am not going to bother to read all this stuff."[47] Ultimately, Senator Hickenlooper did read nine of the loyalty files, Senator Lodge read twelve, and the other members read all of them.[48] Chairman Tydings reiterated that the job of the subcommittee had been investigatory, not to "run down spies and disloyal persons."[49] He described McCarthy's allegations as a "hoax," a "fraud," and a "deceit," proclaiming that "it ought to make the blood of Americans boil, that they have been told these foul and vile charges."[50]

Thirty-five witnesses appeared at subcommittee hearings to give testimony.[51] Earl Browder, for one, testified before the Senate on April 27, 1950. He had been a member of the Communist Party, serving as its leader through the World War II years, but was expelled in 1946.[52] When asked if he knew Dorothy Kenyon, Browder refused to answer. He was asked if he knew Haldore Hanson, a writer and foreign correspondent, and again, Browder refused to answer.[53] Senator McMahon, a Democrat, asked him specifically about Kenyon, then said, "It occurs to me . . . that to withhold an answer to Miss Kenyon and this other gentleman [Haldore Hanson], if you are sincerely interested in not contributing to a smear campaign, that your withholding of an answer on them, if the answer is in the negative, is contributing to that smear. On the other hand, if the answer is in the positive, since those cases are before the Committee, I believe you should answer."[54] Browder responded, "I would say, without the slightest hesitation, that neither one of them ever, in my period of leadership in the organization, the Communists, had any organized connection as members or friends."[55] When questioned further, Browder doubled down. "I would say that regarding the two names you mentioned, to the best of my knowledge and belief, they never had any direct or indirect connection with the Communist Party."[56] Browder asserted that the Communist Party, when he was in leadership, did not try to "convert people in government," as it would have been "foolish and futile."[57] He told the subcommittee he had "no reason to think there are any disloyal persons in the State Department."[58]

In July, Chairman Tydings submitted a report at the conclusion of the subcommittee's investigation. Senator Hickenlooper spoke on the Senate floor, arguing that he, as a minority member of the subcommittee, had not been part of preparing the "so-called" report. He accused the subcommittee of having done "a completely inadequate job in probing the subject-matter" and "that it had wholly failed to call witnesses who should have been called."[59] To rebut this accusation, Chairman Tydings stated that all five members of the committee had met on June 30 to discuss the report.[60]

None of the individuals named by McCarthy were found to be members of the Communist Party. The report found the FBI had conducted "meticulous and comprehensive investigations" and "in no instance have we found in our considered judgment that the decision to grant loyalty and security clearance has been erroneously or improperly made in the light of existing loyalty standards."[61] The fact that infiltration of government agencies by communists was false would undoubtedly assure Americans, but, as the subcommittee members pointed out, the faith of citizens would likely also be "shaken in the security of their Government by perhaps the most nefarious campaign of untruth in the history of our Republic."[62] The report warned about the technique of the "Big Lie" employed in dictatorship regimes, stating that it was being utilized in the US for the first time. The report warned: "We have seen how, through repetition and shifting untruths, it is possible to delude great numbers of people ... We can never hope to preserve for posterity the American dream of freedom by adopting totalitarian methods as an excuse to preserve that freedom."[63]

The subcommittee report gave its endorsement for the loyalty program to continue, stating that it was necessary "to prevent the penetration of our Government by those who would subvert and destroy it" and that federal service "will continue to be a prime target" of those with such an agenda.[64] Approximately 2.5 million federal employees submitted to the loyalty process, of whom 6,412 came under suspicion. Of those, 69 were reinstated after an appeal, with only a total of 201 federal employees failing to qualify. In 1950, the *New York Times* reported that after three years of the loyalty program, not one case of espionage had been uncovered.[65]

It was further concluded that the evidence did not establish Kenyon to have been a communist or otherwise disloyal, although the report chastised her for being "less than judicious in joining certain organizations during the late 1930s and early 1940s."[66] While the subcommittee called Kenyon naive for her affiliations, it also pointed out that "American standards of justice and fair play have not deteriorated to the point that our citizens become disloyal on the basis alone of their affiliations, particularly in the case of Communist fronts which are deliberately designed to deceive and hoodwink the unsuspecting."[67] David M. Oshinsky, in *A Conspiracy So Immense: The World of Joe McCarthy*, writes that although Kenyon was "remarkably casual about lending her name," only in one instance did her membership in an organization—the National Council of Soviet-American Friendship—postdate its designation by the attorney's general as a subversive organization.[68] The conclusion that Kenyon was not a communist received much less press attention than McCarthy's original allegations. The report did little to rehabilitate the reputations of those accused, or to persuade the public of their innocence. Kenyon tried to minimize the damage, putting on a brave face and saying her clients would not desert her.[69]

William O. Douglas, associate justice on the Supreme Court, wrote an essay in the *New York Times* on January 13, 1952, titled "The Black Silence of Fear," criticizing anti-communist hysteria. He wrote, "The mind of man must always be free. The strong society is one that sanctions and encourages freedom of thought and expression." Justice Douglas warned of a society engulfed by fear. "Fear is fanned to a fury. Good and honest men are pilloried. Character is assassinated. Fear runs rampant." He had observed fear in lawyers, saying that individuals who had been accused of communist activity, "all presumed innocent, of course, until found guilty," found it hard to retain counsel. Lawyers had confided to him their fear in taking those types of cases as it could result in losing other clients, thus impacting their ability to make a living; even worse, it could result in their being named "subversive" themselves. Justice Douglas classified this as "a dark tragedy." He described the negative impacts of the past few years as resulting in stereotyped thinking, limits on free public discussion, and "the worst witch hunts we have seen since early days." He urged a reset and a return to embracing civil liberties. "If we are true to our traditions, if we are tolerant of a whole marketplace of ideas, we will always be strong. Our weakness grows when we become intolerant of opposing ideas, depart from our standards of civil liberties, and borrow the policeman's philosophy from the enemy we detest."[70]

A review of Kenyon's papers shows an unsigned note addressed to her lawyer, Theodore Kiendl. It describes how a confidential press source had said that Louis F. Budenz, during his testimony at an executive session of the subcommittee, had sworn that Kenyon was a member of the Communist Party. According to Budenz's testimony, the source reported, Kenyon had been assigned "to stay close to Eleanor Roosevelt and try to guide Mrs. Roosevelt's [newspaper] column along the Party line."[71] The source said the subcommittee voted to keep this testimony secret, but that Budenz could eventually offer his account of events in a public session. It is unknown if Theodore Kiendl ever shared this information with Kenyon.

McCarthy mentioned Kenyon again during a Senate rules subcommittee hearing in 1954. Senator Herbert Lehman asked McCarthy if he had made false charges in 1950 against Kenyon. McCarthy doubled down on his prior allegations, testifying that Kenyon had been a member of the Communist Party. He said that at the time he had been conservative and should have presented evidence that she was associated with fifty-eight front organizations. McCarthy testified, "I didn't know then that she was a Communist. Since then I find she was. According to the testimony of two reliable witnesses, former members of the Communist party, she was a member of the party."[72] He alleged her role was to attach herself to a high-ranking public official and try to influence their writings.[73] McCarthy then named the high-ranking individual: Eleanor Roosevelt. A reporter contacted Kenyon for comment. Her response was concise. "[Senator] McCarthy has exhibited his usual accuracy. There's not a word of truth in what he is reported to have said about me."[74]

A few weeks later, Mrs. Roosevelt responded in her syndicated column. Recognizing that Kenyon did not need her to come to her defense, Mrs. Roosevelt wanted to state that she had known Kenyon for a long time and had worked with her in various organizations. She described McCarthy's witnesses as former communists who were consistently discredited and far from reliable. Mrs. Roosevelt spoke of Kenyon highly, saying she had great respect for her ability and had "always found her honest and courageous."[75] In no uncertain terms, Mrs. Roosevelt wrote that she never tried to influence Kenyon's positions and that Kenyon had never influenced any of her writings.

In response to McCarthy's statements, the chairman of the ACLU board of directors wrote to Senator William E. Jenner demanding that Jenner put it on the record that the ACLU supported Kenyon. According to the ACLU, it was "precisely the kind of reckless accusation which has marked far too many congressional investigations and has produced the public demand for fairer treatment of persons who testify or are named in testimony."[76] Kenyon, meanwhile, advocated for Congress to continue to operate with immunity, but urged Congress to develop rules for investigations where "innocent people cannot, and must not, be smeared."[77] Because fear ruled the day, the desire and the ability to brand someone a communist, she believed, was being abused. "[I]n our fright and our hate," she pointed out, "we call for repressive measures of all sorts, measures not all of which are likely to catch many Communists . . . but are almost certain to snare the innocent and the unwary."[78]

. . .

Since 1950, McCarthy had been in the news accusing individuals of being members of the Communist Party. The Permanent Subcommittee on Investigations for the Eighty-Third Congress (a different subcommittee than that led by Senator Tydings) held executive sessions from 1953 through 1954.[79] McCarthy chaired the Government Operations Committee, as well as this investigations subcommittee. His chairmanship allowed him to continue his smears. For example, McCarthy investigated the US Army for communist infiltration in 1954, holding televised hearings that became known as the Army-McCarthy hearings.[80] On June 9, 1954, one of the army's lawyers, Joseph Welch, made a statement in the televised hearing that led to a sharp decline in McCarthy's popularity. McCarthy had alleged that one of the army's attorneys had communist ties, to which Welch responded: "Until this moment, Senator, I think I never really gauged your cruelty or your recklessness. . . . You have done enough. Have you no sense of decency?" This resounding statement echoed through the nation's television screens, leading to McCarthy's downfall. Enough was enough.

On July 30, 1954, Senate Resolution 301 was proposed to censure McCarthy. The Senate voted on the resolution on December 2, 1954, with sixty-seven senators voting in favor, and twenty-two voting against.[81] The amended resolution resolved that McCarthy had "repeatedly abused the subcommittee and its members who were trying to carry out assigned duties, thereby obstructing the conditional processes of the Senate."[82] Following his condemnation in the Senate, McCarthy was more or less ignored. He died on May 2, 1957, at the Bethesda Naval Hospital from cirrhosis of the liver.[83] Secretary of State Dean Acheson later wrote that McCarthy's name had "enlarged the vocabulary . . . like those of Judge Lynch and Captain Boycott."[84]

Ellen Schrecker identifies the dangers of McCarthyism, writing that it evidenced "how effectively political repression could operate within a democratic society."[85] Institutions which should have held strong in the face of McCarthy's allegations did not. The easy willingness to trample on civil liberties using government mechanisms, on the part both of those who worked within the institutions and of the citizens who supported them, is breathtaking.

In January 2003, the executive sessions of McCarthy's Permanent Subcommittee on Investigations were made public. As the 2003 subcommittee chairman, Senator Carl Levin, and ranking member Senator Susan Collins put it, the McCarthy hearings were "part of our national past that we can neither afford to forget nor permit to reoccur." They noted that the Senate's investigatory power ranks among its highest responsibilities and that McCarthy's chairmanship broke Senate norms. His "zeal to uncover subversion and espionage," Levin and Collins explained, "led to disturbing excesses. His browbeating tactics destroyed careers of people who were not involved in the infiltration of our government."[86] Donald A. Ritchie from the Senate Historical Office wrote that McCarthy "grilled witnesses intensely" with "little patience for due process" or the constitutional rights of witnesses.[87] McCarthyism, Ritchie concluded, became synonymous with "any investigation that flouts the rights of individuals," including smears, guilt by association, and character assassination.[88]

As Kenyon aged, McCarthy was still on her mind. "[He] blighted me," she said. "He ended my public career. I think that's perfectly clear now."[89] Pauli Murray later described the McCarthy allegations as fortuitous, for the experience spurred Kenyon to continue fighting for civil rights at a time when courageous leaders were hard to find.[90] If there was a positive impact, as Murray suggested, the experience gave Kenyon increased motivation to work on civil rights committees and cases, as well as to travel the country giving speeches on topics like women's equality and the promotion of democracy. She had a fervent desire to protect civil liberties wherever they were threatened. McCarthy's accusations also impressed upon Kenyon how necessary it was for individuals to fight against those who operated in bad faith. Kenyon believed civil liberties were never achieved without a struggle, and the price one must pay in that struggle was constant vigilance.[91]

Mildred Adams Kenyon agreed with Murray's description of the allegations as fortuitous. Mildred knew that Kenyon was a fighter for the things she believed in, but communism was not one of those things. The accusations served to place Kenyon in "a group of highly intelligent American citizens that McCarthy sought to bring down," and after her exoneration, Kenyon remained undaunted. She had fought for women and labor prior to the allegations, but afterward she shifted to speaking up for the poor, the unhoused, racial minorities, and the aging. In fact, Mildred speculated that for the remainder of Kenyon's life, her primary efforts were spent in advocacy of minority interests—while practicing law in her spare time.[92]

Kenyon had long held a strong faith in the rule of law and fair play, and McCarthy had violated both. Members of the public labeled her a traitor—without any due process. Kenyon described it this way: "Out of the blue sky came the red thunderbolt to strike us all. And although we all instantly and vehemently denied the charges, the truth, as is well known in such cases, never catches up with the lie, and we will all of us be branded, to a certain extent at least, forever."[93] Kenyon's friend and client Dorothy Dunbar Bromley said Kenyon "never felt sorry for herself on any score—except for the McCarthy onslaught."[94]

McCarthy's impact was far-reaching within Kenyon's immediate family as well. Her nephew Edward Kenyon was a senior at Harvard when McCarthy's allegations became public. He found out from the front page of a newspaper. Edward went to law school and ultimately applied for a commission in the Navy. When his application was denied, he filed a FOIA request to find out why, eventually learning that it had been based on his familial association with Kenyon. Edward also speculated that Kenyon & Kenyon, the law firm where Kenyon's brothers worked, lost patent clients because of the brothers' vigorous defense of Kenyon.[95] Edward explained that, at the time, Americans were so afraid of communists that they "believed somebody [i.e., McCarthy] who came along and said . . . there were people out there who were going to take away our country and take away our way of life. And he had no basis for anything he said."[96]

Fred J. Cook wrote, "McCarthyism did not die with McCarthy."[97] On that point, Kenyon concurred. Writing about the McCarthy episode before her death, she recognized her place in history. She feared that the younger generation had forgotten the McCarthy days—if in fact they had ever heard of them. She urged vigilance against others who would create the same kind of chaos.

> It seemed there was no one to stop him. Government was weak; Congress, except here and there, was frozen; the parties were weak. . . . The fight is not yet over. Barry Goldwater is still around; Republican Senators are gathering up the ultra-conservatives to themselves; America Firsters, the Know Nothings, the Red Baiters, divisive groups of all sorts are hardening themselves, building up for another McCarthy, tyrannical of necessity and therefore the kiss of death to free democracy as most of us understand the terms. McCarthyism hasn't left us yet. We have the brains to prevent this if we try. Have we the heart, the courage, the decency to do so?[98]

Kenyon warned of the cyclical nature of history, hoping future generations would be able to stop the type of unfettered damage another McCarthy would cause. Although Kenyon was both emotionally scarred and economically damaged by the McCarthy affair, the experience did not "dim her self-confidence" or stop her from advocating for the causes she supported.[99]

One of the causes she cared deeply about was protective legislation. Kenyon felt laws that specifically applied to women were necessary to protect them in the workplace. This belief pitted her against other women's rights activists who wanted an end to protective legislation. Although those active in the women's rights movement did not always agree on the same priorities or the suitable pathways to achieve their end goals, they shared the desire for women to be free to make their own choices in their lives and occupations.

SEVEN

# *Not a Feminist*

## ORGANIZING FOR PROTECTIVE LEGISLATION

While the Constitution protected men's right to live for themselves, the law could push women to live for others.

JILL ELAINE HASDAY,
*We the Men*[1]

IN THE NINETEENTH CENTURY, laws were written by men. Yet women were working behind the scenes in their communities to obtain the social change they wanted to see. Women's clubs and organizations "functioned as a kind of early warning system, recognizing emergent problems before they were identified by the male-dominated political process."[2] They advocated on behalf of a multitude of causes, ranging from broad societal issues such as the abolition of slavery and prison and educational reform, to more focused concerns such as the ability to keep wages earned and to own property, the right to divorce, and the right to wear pants.[3] It is important to understand the history of women's organizing, as there was a clear divide in the women's rights movement from the start. For example, the suffrage movement itself was divided between those who wanted women to vote and those who wanted to preserve traditional domestic roles in which only men made political decisions, as well as those who wanted to include Black women and those who did not. And as women entered the workplace there was disagreement regarding how, or even if, the law should provide protection for them. Some wanted radical, revolutionary change, while others wanted to work within the existing legislative and judicial frameworks to obtain slower, enduring change.

Two women active in the abolitionist movement, Elizabeth Cady Stanton and Lucretia Mott, became determined to improve the legal status of women. They organized a Woman's Rights Convention to take place in Seneca Falls, New York, in July 1848. Stanton drafted a Declaration of Sentiments before the convention that asserted "all men and women are created equal" and stated, "[t]he history of mankind is a history of repeated injuries and usurpations on the part of man toward woman, having in direct object the establishment of an absolute tyranny over her."[4] This declaration, coupled with the convention, inspired women to link economic dependence with the ability to exercise political rights.[5]

The listed complaints included the deprivation of women's right to vote; the taking of women's wages and other property; the monopolization of well-paying jobs by men, leaving women little economic opportunity; and the destruction of women's confidence and self-respect, resulting in dependence on men.[6] More than three hundred individuals met in Seneca Falls to discuss equality, but no Black women were in attendance.[7] Frederick Douglass, a Black abolitionist supportive of women's rights, was there.[8]

Because of exclusion from women's clubs and associations, Black women created their own networks. Josephine St. Pierre Ruffin was the first president of the National Association of Colored Women; she said the organization was "for the good of women and men, for the benefit of all humanity."[9] Sarah Tompkins Garnet, the first Black woman principal in New York City's school system, started the Equal Suffrage League for Black women to organize to secure the vote.[10] Black women suffragists recognized that the enfranchisement of Black women would be necessary in the fight to obtain racial equality.[11]

Women demanded the right to vote on street corners, in public meetings, and through marches. Author Mildred Adams Kenyon (Kenyon's sister-in-law) explained that demanding the right to vote "ran in direct contradiction to Victorian customs . . . [and] generated enough emotional heat to divide families and turn supper tables into battlegrounds."[12] The public was suspicious and distrustful of those attempting to stir up support to change the status quo.

Elihu Root, a lawyer who would serve as senator, secretary of war, and secretary of state (and the father of Sec Root), gave a speech at the New York State Constitutional Convention opposing suffrage in 1908. He argued that voting was not a natural right and politics was no place for women:

> Woman rules [today] by the sweet and noble influences of her character. Put woman into the arena of conflict and she abandons these great weapons which control the world, and she takes into her hands, feeble and nerveless for strife, weapons with which she is unfamiliar and which she is unable to wield. Woman in strife becomes hard, harsh, unlovable, repulsive; as far removed from that gentle creature to whom we all owe allegiance and to whom we confess submission, as the heaven is removed from the earth. . . . [I]n the

> divine distribution of powers, the duty and the right of protection rests with the male. . . . The true government is in the family. The true throne is in the household. The highest exercise of power is that which forms the conscience, influences the will, controls the impulses of men, and there [today] woman is supreme and woman rules the world.[13]

It was not only men who opposed women voting. Some middle- and upper-class women felt threatened by the idea of suffrage, believing their societal positions would be diminished.[14] Elite women opposing suffrage were coming from a very privileged position, with little regard for the issues of working women. Within these middle- and upper-class families were immigrant or Black domestic workers who kept the family home running.[15] Some wealthy women openly advocated for the disenfranchisement of Black women, while others simply could not identify with their plight and made no effort to change their opinions.

When the universal right to vote was won in 1920, most women knew the fight to fully exercise their rights was just beginning. While the ultimate impact in the years following ratification can be debated, Joan Hoff-Wilson writes that the Nineteenth Amendment is the "only successful attempt to include women by gender in the Constitution."[16] A newspaper article painted a somewhat poetic picture of what women faced after winning the vote: "The big fact remained that women were still 'the governed half of society.' And so they have been standing with reluctant feet where the citizenship brook and the equality river meet, looking out of the corners of their eyes at the river and wondering whether to venture thereon was worth the price they would have to pay."[17]

Women found themselves without the power they thought they would have, while lacking confidence in their abilities. In "Now We Can Begin," an essay intended to encourage activists not to lose their focus, Crystal Eastman, an advocate for labor and women's rights, wrote:

> What is the problem of women's freedom? It seems to me to be this: how to arrange the world so that women can be human beings, with a chance to exercise their infinitely varied gifts in infinitely varied ways, instead of being destined by the accident of their sex to one field of activity—housework and child-raising. And second, if and when they choose housework and child-raising, to have that occupation recognized by the world as work, requiring a definite economic reward and not merely entitling the performer to be dependent on some man.[18]

Obtaining the right to vote brought some political power to women, but by no means did women form a monolithic voting bloc. Married women tended to vote similarly to their husbands. Few women ran for office, and fewer women voted than men.[19] Black women continued to face disenfranchisement based on their race. States passed laws, like poll taxes or literacy tests, that discriminated against Black women and men both.[20] Jim Crow laws imposed grandfather clauses regarding voting, where a voter would have to provide evidence that their ancestors voted before 1867—an impossible hurdle for many Black voters due to the stain of slavery.[21] It would not be until the Voting Rights Act was signed by President Johnson in 1965 that voting became more equitable and accessible for Black citizens.[22]

Kenyon recognized that the momentum shifted after the Nineteenth Amendment, writing, "We got sidetracked and discovered to our astonishment that when you got the vote you were not thereby made a full-fledged citizen. It was a horrible discovery. After 1920, a genuine wave reaction set in."[23] Though the post-suffrage years were met with some lethargy and increased efforts to chip away at voting rights, many reformers hung on to their idealism and set their sights on pushing forward the cause of women.

• • •

Feminism as a US movement arose in the 1910s as women organized to redefine society's definition of womanhood.[24] The term "feminist" was derived from the French *féminisme* of the late nineteenth century.[25] Feminism was ideologically on the left of the political spectrum, with socialist women being the first to embrace it.[26] Some women rebuked the feminist label because of its implied affiliation with communism.[27] A 1915 *New York Times* article critical of the feminist movement started with this sentence: "The woman's movement is a movement toward national suicide."[28]

The white privileged women who dominated the feminist space had little self-awareness about their own race and class biases.[29] Although their intentions were noble, they were missing a critical piece: the ability to listen to, learn from, and follow those who were most impacted by oppressive societal conditions. A group of women living in New York's Greenwich Village came together in 1912 to brainstorm how to reform the "social and economic structure of American life."[30] Calling themselves Heterodoxy, they disavowed Victorian notions of what women should be while embracing the unorthodox.[31] Members included

Eleanor Roosevelt, Crystal Eastman, and Elizabeth Gurley Flynn.[32] They met weekly to share their personal experiences and brainstorm ways to create a new consciousness regarding women. The *New-York Tribune* described Heterodoxy as the "real star chamber council of the thinking women of New York."[33] In her book *American Moderns*, Christine Stansell writes that, particularly in New York, "intellectuals and artists developed a view of themselves as a select group uniquely equipped to speak to and for the poor and voiceless."[34] Greenwich Village is where NYU School of Law is located, so it is likely that Kenyon was exposed to their ideals.

In 1914, the "Mother" of Heterodoxy, Marie Jenney Howe, organized two meetings to spread public awareness. The first was around the topic of "What Feminism Means to Me." The *New York Times* described it as the "first feminist mass meeting ever held."[35] Men in the audience outnumbered the women.[36] The ideas of habit and custom were argued to have outlived its usefulness and needed to be reformed. In her speech, Howe said that "while men were held in a prison by convention, custom, and tradition, women were confined to one room in the prison and had to watch the men walk about in the corridors in comparative freedom."[37]

The second meeting invited speakers on different subjects, including the right to work and organize and the right of a mother to a profession.[38] Howe assured men that women had no interest in telling them what they could or could not do, but they expected similar courtesy. "We do not put any fence around men, but we insist that they shall not put any fence around us, either. We want to remove the fence they have put around us, and which is crumbling and decaying. But they object, because we might destroy the vines that have clambered over that rotten old fence, and the flowers and poems that grow on that vine. They do not see the human lives behind that fence."[39]

The members of Heterodoxy considered an egalitarian society as one that would be communal, where neither sex nor class would play a role.[40] They were living in New York City, where industrialization had exploited workers in jobs that did not pay enough for them to leave the slums and tenements. Cheap labor and sweat shop conditions provided great profits for the owners but kept workers impoverished. Child labor was on the increase and there were few, if any, regulations on corporations regarding employment or environmental abuses. Workers received low wages and suffered frequent accidents in the workplace, often resulting in fatalities. Heterodoxy members were advocating for a reformation of industrialization, the driving force behind capitalism.

Lower-class women were skeptical about the idea of feminism. These working women would not have defined equality in the same way that middle- or upper-class women did. Early feminists were espousing the view that work outside of the home would be liberating, yet working women understood that work outside of the home could be dehumanizing. It would not be a liberation for them to have equality with men because they were working side by side with men who likewise had no economic or political power.[41]

Women had historically worked in domestic service, but as industry expanded to manufacturing and mills, they entered the factories.[42] Between 1880 and 1890, New York City's population exploded, along with other major cities like Philadelphia and Chicago.[43] Society was rapidly changing with new developments, such as gas lighting, connected water systems, indoor plumbing, and railroads connecting rural areas.[44] The 1880 US census shows that labor included a million children under the age of fifteen.[45] By 1890, one million women worked in factories, even outnumbering male employees in clothing factories.[46]

Women were working twelve-hour days for extremely low wages, in unsanitary conditions, so equality to them looked different than it did to middle- and upper-class women.[47] In a letter to the *New York Times*, Margaret Doane Gardiner wrote in 1910 that she was a working woman and when activists talked about equal pay, they were missing a fundamental point: "[W]ho do you think would employ us if they had to pay us the same as men?" Rather, she said, "to get employment [a] woman must offer her services at a reduced rate."[48] For example, twenty scrub women employed by Harvard University were fired in 1929 when Massachusetts ordered their hourly pay to be increased by two cents.[49] The working woman accepted unequal pay as the price of admission to the workplace, as it was believed they were better off making low wages than being unemployed. They understood that if they did not work, they did not eat—a reality that upper-class women could not truly grasp.

In 1912, an unmarried woman wrote a letter to the editor of the *New York Times* describing her life as a working woman. She lived in a boarding house, as she could not afford a home of her own, and worked in a factory every day for ten hours, earning just enough to pay for her room and board and some decent clothes. She argued that if a woman's place is at home, then all women should be furnished with one, and ended by observing, "Things are not well, and women are beginning to think."[50] Other letters to the *New York Times* expressed similar sentiments. Anna H. Wheeler wrote that men "have no idea of the thoughts that are tearing the feminine mind asunder. . . . Some of us are sound asleep yet, but the walking delegate is about, and many of the sleepers are already rubbing their eyes."[51]

A movement was brewing. Women were organizing to enact protective legislation addressing labor conditions for women and children.[52] The National Consumers' League focused on developing model laws that could remedy poor working conditions.[53] To help reform efforts, activists gathered data about what was occurring in factories. The Pittsburgh Survey was a sociological study conducted in 1907 in Pittsburgh, Pennsylvania, to inquire into the impacts of industrialization. Much of the field work was completed by women.[54] The survey found egregious instances of child labor, low wages, seven-day work weeks, twelve-hour days, prolonged daily standing with no seating options, minimal breaks, lack of clean drinking water, lack of ventilation, and hundreds of workplace accidents resulting in death.[55] It served as a foundation for progressives to lobby legislatures for change, such as minimum wage laws and eight-hour days.

It may be difficult for Americans today to understand how divisive these proposals were at the time. In the early twentieth century, notes Susan Ware in *Partner and I: Molly Dewson, Feminism, and New Deal Politics*, "the federal government did almost nothing to protect the economic and social welfare of American citizens; the few attempts by states to regulate working conditions were usually struck down by the courts as an unconstitutional restraint of trade and the freedom of contract."[56] It should be noted that those pushing for protective legislation desired it for all workers. However, when legislators balked at interfering with the rules of the workplace, activists took what they could get—protection for women with the hope it could later be expanded to include men. As states passed protective legislation, statutes were challenged on appeal.

In 1908, *Muller v. Oregon* examined whether an Oregon statute that limited women to a maximum of ten hours during a workday violated the Fourteenth Amendment. At this time in society, women's bodies were seen as "delicate mechanism[s]" and industrial work was considered especially dangerous to their weak constitutions.[57] Louis D. Brandeis, who would go on to serve as an associate justice of the US Supreme Court, represented Oregon.[58] Through an extensive 113 pages, Brandeis used domestic and foreign case studies, along with legislative action pertaining to wages from a period of over sixty years, to show that women working more than ten hours a day suffered from an observable cycle of overwork. Though standard today, this use of sociological data was new.[59] It is important to note that Josephine Goldmark, Brandeis's sister-in-law and a leader in labor reform, compiled most of the research for the brief and deserves credit for the Supreme Court's shift in examining socially relevant factors as evidentiary support in brief-writing.[60] Florence Kelley of the National Consumers' League co-authored the brief with Goldmark. Kelley earned her law degree from Northwestern University in 1894 and went on to advocate for protective legislation for women.[61]

The Court unanimously supported protective legislation in *Muller v. Oregon*, stating that women's physical structure justified special laws. The Court said it was obvious that physiology, together with maternal obligations, placed women "at a disadvantage in the struggle for subsistence."[62] The perceived differences between the sexes, as evidenced in *Muller*, coupled with the societal importance of childbearing, created the need for patriarchal constitutional and statutory provisions relating to the ability of women to work certain jobs. Thus, the Oregon statute limiting the hours women could work was upheld. It may appear that protective legislation leaned into negative stereotypes of women, such as that they were weak and in need of protection. It may even seem like an acquiescence to Blackstone's *Commentaries*. But by deploying those stereotypes, women were able to gain a foothold in the workplace and pull themselves out of impoverishment.

In her book *Women's Rights*, Christine Lunardini writes that *Muller* was a landmark decision because it was the first instance of "sociological jurisprudence."[63] The Court examined, and was receptive to, statistics evidencing the negative impact poor working conditions had on women. The Court would now consider sociological data in its review of cases. *Muller* gave hope that women, especially those in the lower class, could benefit from protective legislation.

Yet *Muller* did not act as a magic wand. Exploitative and unsafe conditions continued to exist. A tragic example can be found in the Triangle Shirtwaist Factory fire of 1911. The factory was on the eighth, ninth, and tenth floors of a New York City building. Here, hundreds of women worked at machines, practically on top of one another, for long hours with minimal breaks.[64] The fire department had previously reported that the building was not safe due to lack of exits, but the warning went unheeded. Months before the fire, the Ladies' Waist Makers Union had called a strike complaining about the dangerous factory conditions. The strike was unsuccessful, and people returned to work.

Fifteen hundred machines were packed into the three floors of the factory, with only one fire escape for the approximately five hundred employees working that day. The fire started around 5 p.m. As it spread, workers jumped from the windows, with reporters confronting fifty-three bodies on the street upon their arrival. Nets were held for workers to jump into, but they were stretched beyond appropriate use, with firemen and passersby "crushed to the pavement by the rain of falling bodies."[65] A total of 146 employees died in the fire.[66] The owners of the factory, Max Blanck and Isaac Harris, were indicted for manslaughter in the first degree. At trial, however, the jury found the defendants not guilty.[67]

Demands were made on the legislature to pass an employers' liability act and require fireproofing of large buildings.[68] Frances Perkins, a social worker who would go on to serve as secretary of labor in the Franklin D. Roosevelt administration, worked to create the New York Factory Investigating Commission to scrutinize conditions in industrial workplaces.[69] This innovative commission served as a model for other states and resulted in the New York legislature revising occupational safety and health codes and adopting worker's compensation.[70]

Lobbying for protective legislation continued, with Massachusetts becoming the first state to pass a minimum wage law in 1912.[71] In 1918, Congress passed a law setting minimum wages for women in the District of Columbia.[72] The Children's Hospital filed suit to block enforcement of the law. The Supreme Court of the District of Columbia upheld the law, and the US Court of Appeals affirmed the lower court's ruling. The minimum wage law was challenged in the US Supreme Court in *Adkins v. Children's Hospital*, and the Court reached its decision in 1923, saying that such laws violated the Due Process Clause of the Fifth Amendment by interfering with the right to contract.[73]

Things had changed politically. The Nineteenth Amendment had been passed, changing the "contractual, political, and civil status of women." Except for legislation considering physical differences, the Court now declared that there was no further need of "special protection" for women and that adult women should not be subject to restrictions on their right to contract when men were not also subject to that restriction.[74]

The problem was that women did not have the same bargaining power to negotiate wages as men did. Chief Justice (and former president) William Howard Taft dissented in the opinion, writing that employees in the class receiving lesser pay "are not upon a full level of equality of choice with their employer, and, in their necessitous circumstances, are prone to accept pretty much anything that is offered. They are peculiarly subject to the overreaching of the harsh and greedy employer."[75] Taft recognized that the Nineteenth Amendment gave women political power, but it "did not change the physical strength or limitations of women upon which the decision in *Muller v. Oregon* rests."[76] Justice Oliver Wendell Holmes Jr. also dissented, writing that the Nineteenth Amendment did not preclude the legislature from considering the differences between the sexes and drafting laws accordingly. Efforts to pass minimum wage legislation at the state level were chilled as a result. *Adkins* would eventually be overturned in *West Coast Hotel Company v. Parrish*, decided by the Supreme Court on March 29, 1937.[77] Here, the Court signaled that it would no longer invalidate legislation that attempted to regulate business. Instead, states could use their police power to restrict an individual's freedom to contract. Empowered by the ruling, New York passed a minimum wage law the very next month.[78]

Most Americans saw women in the workplace as a direct threat to men, especially women who were married yet worked.[79] The common view was that married women did not need to work and should remain out of the labor force. By working, married women were double dipping financially and taking positions away from those who really needed the job. This belief was also held by employers and legislators. For example, General Electric fired women workers if they married; Ford preferred hiring males with dependents over women.[80] In New York, a woman teacher who married and had a child could not return to her job following the birth. It was a further policy in the school system that a married woman would not be hired unless she had been separated from her husband for three years or had been widowed.[81] Additionally, the Economy Act of 1932 required departments in the federal government to fire employees whose spouse also worked for the government. It was typically the wives who would lose their jobs, as men earned a higher wage.[82] To ensure that women did not sidestep the law by using other names, the federal government required women in federal employment to take their husband's name.[83] Some states also required women to take their husband's name upon marriage as a requirement of common law.[84]

By 1940, twenty-six states had passed statutes prohibiting or limiting the employment of married women in state government jobs.[85] A Gallup poll taken on October 31, 1945, asked, "If there is a limited number of jobs, do you approve or disapprove of a married woman holding a job in business or industry when her husband is able to support her?" Eighty-six percent of those polled disapproved.[86]

Protective laws had been enacted over the years that recognized the differences between men and women, and because of those fundamental differences, women were treated as a separate class. Alice Paul, author of the 1923 Equal Rights Amendment (ERA), opposed those blanket restrictions and wanted women treated as individuals. She proposed the amendment to read simply: "Equality of rights under the laws shall not be denied or abridged by the United States or by any state on account of sex."[87] In her mind, the ERA was the way to secure equality, arguing that all legal distinctions between men and women should be eliminated, as they kept women from pursuing the same economic opportunities that men enjoyed.[88] Paul led the National Woman's Party, whose members were referred to as equal rights feminists.[89] The group solidified its claim to the feminist label from the 1920s through the 1960s as it lobbied narrowly for the passage of the ERA.[90] By means of the constitutional amendment, the equal rights feminists wanted to wipe out protective legislation in one broad sweep.

Opponents of the ERA, sometimes called social feminists, understood that protective laws were necessary in providing a foothold for women in the workforce. The special conditions experienced only by women, like childbearing and child-rearing, acted as handicaps and limited a woman's ability to compete equally with men. Social feminists argued that sex-based differentials in the law should be eliminated through specific statutory reform, not a broad constitutional amendment.[91] The League of Women Voters' first president, Maud Wood Park, recalled that the league had a goal of gradualism that did not seek "to lead a few women a long way quickly, but rather to lead many women a little way at a time."[92] Dorothy Straus, Kenyon's law partner, warned that "sudden and violent advances have invariably been followed by repression."[93] Kenyon herself believed that sex equality correlated directly with economic conditions.[94] She, too, wanted women treated as individuals but did not believe the ERA would be effective in that regard. Instead, women needed to be hired and over time prove their worth to employers, thereby changing hearts and minds.

Labor unions wanted protective legislation to remain in place because it would ensure continued employment for workers, a view shared by the ACLU due to its alliance with organized labor. Working women were making progress at winning safeguards that met their unique needs. Men, through unions, had already won shorter working hours and higher wages. Women did not have the bargaining power those male workers did, but protective legislation would provide them the edge they needed to advocate for, and obtain, similar benefits. The American Federation of Labor and Congress of Industrial Organizations would assert that special labor legislation for women was a positive advancement in reducing discrimination against women in the workplace.[95] Cynically, protective legislation tended to limit what women could do, which unions appreciated because it maintained job security for male employees. Men would be needed to fill the gaps that women were prohibited from occupying vocationally.

Nancy Cott, in *The Grounding of Modern Feminism*, argues that both sides of the sex equality debate had correct opinions. The social feminists were right in that protective laws would, at that time in history, serve the "greatest good to the greatest number of women workers."[96] They were trying to work within the existing labor restraints imposed on women by employers and to protect women from exploitation, both admirable goals. The equal rights feminists were right, however, in that protective laws could hamper the ability of women to have their work appropriately valued. They wanted to envision a new labor market, one that culminated in burning down the systems that were based on sex inequalities. But how do you meet these goals, for either side, when women are so varied in their needs? Economics, class, sex—they were clearly intersectional. The social feminists were moving slowly, being considerate of those intersections. The equal rights feminists wanted rapid, revolutionary change.

What was needed was a consensus: to use litigation to obtain judicial relief, or to pursue constitutional change through legislative reform. In the end, it was uncertain who could be trusted more to provide relief from sex-based differentials in the law—judges or legislators. The debate about protective legislation would last for decades. Women had varying principles and desires, and there was no one-size-fits-all path forward to achieve them. Crucially, activists in the early twentieth century failed to recognize how the suffrage campaign had divided women into warring factions, rather than bringing them together.

. . .

The 1932 election of Franklin Delano Roosevelt helped bring back momentum to the women's movement. President Roosevelt placed women in political positions, though he failed to appoint any as his close advisors.[97] Even so, excitement was bubbling as President Roosevelt relied on the support of educated women for guidance. He appointed Frances Perkins as secretary of labor, the first woman to serve in a presidential cabinet.[98] As William H. Chafe puts it, "Who better . . . to administer and implement these programs than . . . the same women who had comprised Eleanor Roosevelt's community in New York."[99] Susan Ware astutely notes that this was the first time "women had a crack at national power and influence . . . in areas traditionally reserved for men."[100] She argues that the success women were having in the New Deal era regarding public leadership is proof that feminist activity did not die in 1920 after the Nineteenth Amendment. Dorothy Sue Cobble labeled the post-depression feminists of the 1930s as "labor feminists," calling the group the daughters and granddaughters of the "social feminists" of the Progressive Era.[101]

As the country emerged from the Great Depression, policies were put in place to meet the needs of the electorate. In President Roosevelt's first hundred days in office, his administration pushed through legislation to help the banking system and stimulate the economy, while establishing public works programs that would put people back in the workplace.[102] These types of policies could be traced back to what women's associations and reform groups had been addressing. The New Deal era also ushered in legislation like the Social Security Act of 1935, which provided a social insurance program for retired workers above age sixty-five, and the Fair Labor Standards Act of 1938, which set minimum wage and maximum working hours. As President Roosevelt put it when he sent the bill to Congress in May 1937, America should be able to give "all our able-bodied working men and women a fair day's pay for a fair day's work."[103]

By 1945, twenty-six states had passed minimum wage laws, and forty-three states limited the maximum hours women could work.[104] The efforts to regulate workplace conditions, particularly in industry, were having positive impacts. Women's employment was increasing, and they were also experiencing higher rates of promotion. It is important to remember the labor legislation enacted under the Roosevelt administration did not happen overnight. Its passage built on the decades of hard work and lobbying efforts by many women on a state-by-state basis to address exploitative labor practices.[105] Women like Kenyon who had been college educated during the Progressive Era were primed to participate in reform on the level of the New Deal. It was their opportunity to show what they could do in the political arena. They were demanding that government address the social needs of those in their communities. As Dorothy Straus wrote, "[W]e are not feminists primarily; we are citizens."[106]

Continuing her mission to educate the public, Kenyon wrote an article, "The Awakening of Women," about the history of the women's movement from Seneca Falls (1848) to the late 1940s. She emphasized the importance of a liberal arts education for women and continued to advocate for more women in government: "Government needs to be fertilized by women; the woman's point of view, if there be one, and certainly women's brains are badly needed in every type of skill at every level." She stated her belief that the entire point of the woman's movement was to "open the doors to all of women's potentialities, as mothers and everything else." Kenyon stressed that the important work of housewives should not be forgotten. "[L]et's recognize that human beings differ greatly in their abilities (but practically not at all along sex lines) and that the best and most normal thing is for men and women to work and play together, not only in making babies and homes, but in everything else besides."[107] The article echoed a common theme in Kenyon's correspondence through the years: that women be seen as human beings, entitled to all human rights.[108] She believed that for women to obtain true equality, societal institutions would have to fundamentally transform, and that it would be up to each subsequent generation to continue that work.

In 1948, a celebration was held to commemorate the hundredth anniversary of the Seneca Falls convention.[109] More than two thousand people attended, listening to speeches on contemporary issues impacting the legal status of women. The US post office marked the occasion with a three-cent commemorative stamp, paying homage to "the progress of women during the past 100 years."[110] Kenyon was a keynote speaker at the celebration and urged the audience to focus on the work ahead, while celebrating past accomplishments. She reminded them that, with women underrepresented in the halls of government, it was imperative to use the vote to place "qualified women in all posts of government." She recognized that some things were changing: wife beating had "gone out of fashion," the word "obey" was disappearing from marriage vows, legal disabilities of married women were being removed from statutes, and property laws were being modified, albeit slowly.[111]

Despite working for decades to advance the cause of women, Kenyon, like many women activists of her generation, never made peace with the feminist label, or with feminists. Although during the time she was working at Straus & Kenyon she was described as "an ardent feminist, a strong advocate of the rights of labor and a staunch upholder of the civil liberties of the individual," her own writings denounce the feminist title, finding the idea antagonistic.[112] Instead, she believed that progress required the slow passage of time coupled with the persistent achievements made by professional women.[113] Kenyon separated equality from feminism, to the dismay of many active within the feminist movement.

In the 1970s she expressed her frustration with the second-wave feminists to one of her ACLU colleagues:

> The truth is I don't know how to handle this liberation of women problem. Apparently you must be either (1) an offensive feminist, which God knows I am not (I adore men *if they have brains*; and find women excruciatingly dull by comparison) or (2) a soft spoken, deferential, slightly flirtatious piece of femininity, which I also, alas, am not. I try to steer a middle course by taking the court jester role, making fun of men, mocking, teasing and so on—not dignified but calculated to amuse you and hold your attention for a few minutes at least, which is about all I ever get. But when I get angry, I go berserk and lose my judgment entirely. I know exactly how the Black Panthers feel, ignored, passed over, segregated (intellectually at least) and frustrated until they are ready to kill. . . . What I am trying to assert is my own female right to recognition as another human being.[114]

This was not a rare mindset for women of Kenyon's age. An article in *Time* magazine provides some context, describing the "new feminists" as viewing the United States as "a rigid, male-dominated society which, deliberately, or more often unconsciously, perpetuates arrant inequities between men and women—in pay, kinds of jobs and, more subtly, self-expression."[115] It depicted older women like Kenyon as being skeptical, or even hostile, to the movement.

As Samantha Barbas submits, Kenyon "dedicated herself to transforming both popular and official understandings of the Constitution through a dual program of impact litigation and social activism."[116] Kenyon spent years traveling across the country, giving public talks that encouraged the advancement of democracy and equality. Her writings and speeches promoted her causes, which aligned with later second-wave feminist organizing. Although she did not embrace feminism herself, the feminist ideals she expressed in her speeches and writings encouraged the expansion of feminism as a widespread social movement.

In the end, Kenyon favored educational efforts to advance the cause of women over radical methods of protest. She wanted to change habits and customs among men who held unconscious biases against women, with roots in Blackstone's writings.[117] She was often at odds with other progressives about how best to move forward. Ultimately, Kenyon was able to use her position on the ACLU national board to champion the causes she considered important, influencing the ACLU's direction through a critical time in its development. Often the lone voice in the room, she urged the other board members to focus their time, attention, and strategies on eliminating sex discrimination. It eventually worked, but it took a lot of patience and effort on Kenyon's part. It would also require the help of another trailblazing lawyer—Pauli Murray.

EIGHT

# *A Glorious Rebel*

## THE IMPORTANCE OF THE ACLU

> These many years I have been a Cassandra crying out in the ACLU wilderness against . . . man's inhumanity to women.
>
> DOROTHY KENYON

KENYON SERVED ON THE ACLU national board of directors from 1931 to 1972.[1] She enjoyed working with the ACLU, which she described as standing "on the frontiers of freedom for everybody."[2] Her official title was vice chair and corporate secretary, but she wanted it changed to Member, Board of Directors, and Officer, ACLU.[3] She requested this variant because of the word "secretary," saying, "Somehow or other I have an aversion to being called the secretary of anything, a female inferiority complex I suppose."[4] Her committee service included the Executive, Constitution, Free Speech, and Due Process committees. She especially enjoyed attending the Executive Committee meetings, calling it "a psychological lift to go."[5] She also chaired the Committee on Women's Rights, later renamed the Equality Committee, which fought both race and sex discrimination.[6] She enjoyed taking the reins and creating progressive policy in the areas of labor, civil rights, and social justice.

Prior to joining the ACLU, in 1929, Kenyon testified before a congressional subcommittee about the ERA, saying that enacting it would be "like a blind man with a shotgun" because "[n]o lawyer can confidently state what it would hit."[7] Because of her strong opposition, she persuaded the ACLU national board to stand with her. Yet over time she grew to see the need for the ERA. Ultimately, she helped lead the ACLU's policy shift from supporting protective labor legislation to supporting the ERA, a process that took decades of discussion and argument.

. . .

In the summer of 1917, Crystal Eastman was recruiting attorneys. Eastman, a graduate of NYU's School of Law and a member of Heterodoxy, had written New York's first worker's compensation law while serving as the only woman on the New York State Employers' Liability Commission.[8] She had long advocated for a restructuring of society and its value system. Like many women in her generation, Eastman believed that women had a better grasp of avenues to peace and humanitarian reform.

That year, Congress had passed the Espionage Act, targeting disloyal Americans, specifically around speech that was deemed harmful to the war effort.[9] Any modes of dissent were to be suppressed—which offended those in the Progressive movement. Eastman wanted to take on this intolerance of dissident speech against the war and, together with Roger Baldwin, worked to form a bureau that would provide legal advice for those whose civil liberties had been violated, specifically conscientious objectors and war resisters.

On July 3, 1917, the National Civil Liberties Bureau was unveiled, and it quickly became busy with litigation because of the Espionage Act.[10] In 1920, following the end of World War I, the bureau was reorganized into the ACLU. The original ACLU national committee members included, among others, Felix Frankfurter, Jane Addams, Elizabeth Gurley Flynn, and William Z. Foster from the American Federation of Labor.[11] Baldwin served as executive director from 1920 to 1950. As reported by the *Washington Post*, the ACLU would "champion in the highest courts the civil liberties of persons and organizations."[12]

Today, protecting free speech is seen as a fundamental part of American democracy, but during this time in history the fight to protect the First Amendment from government interference was sporadic.[13] One focus of the ACLU's agenda was to protect the right to protest, particularly surrounding labor organizations. In 1925, expanding its mission to include protection of other civil liberties beyond the First Amendment, the ACLU focused attention on opposing a deportation bill, restoring civil rights to those convicted under the Espionage Act, establishing the right of individuals advocating for birth control to assemble, establishing civil rights for those in non-union coal-mining districts, raising funds for free-speech defense cases, and sponsoring free-speech debates in colleges and high schools.[14]

The ACLU was "one of the first predominantly white, liberal organizations to pursue racial equality."[15] It investigated lynchings in the 1920s and spoke out against racist mob violence by the Ku Klux Klan.[16] It also started working with the National Association for the Advancement of Colored People (NAACP) on cases, lobbying all the while for a federal anti-lynching law.[17] Yet Congress repeatedly failed to move on such civil rights legislation.

The ACLU board's stance on sex-based discrimination was less well defined. The board would have to reconcile whether sex discrimination cases deserved equal strategic energy with race discrimination cases. That discussion began with the ERA.

In her position on the ACLU board, Kenyon advocated for a case-by-case method of achieving sex equality. In 1943, she published an essay in *Woman's Day* magazine explaining her continued opposition to the ERA, writing:

> It is a great tragedy, at a time when there is so much work crying to be done in the world, that women must be divided on this issue and must waste precious time debating with one another the dubious merits of this perennial proposal. I console myself with working strenuously for the advancement of women all along the line, helping women doctors get commissions in the armed forces, fighting the mandatory joint income tax proposal for husbands and wives, fighting for the establishment of the principle of equal pay for equal work, fighting to get qualified women appointed to policy-making positions in public affairs, seeking to be as good a lawyer and judge as I can possibly be in the hope of thereby securing greater recognition for women in the professions. . . . I am opposed to the Equal Rights Amendment because I think that it would endanger progressive legislation in the fields of home and labor.[18]

In personal correspondence to her friend C. C. Burlingham, however, Kenyon was wavering. She wrote, "I am not a bit sure whether I am on the side of the angels or not. . . . Isn't it awful not to know one's own mind?"[19]

Despite her private indecision, Kenyon stood firm in her public opposition to the ERA. Kenyon argued that discriminatory laws in the areas of marriage, divorce, property ownership, and jury service should be struck down, and favored using the Equal Protection Clause of the Fourteenth Amendment to litigate those issues. She suggested the ERA would not magically end discrimination against women in employment or provide them the upward mobility and equal pay they had been seeking. Kenyon also had strategic reasons for believing it would be better if the Supreme Court recognized equality under the Fourteenth Amendment, rather than relying on legislators to pass a constitutional amendment. Specifically, she found the idea of putting the ERA into the Constitution for courts to interpret as "nondemocratic," remarking that "such an amendment might be twisted into all sorts of anti-social meanings. No one knows what interpretation would be given it in the future. It would leave the rights of women to be decided by what might be a group of reactionary judges."[20]

In 1944, the ACLU established the Committee on Discrimination Against Women in Employment. Kenyon was elected chair, a position she retained until 1970. In that same year, the ACLU successfully challenged a Massachusetts law prohibiting married women from teaching in public schools and focused on lobbying Congress for a bill to provide women equal pay for equal work. In 1945, the committee would be renamed the Committee on Women's Rights, with a focus on defeating the ERA because it would "nullify protective labor laws."[21]

As she had suggested in her *Woman's Day* piece, Kenyon felt time would be better spent trying to modify sexist habits and customs rather than debating the passage of the ERA. She pointed out that the Reconstruction Amendments, which included the Fourteenth, had not brought equality to Black citizens, so there was no guarantee the ERA would create equality for women.[22] She thought the idea that the ERA would suddenly change the nation's habits and customs was expecting an impossibility, and argued that the only way to obtain true equality was in the hard, slow way of changing public attitudes, which took time but could be specifically directed to correct inequality.[23] The ACLU board adopted a memorandum on women's rights in July 1945 that reiterated Kenyon's beliefs. The memorandum opposed the ERA, stating that "such an amendment, couched in vague and sweeping language, while emotionally attractive, is bound to lead to great confusion and uncertainty in its application. . . . It is sure to jeopardize a great body of valuable social and labor legislation without producing anything significant in the field of civil liberties in its stead."[24]

Kenyon would go on to join the National Committee to Defeat the Un-Equal Rights Amendment and to Promote Equal Opportunities, chaired by Mary Anderson, former director of the Women's Bureau at the Department of Labor.[25] Other labor organizations at the time opposed to the ERA included the American Federation of Labor, American Federation of Teachers, League of Women Shoppers, National Consumers' League, National Women's Trade Union League of America, and the United Steel Workers of America.

Writing for the ACLU's *Civil Liberties* magazine in 1953, Kenyon remarked that "[d]ifferential legislation, non-discriminatory but on the contrary equalizing in its effect . . . can be a valuable tool for freedom and should not be lightly thrown into the discard."[26] Two years later, Kenyon provided the ACLU board with a restatement of the ACLU's position in favor of women's rights that she had written, which reiterated why the ACLU should oppose the ERA. She noted that the remnants of Blackstone's *Commentaries* had been removed from statute books over time, as evidenced by the fact that only a few states now excluded women from jury service, preferred fathers as guardians in the case of divorce, or required a wife to obtain her husband's consent before engaging in a business.[27] The restatement was subsequently ratified by the board, which asserted that nondiscriminatory differential legislation was in some circumstances essential and that litigation under the Equal Protection Clause of the Fourteenth Amendment should be pursued.[28]

The ACLU continued to debate and discuss the ERA. The only way the board would consider supporting it was if it was revised to preserve protective legislation for women.[29] The ERA had been introduced in every Congress since its writing, with hearings held by the House of Representatives and the Senate in 1948 and 1956.[30] It passed twice in the Senate with the Hayden rider, which was intended to preserve protective legislation for women but in fact resulted in killing the amendment.

• • •

In 1961, President John F. Kennedy created the Commission on the Status of Women (CSW) to develop "plans for fostering the full partnership of men and women in our national life."[31] Esther Peterson, head of the Women's Bureau, suggested the group be created to dissuade pro-ERA activity.[32] President Kennedy, having been criticized for failing to appoint any women to his cabinet, saw Peterson's suggestion as a way to win back women voters. Peterson worked behind the scenes to stack the committee with individuals who opposed the ERA.[33]

Pauli Murray's direct involvement with the women's rights movement began when she was appointed to the CSW on the recommendation of its chair, Eleanor Roosevelt, whom Murray had known for some time.[34] Susan Ware notes, "Pauli Murray was involved in all the major developments that historians write about when they try to make sense of the twentieth century, especially the movements for social change that have been so central to its history."[35]

Murray had faced many obstacles on her journey to becoming a lawyer. After graduating from Hunter College, she applied for graduate admission to the University of North Carolina in 1938, only to receive a rejection letter saying, "[M]embers of your race are not admitted to the University."[36] Murray sent a letter to President Roosevelt, with a copy to the First Lady, expressing her frustration about racial discrimination. On December 19, 1938, Eleanor Roosevelt wrote Murray back saying she had read her letter and understood her feelings but that "great changes come slowly."[37] The First Lady said it was sometimes better to fight hard with conciliatory methods; the South was changing, she believed, and urged Murray not to push too fast.

When Murray was ultimately admitted to Howard University School of Law in 1941, she was shocked to encounter derogatory jokes about women, as well as the exclusion of women from the school's legal fraternity. Murray began developing the idea of Jane Crow, which referred to the stereotypes and customs that have "robbed women of a positive self-concept and prevented them from participating fully in society as equals with men."[38] She argued that racism and sexism in the United States shared common origins and reinforced one another; "the successful outcome of the struggle against racism," she wrote, "will depend in large part upon the simultaneous elimination for all discrimination based upon sex."[39] Eventually, Mary Eastwood and Murray would co-author a law review article titled "Jane Crow and the Law: Sex Discrimination and Title VII," in which they "equated the evil of antifeminism (Jane Crow) with the evil of racism (Jim Crow)."[40]

Murray pushed herself in her studies and placed first in her class, winning a Rosenfeld Fellowship that would allow her to pursue postgraduate study at Harvard upon receiving her law degree. She was informed, however, that she was "not of the sex entitled to be admitted to Harvard."[41] She promptly appealed to the Harvard Board of Overseers, pointing out that her sex was an immutable characteristic. Harvard was unmoved. After receiving her law degree in 1944, she studied at the University of California, Berkeley, where she received her Master of Law degree. *Mademoiselle* magazine named Murray one of the ten outstanding American women of 1946.[42]

When Murray tried to land a job in New York City she had trouble, though her qualifications were exemplary. There were two stumbling blocks: she was both Black and a woman.[43] She was referred to Kenyon, who was in private practice at the time. Though Kenyon had no job to offer, she did offer advice:

> The legal profession is a long hard battle for a woman. We are still only barely tolerated, and you're facing the same problem now that my generation of

> women lawyers had to contend with after World War I. A few of us got a foot in the door during the war, but when it was over the men began pushing us out again. All I can tell you is what I've observed over the years, that if a woman has the guts to stick it out she somehow survives.

Kenyon reassured Murray that her difficulty in obtaining employment had more to do "with an entrenched bias against women in the legal profession" than with her qualifications.[44]

Murray eventually opened her own office for the general practice of law at 225 Broadway in New York City in July 1948.[45] She went on in 1956 to join Paul, Weiss, Rifkind, Wharton & Garrison in New York City as an associate, the only woman attorney at the firm.[46] She left in 1960 to take a position in academia.

After being appointed to President Kennedy's CSW in 1961, Murray was asked by its Committee on Civil and Political Rights to examine legal strategies to address the status of American women.[47] She spent months writing the memo, which highlighted jury service as a current example of sex discrimination. While conducting research and preparing her argument, Murray requested a copy of the amicus brief Kenyon had submitted to the Supreme Court in *Hoyt v. Florida* where Kenyon argued, unsuccessfully, that sex discrimination in jury service violated the Equal Protection Clause. Murray wanted to develop a litigation strategy much like Kenyon's in *Hoyt* where the Fourteenth Amendment would apply to sex-based differentials in the law. Although she knew such strategies had failed in the past, nevertheless she wanted to argue that sex and race were similar and that classifications by sex, as by race, were discriminatory. If the law accepted this argument, women could potentially achieve the same full citizenship that men enjoyed, including economic independence.[48] It would create a new consciousness around how women were treated both in the home and in the workplace, as well as provide new judicial remedies.

While Murray was working with the CSW, Kenyon testified before the House Committee on Education and Labor, Subcommittee on Labor, about the proposed Equal Pay Act. In her testimony, Kenyon reminded the subcommittee that she had proposed the first resolution on equal pay for woman at the UN. She asserted that women were "seriously discriminated against," especially in the economic arena "where changing economic conditions and old habits and customs clash," catching women in the middle. Kenyon chastised the US Supreme Court for failing to apply the Equal Protection Clause of the Fourteenth Amendment to women and urged the subcommittee not to wait on the Court to do what they could do legislatively. Kenyon testified that the reasons for paying women less than men did not "make sense nowadays and I doubt if they ever did. People should be paid on an equal basis for the work that they do, whether [B]lack or white, man or woman, no difference is tolerable."[49]

In December 1962, the CSW published Murray's memo, "A Proposal to Reexamine the Applicability of the Fourteenth Amendment to State Laws and Practices Which Discriminate on the Basis of Sex Per Se."[50] A comprehensive analysis of judicial decisions involving sex-based differentials within the law, it emphasized the need for a "reexamination by the courts . . . of state laws and practices that discriminated solely on the basis of sex."[51] Murray recommended that, instead of seeking constitutional reform through passage of the ERA, a litigation strategy that employed the Fourteenth Amendment might be more effective in overcoming sex discrimination. By using very specific cases to persuade the Supreme Court to apply the Equal Protection Clause to sex-based differentials, she argued that protective labor laws could remain in place. Relying on Kenyon's arguments in *Hoyt*, Murray realized that the strategy could link the civil rights and women's rights movements, thereby acting as an alternative to the counterproductive arguments around the ERA that had historically served as a roadblock to securing equality.[52] If the Court would interpret the Fourteenth Amendment in the way that she, and Kenyon before her, proposed, there would be no need for the ERA.

Murray wrote to a fellow member of the CSW, representative Edith Green, expressing the need for unity. She acknowledged that the ERA—which she was not opposed to in substance—had divided activists and wasted energy that could already have been used to obtain equality.[53] Focusing on judicial reinterpretation of the Fourteenth Amendment to bring about change, she suggested, would not necessarily prevent the eventual enactment of the ERA, should that be necessary. But perhaps the litigation strategy she proposed would bring about the same type of change sought by the ERA, simply on a deliberate, case-by-case basis.

Murray's memo became part of the final CSW report for 1963. Having been persuaded by the proposed litigation strategy, the commission did not take a position in favor of the ERA; rather, it advocated for a legal end to discrimination in the workforce, jury service, property rights, and politics.[54] The report inspired governors to appoint commissions to ask similar questions regarding the status of women in their own states.[55] The report also recommended "revaluing household and reproductive labor through social supports, including paid maternity leave, universal childcare services for women whether they were working outside the home or not, and changes in Social Security that would allow housewives to build up equity as if they were earning wages."[56] By the time the CSW issued the report, President Kennedy had already signed the Equal Pay Act on June 10, 1963. The report was important, however, because it helped focus the agenda for second-wave feminists. It documented the often inferior treatment women received, and made recommendations that could spearhead legislative change.

The ACLU was gratified by the CSW's report, having long considered the Fifth and Fourteenth Amendments "the fitting instruments for women's protection in defense of their rights."[57] In a letter of appreciation and support to Murray, Kenyon wrote, "I couldn't agree with you more that [the equality clause of the Fourteenth] Amendment is ideally fitted to deal with discriminations against women if only the Judges could be made to see it."[58] Kenyon also wrote to the CSW endorsing Murray's memo. "Miss Murray's analysis heartens us," she said, "in our belief that the equality clause of the XIV Amendment looks like the best constitutional instrument at hand for the reflection of the social changes involved in the changing status of women."[59]

One year later, the federal government enacted the Civil Rights Act of 1964, which outlawed discrimination based not only on race but also on sex, a category added to the legislation by Congressman Howard W. Smith of Virginia. Some believe Smith, a segregationist and opponent of the bill, added the language as a joke.[60] Others credit the work of activists able to persuade Congress to move forward on the issue of women's equality.[61] Jill Elaine Hasday, in her book *We the Men: How Forgetting Women's Struggles for Equality Perpetuates Inequality*, recognizes the importance of remembering the relentless work of women in obtaining the sex discrimination prohibition in Title VII. She wrote, "The womanless story about the origins of the sex amendment that many courts and commentators have told for decades erases women's struggles for their own equality, much like the judiciary's spontaneous enlightenment stories do."[62] Women advocates were "active participants rather than passive bystanders" in passing the landmark legislation.[63]

Title VII of the Civil Rights Act outlawed workplace discrimination based on sex, race, color, national origin, and religion. Described as viewing race and sex discrimination as "twinned legal harms," it addressed many of the concerns of ERA opponents by codifying protections for both men and women in the workplace.[64] This changed the legal landscape regarding discrimination for various classes, and Kenyon was ready for whatever litigation battles would come. As Harriet Pilpel, a lawyer and fellow member of the ACLU national board, described it, Kenyon was "the best-informed human being in the United States . . . on the progress of test cases or . . . any kinds of action under the sex provision of Title VII of the Civil Rights Act of 1964."[65]

. . .

In 1965, Kenyon and civil rights leader James Farmer sponsored Pauli Murray's appointment to the ACLU national board of directors. Murray would serve on the board until 1974.[66] Citing discrimination she had experienced as a Black woman, Murray helped Kenyon convince the ACLU board that litigation addressing both race and sex should be a priority.[67] Undoubtedly, Kenyon thought the priority the ACLU put on battling racial discrimination was important; "[i]f one is blind to color at this point in history," she said, "one can deny knowledge of all racial imbalances."[68] However, she wanted the ACLU to place equal importance on, and funding behind, efforts to battle sex discrimination. In this, Kenyon and Murray had to work to convert the male members of the executive board to their position.

Kenyon and Murray, it turns out, were kindred spirits. Kenyon described the two of them as a "heady pair—each with our own special brand of intensity and determination to overcome."[69] Kenyon would describe Murray and herself as the perfect team, "she out in front with her double discriminations, I at the rear with my years of experience behind me and the prayer that the younger ones may start out differently from us."[70] Kenyon had waited decades for the opportunity to convince the board to move forward on sex discrimination cases. Murray's joining the board, along with the recently passed federal legislation, created the opportunity she had long desired.

On October 13, 1966, Kenyon wrote Murray to say that she was considering a lawsuit against employers who failed to give equal promotional opportunities to women, legally limited as they were to working a maximum of eight hours per day.[71] Kenyon told Murray they needed to find a strong case that would convince the Supreme Court that judicial reinterpretation of the Fourteenth Amendment was critical to eliminating sex discrimination. In an essay for the ACLU voting membership, Kenyon wrote of her ongoing fight to expand the interpretation of the Fourteenth Amendment. "I recognize that I have not yet converted all board members to my eminently logical and rational view of sex, namely that women are not just human beings with delightful different sex characteristics but are also human beings *with minds*, just like other people's as well. I promise to continue my efforts to convert you to this view."[72]

At a meeting of the ACLU Equality Committee in December 1967, Murray persuaded the group to reexamine its policy on sex discrimination, taking Title VII into account. She argued that they were seeing an "upsurge in the numbers of groups in addition to blacks who feel discriminated against in American society" and noted that women were now bringing pressure to eliminate state labor laws that affected only them as a class.[73] Women, she claimed, made up one third of the total workforce, with only 20 percent of the average woman's life span dedicated to child rearing. Thus, laws that restricted, either directly or indirectly, women's ability to work (by prohibiting them from working overtime hours at night, for example, or from working jobs that required lifting certain amounts of weight) meant that women could not compete with men for improved wages. She also pointed out that legislation to protect "low-skilled, low-paid workers" from potential exploitation impacted men as well, and that legislation should be tailored to apply to both men and women in this category.[74]

A member of the Equality Committee recommended that the legal department of the ACLU get involved in these types of cases. Kenyon, however, disagreed, saying that the ACLU staff had "little experience in this field.."[75] Instead, she suggested that Murray and she, for whom these issues had "been the center of interest" for several years, handle such cases; after all, they were the experts on women's rights at the ACLU. The discussion continued a month later, when Kenyon said the goals of labor and the ACLU "should be to try to bring all workers, not just one category, up to the same level."[76]

This was a difficult time for Kenyon on the board. In a January 6, 1969, letter to the directors, Kenyon apologized for a "temper tantrum" she threw at a prior meeting. Not only had she flung her papers on the table, but that action resulted in water splashing on a fellow board member. She stated her tantrum was a result "of tensions and frustrations common to many minority groups and individuals these days," and reiterated her position that "[t]he old labor laws, for women only, have fulfilled their purpose and run their course.... The old outmoded laws, which are not protective as to one group of women workers but discriminatory as to others, can be phased out." Kenyon ended her letter, "I am far from being a feminist and am not greatly interested in women, certainly not nearly as much as I am in men. But I do care passionately for fair play, even for women and children. I am delighted that the Yale boys are so pleased at the coming of the girls to Yale" (a reference to Yale College's 1969 decision to admit its first class of women students).[77] Kenyon was seen as the expert on women's rights on the ACLU national board. As she aged, however, she would find that her experience was underappreciated—no doubt adding to her frustrations.

A few months later, new ACLU guidelines were circulated that imposed age limits on board members. To meet the goal of diversifying board membership in terms of ethnicity and geography, the Nominating Committee was considering limiting the slate to sixteen individuals and not renominating Kenyon or Osmond Fraenkel, two at-large members, both of whom had reached the age of eighty.[78] It appears there was no other legitimate reason to push them off the board, just age. Fraenkel had been in Kenyon's class at Horace Mann High School, and they had served together on the ACLU board for over thirty years.[79] Kenyon, taken aback by the ageist implications of this proposal, wondered if it was a good idea "in a civil liberties organization, where the individual is all important, to apply an automatic robot-like rule like this?" Kenyon implored the Nominating Committee to refrain from establishing an age restriction and to allow all candidates on the ballot to "take their chances in the democratic process of the vote." As she put it, "I would rather go down on a vote than be asked to step out for age."[80]

Predictably, Kenyon was able to count on Murray for support. In a memo to the board, Murray dissented from what the Nominating Committee was attempting to do. Because no other at-large member of the ACLU national board was approaching the age of eighty for several years, Murray pointed out, this action had all the appearances of singling out just two board members. Murray argued that the use of age was not only discriminatory, it was also "particularly repugnant to one of the basic principles for which [the] ACLU stands and to its emphasis upon the individual as all-important who should be judged on the basis of individual merit."[81] She cited the benefits to the board of continuity and experience; this cruel action, she said, seemed to penalize Kenyon and Fraenkel for their loyalty and steadfastness.

Murray knew this experience was difficult for Kenyon. She described the ACLU as Kenyon's religion.[82] However, all was not lost. Murray, together with other supporters, put the names of Kenyon and Fraenkel on the slate by petition, which led to their successful reelection to the board in the summer of 1969.[83] With that resolved, Kenyon shifted her attention to changing the ACLU's official position on the ERA.

• • •

At an Equality Committee meeting on April 1, 1970, Kenyon described how she had long worked to "achieve adoption of her belief that women should be considered as simple human beings and should not be classified in a category unto themselves."[84] She continued to argue that the proper vehicle for the protection of women was not the ERA but the Fourteenth Amendment. However, with the passage of the Equal Pay Act and Title VII, and after her loss in *Hoyt v. Florida*, Kenyon eventually came to advocate for the ERA. This shift encouraged the ACLU ultimately to throw its support behind the amendment. In explaining her change of mind, she expressed concern for the composition of the Court when she wrote: "And now the Supreme Court . . . is prepared to give us worse decisions. We cannot wait for the return of sweet reason and fair play. We must grab what we can." She stressed both the historical and future importance of this position, stating that "the Equal Rights Amendment is as good as anything in sight and we must use what we have in these dreadful days. For women, white and [B]lack, know now that they are people and they will not forget."[85]

In considering why the Supreme Court had not yet applied the Fourteenth Amendment to sex-based discrimination cases, Kenyon placed some of the blame on her old friend Justice Felix Frankfurter.[86] She had already disagreed with him on two major cases, *Goesart v. Cleary* (1948) and *Hoyt v. Florida* (1961). Justice Frankfurter wrote the majority opinion in *Goesaert*, which held that the Equal Protection Clause did not prohibit states from drawing sharp lines between the sexes regarding certain types of employment.[87] The Michigan legislature, for example, had enacted a statute that generally prohibited women from working as bartenders (wives and daughters of bar owners being an exception). The Court upheld the statute's constitutionality, and pointed to its function of protecting against moral problems that could arise from women working in such an environment. Justice Frankfurter wrote, "Michigan evidently believes that the oversight assured through ownership of a bar by a barmaid's husband or father minimizes hazards that may confront a barmaid without such protecting oversight." Because there was a moral reason for the law, he did not consider it discriminatory, and he urged the Court not to "give ear to the suggestion that the real impulse behind this legislation was an unchivalrous desire of male bartenders to try to monopolize the calling."[88] Frankfurter's majority opinion, dismissive as it was of the women's concerns, only empowered unions and lawmakers to support sex-based restrictions on women in the workplace.[89]

Justice Frankfurter was also on the Court for Kenyon's amicus brief in *Hoyt*, where Florida's statute restricting women from mandatory jury service was unanimously deemed reasonable.[90] The opinion noted that because women were still regarded as the center of home and family life, they should not be compelled to serve on juries. This finding merely reinforced the (all-male) Court's opinions from other sex discrimination cases up to that point. As noted by Philippa Strum, *Muller, Goesaert,* and *Hoyt* all supported the Supreme Court's "perpetuation of treatment of women as less than full persons within the meaning of the Constitution."[91]

Notably, Justice Frankfurter rejected Ruth Bader Ginsburg when, in 1960, she applied for a judicial clerkship with him at the Supreme Court, "horrified" at the idea of a woman working in such a capacity.[92] Given his views on women, Kenyon would happily celebrate Justice Frankfurter's retirement from the Court in 1962. Writing to a friend, she said: "The fight must be directed to educating [the Court]. And it's easier now that Felix Frankfurter is gone. Thank God. Reason will rise to the top someday."[93] Clearly, her "friendship" with Frankfurter had soured over the years.

To reach consensus on the ERA, the Equality Committee agreed to form a special subcommittee to draft a sex discrimination and protective labor legislation policy recommendation for the ACLU's national board. Kenyon, of course, served on this subcommittee. The language it ended up proposing included support of litigation that used the Fifth and Fourteenth Amendments to the US Constitution for "the purposes of eliminating discrimination based on sex" in various areas of the law.[94]

Kenyon was optimistic that the Supreme Court would come around to her interpretation of the Fourteenth Amendment. As she wrote to a friend, "the Supreme Court doesn't agree with me (yet), I answer you that the Supreme Court is wrong *not me*. The fight must be directed to educating them."[95] But she was tired of waiting for the Court to see reason. Thanks to labor legislation passed at the federal and state levels that diminished the need for protective legislation, and to the fact that unions were now allowing women to join, Kenyon felt increased comfort about supporting the ERA.

Kenyon remarked to the *New York Times*, "[W]e better have the Equal Rights Amendment in a hurry because I'm afraid the Supreme Court is going in a backward wave for the next 20 years."[96] The protective laws for which Kenyon had so fiercely advocated she now saw as outdated. Originally instituted to protect women in low-paying positions from exploitation, Kenyon urged that statutes be amended to provide employment-related protections for both men and women.[97] Until the Supreme Court agreed with her interpretation regarding the Fourteenth Amendment, Kenyon believed that passing the ERA would at least "stir up the men" and "annoy" the Court.[98]

In 1970, sex-based differentials in the law still existed across the country. For example, state laws prohibited women from working in certain professions, alimony could not be awarded to ex-husbands, women had to obtain court approval before they could begin a business apart from their husband, women were excluded from the Selective Service Act, women were excluded from jury service, Social Security provided higher benefits to men, state laws preferred the father as the custodian of minor children, and female criminal offenders incurred higher sanctions in criminal cases than males for the same offense.[99] There was still much work to be done regarding equality of the sexes.

On August 26, 1970, at age eighty-two, Kenyon marched alongside thousands in the Women's Strike for Equality parade in New York City. Locked arm in arm with Betty Friedan, women's rights activist and the first president of the National Organization for Women, Kenyon refused to ride in the car provided for her and walked down Fifth Avenue instead. Kenyon participated because she wanted the young activists to know that she was with them.[100] The march brought together fifty-four separate groups concerned with issues like equal pay, reproductive choice, and equal rights, making it the largest women's rights protest since the suffragists took to the streets and earning first page attention in most major newspapers.[101] The march also celebrated the fiftieth anniversary of the ratification of the Nineteenth Amendment.

In September 1970, the New York City Commission on Human Rights held an entire week of hearings on the status of women's rights. The testimony covered issues like sex discrimination, quotas for women, and bias against working women. Kenyon was there, and brought the plight of women, particularly the most vulnerable, to the attention of policymakers, urging them to "never forget that an enormous part of the discriminations we are concerned with hits people who have no backing and no resources the hardest of all." She then drove the point home, saying, "The women that I really care about are not the women on the top who want something fine and powerful for themselves, [but] . . . the poor women and the old women."[102] Kenyon received a copy of her transcript in the mail afterwards with the request that she edit it for publication in a trade paperback. Eleanor Holmes Norton, the commission chair, included a handwritten note saying the book could not go to press "without your unique prose, Dorothy!"[103] Norton would go on to head the US Equal Employment Opportunity Commission, then serve as congresswoman for the District of Columbia.[104]

Kenyon had spent decades, even within the ACLU, arguing that women needed to be seen as humans. Yet she and Murray still found instances of exclusion. In September 1970, they received a packet of materials for an upcoming board meeting; among the contents were a memo from the ACLU board with arguments for and against the ERA and an analysis of the amendment's probable effect on state minimum wage laws for women. [105] The memo was based on testimony given by four constitutional law experts, all men, before the Senate Judiciary Committee.[106] On September 23, 1970, Kenyon and Murray sent a joint telegram to the entire board in response: "Board materials include paper on Equal Rights Amendment written by four *men* law professors and (inadvertently) not one syllable from any women. We are aghast at such gallant effrontery. Hell hath no rage greater than a woman scorned. Beware of more materials."[107]

The next day, Kenyon and Murray sent a memo of their own to the board, advising a dual strategy of proceeding with litigation under the Equal Protection Clause while also supporting the ERA.[108] Recent Supreme Court appointments, they wrote, had resulted in an influx of strict constructionists, making it unlikely that the Court would accept any arguments claiming that the Fourteenth Amendment pertained to sex discrimination. They went on to remind the group that women had been waiting over a century for constitutional rights, and they could not wait any longer. Both the ERA and the Fourteenth Amendment, they noted, could serve to achieve the equality they sought.

Their argument worked. The Equality Committee suggested that the ACLU not attempt to abolish laws that afforded desirable outcomes for women in the workplace but rather should focus on extending protection against discrimination to men. Protective legislation, they emphasized, was now a hindrance. With protective laws prohibiting women from working overtime on the books, women were prevented from taking positions that required longer hours. Essentially, men could choose to work for extra money, but the state had declared that women could not. The committee's memo to the board of directors made this point plainly. "By protecting women, such laws actually relegate women to the bottom of the economic heap. It is not only middle-class, career-minded women who aspire to advancement; many a woman who must support dependent children would be glad to have the extra overtime money."[109]

On September 27, 1970, the ACLU board of directors endorsed the ERA by a vote of 52–1.[110] A few days later, the organization issued a press release announcing its support of the ERA and urging senators to vote for it. The statement noted the ACLU's frustration that the Supreme Court had "refused to apply the [Fourteenth] Amendment against sex discrimination because it has interpreted the Amendment in light of conditions prevailing at the time of its adoption. In 1868, women were not 'persons' in the legal sense." Given the Court's constructionist leanings, the ACLU thought that the ERA was essential to achieve "full equality of all individuals, on which rests the entire democratic experiment."[111] Even as the ACLU shifted its position to support the ERA, Americans were now polled for the first time about the amendment. Fifty-six percent of respondents declared they were in favor of the ERA.[112] The Senate, however, took little heed of this public popularity or of the ACLU's position. It failed to schedule a vote on the amendment before its fall adjournment.[113]

Even though Congress did not manage to accomplish a vote on the ERA in 1970, Kenyon was unwilling to give up the fight. Writing for the *Chelsea-Clinton News*, Kenyon continued her advocacy in favor of the ERA:

> The crux of the matter is Equal Rights. Women still occupy the same anomalous position that they did in 1868—*different* from other people, non-persons, outside the pale. Yet they are *different* only in the sense that they and men are *different* from one another, each being essential to the other. It would be just as wrong to put men beyond the pale and say that they, not women, are the non-persons, because *different*. Both positions are wrong; and this one only betrays the prevailing male chauvinistic mind, which always sees itself on top.[114]

Kenyon wrote Senator Edmund S. Muskie in 1971 asking for support and reminding him that women had been treated carelessly and outrageously throughout the centuries. However, she clarified, "[D]on't take me to be a feminist. . . . I am for human rights and that happens to include men as well as women. The XIV Amendment is where we belong. But the Supreme Court has rejected us. A Constitutional Amendment would benefit both sexes and I believe greatly ease existing tensions."[115] In a letter to her friend at the Citizens' Advisory Council on the Status of Women, Kenyon reiterated that the Fourteenth Amendment was the proper channel for eliminating sex-based differentials in the law, but that the Supreme Court had "stubbornly persisted in its notion that women are 'different' from everybody else, and therefore can never hope to be equal but must be 'protected' by men instead. . . . I therefore think the Equal Rights Amendment is our best move now and that we must all combine to work for it."[116]

• • •

Kenyon's shift in thinking, and her suggestion that ACLU priorities be redirected, helped determine some of what happened before the US Supreme Court in the 1970s. By now, law professor Ruth Bader Ginsburg was collaborating with the ACLU on sex discrimination cases. While an undergraduate student at Cornell, Ginsburg had been a research assistant for Dr. Robert E. Cushman, a government professor and constitutional law scholar. Dr. Cushman influenced Ginsburg's way of thinking regarding civil liberties and encouraged her to become a lawyer. As part of his mentorship, he discussed the actions of Senator Joseph McCarthy, convincing Ginsburg of the important role lawyers played in the areas of First and Fifth Amendment law.[117] Ginsburg later wrote, "The McCarthy era was a time when courageous lawyers were using their legal training in support of the right to think and speak freely. That a lawyer could do something that was personally satisfying and at the same time work to preserve the values that have made this country great was an exciting prospect for me."[118]

Ginsburg chose to work with the ACLU because it offered her the ability to handpick strong cases to litigate. Additionally, she "wanted to be a part of a general human rights agenda."[119] Ginsburg later said serving as a volunteer lawyer for the ACLU allowed her to "help advance the vibrant idea of the equal stature and dignity of men and women as a matter of constitutional principle."[120] The case of *Reed v. Reed* would give her this opportunity as she took on the role of principal author of the ACLU's brief.[121] In that case, after Sally Reed's teenage son died by suicide, Sally applied to administer his small estate. Cecil Reed, the teenager's father, who was estranged from Sally, later filed to be administrator as well. An Idaho statute at the time favored men over women to serve in this capacity, even when the woman petitioned the court first, so Cecil was appointed. Protesting the decision as unfair, Sally sought legal representation. Her counsel, Allen R. Derr, appealed the case to the Idaho Supreme Court. The ACLU reached out to Derr after reading about that court's ruling, which said the Equal Protection Clause did not invalidate the statute preferring males over females as estate administrators.[122] They had been looking for just such a case, one allowing them to take on sex-based classification. Derr wrote that he would welcome the ACLU's assistance.[123]

Before submitting the *Reed* brief to the Court, the ACLU provided Kenyon and Murray with a final draft and asked to include them as coauthors of the document.[124] Ginsburg felt strongly that they should be recognized due to their advancement of the Fourteenth Amendment litigation strategy. They gave their consent to be listed as authors. Ginsburg would later write that she added their names to give credit to arguments of theirs that, until the 1970s, the Court was not prepared to hear.[125]

Response to the brief was very positive. Congresswoman Martha W. Griffiths, the second woman from Michigan elected to the US House of Representatives, received an advance copy from ACLU legal director Melvin Wulf.[126] Griffiths and her husband, Hicks, had studied law together at the University of Michigan Law School and were the first married couple to graduate from there.[127] In a note thanking Wulf for the well-written brief and the work the ACLU was doing on behalf of women, she expressed a desire to resign from humanity if the brief was unsuccessful; but, she said, she had full confidence in the ACLU.[128] Wulf wrote to Derr saying that the brief was "one of the very best . . . to come out of our office" during his time with the organization.[129]

The good spirits did not last long. A breakdown in cooperation occurred between the ACLU and Derr prior to the oral argument. Wulf wanted Eleanor Holmes Norton to argue the case, both as an experienced constitutional lawyer and as head of the New York City Commission on Human Rights.[130] He argued that *Reed* had "profound constitutional significance" and that he felt a "duty to the public in general and the Supreme Court in particular to see that the case is argued in such a way as to maximize the results."[131] By this point, Derr had begun avoiding Wulf's calls and letters. Wulf's correspondence to Derr took on an increasingly irritated tone. In September 1971, one month before the scheduled oral argument, Wulf wrote inviting Derr and Sally to come to New York so he could attempt to persuade Sally to let the ACLU argue the case. If they were unwilling to do that, he said at least Derr needed to come to New York to practice his argument, writing: "Since you have never argued before the Supreme Court, you really have no idea what is in store for you."[132] Now with three weeks to go, Derr wrote back saying he would be willing to split his oral argument time with the ACLU; unfortunately, his offer came too late, and the clerk of the Court denied the request.[133] Wulf did not hold back his displeasure, writing in a letter to Derr:

> Though my strenuous efforts to persuade you to let the case be argued by a woman were prompted primarily by my good faith belief that a competent woman attorney would enhance the presentation, there was always in the back of my mind the fear that you were not competent to do the job. My fears were based on the brief you filed in the *Reed* case in the Idaho Supreme

> Court. It is, in a word, an awful piece of work which demonstrates total ignorance of the equal protection clause and of the cases involving sexual discrimination; it also demonstrates that you had no interest in learning anything about those two subjects in order to present them intelligently to the Supreme Court of Idaho. Now you're going into the big leagues with a big league brief and I have no reason to believe that you are any more prepared to handle the case competently now than in the Idaho Supreme Court. And I must say that having devoted weeks of hard work to our brief, I'm not looking forward to the case being incompetently argued before the Supreme Court of the United States just because you want what you imagine will be some glory or ego satisfaction.[134]

Following the oral argument, Wulf wrote Derr calling it "one of the worst in the history of the Supreme Court."[135]

Despite Derr's poor performance, the US Supreme Court under Chief Justice Warren Burger issued a unanimous decision overturning the Idaho law that preferred men over women as administrators—the first time it had overturned a law in response to a woman's complaint of sex discrimination. The Court agreed that women would be protected under the Equal Protection Clause of the Fourteenth Amendment and that there must be a rational relationship between a sex-based differential in the law and a legitimate state interest for the law to succeed.[136] Following *Reed*, the Burger court "showed consistent hostility to laws that facially discriminated against women."[137] As Linda K. Kerber notes in *No Constitutional Right to Be Ladies: Women and the Obligations of Citizenship*, sex discrimination was now viewed as a burden, not a privilege, and this new perspective "challenged law and custom in virtually every sector of American life, from the workplace to schools to intensely private matters of sexuality."[138]

Building on the *Reed* victory, the ACLU national board asked the Equality Committee to design a program aimed specifically at women's rights, and appropriated $50,000 from the ACLU's general account to fund it.[139] This would ultimately become the Women's Rights Project, which Ginsburg and Brenda Feigen would co-coordinate.[140] Ginsburg was tapped by ACLU executive director Aryeh Neier because she had been "on the fringes of the ACLU for some time."[141] She also had a personal connection with Wulf, both of them having attended the same summer camp as children.

Philip Hirschkop, Pauli Murray, Eleanor Holmes Norton, Suzanne Post, Faith Seidenberg, and Gloria Steinem were among the original members of the Women's Rights Project's advisory committee.[142] The project's activities included offering assistance to ACLU affiliates in sex discrimination litigation, informing ACLU affiliates about pending cases, and serving as counsel in cases of national significance. The project considered its chief priority to be persuading the Supreme Court to reverse decisions affirming sex-based differentials in statutes. The ACLU board declared "women's rights its top legal and legislative priority."[143]

Ginsburg recognized that, since the beginning of women's rights litigation, lawyers were representing clients without considering the larger picture. She felt strongly that courts needed to be educated about the ways in which sex discrimination could hurt both sexes. And so she waited for the right case to come along, one that would effectuate enduring change.

One important case was *Weinberger v. Wiesenfeld*, decided by the US Supreme Court in 1975. In that case, the petitioner, Stephen Wiesenfeld, was a widowed father whose wife, the primary breadwinner of the family, had died in childbirth. He wanted to stay home with his son and not work full-time; however, since he was a male, he was not entitled to his wife's Social Security benefits. Ginsburg represented Wiesenfeld, demonstrating to the male justices on the Court how sex discrimination impacted both men and women. Another unanimous decision came down, the Court ruling that the sex-based distinction in Social Security death benefits violated due process.[144] Ginsburg later wrote, "Using sex as a convenient shorthand to substitute for financial need or willingness to bring up a baby did not comply with the equal protection principle, as the Court had grown to understand that principle."[145]

Even with such successes at the US Supreme Court, there was still confusion surrounding sex discrimination. In an article for the *New York Times*, Ginsburg advocated for equal rights for women, arguing that before the Supreme Court applied the Fourteenth Amendment to sex discrimination cases in *Reed v. Reed*, it had treated each sex discrimination case in isolation.[146] This ad hoc approach to decision-making in sex discrimination cases should, she said, be replaced with a clear and consistent framework, such as the Fourteenth Amendment provided for in race discrimination cases. If the Court could not do that, she argued, then the ERA should be passed. In 1981, Ginsburg continued advocating for the ratification of the ERA. Without it, she said, "the controversy will drag on as case by case is reviewed, ideally by legislators, but if they default, then by judges. . . . We believe in racial equality, we believe in free speech. We have recorded those beliefs in the Constitution, our fundamental instrument of government. We are advancing toward the belief that men and women should be seen as equal before the law. We should record that basic principle in the Constitution."[147]

The ERA passed in the Senate and went on to the states for ratification in 1972.[148] Virginia became the thirty-eighth state to ratify in 2020; however, the states had missed the ratification deadline, which had been extended to 1982.[149] Litigation is ongoing around the status of the ERA. As of 2026, it is not part of the US Constitution.

• • •

According to Susan M. Hartmann, by the mid-1970s the ACLU had become the "premier litigator for women's rights and defender of reproductive freedom."[150] Ginsburg would brief ten sex discrimination cases before the US Supreme Court in the 1970s, and give oral argument in six.[151] She would ultimately be recognized as the "founding mother" of modern constitutional sex equality law because of her advocacy before the Supreme Court.[152] Ginsburg's successes in convincing the Court to apply the Equal Protection Clause to sex-based differentials during this decade can be traced directly to Kenyon's litigation strategies.

The ACLU provided Kenyon an ideal platform from which to lobby on behalf of the issues that were important to her. While she did not consider herself an interpreter for the women's movement, she described herself as sympathetic to the cause, and specifically to the effort to remove "the many crippling discriminations against women particularly in the economic field."[153] As she put it, she and her fellow activists were engaged in "the battle to coax women out of their cocoon of submission to men's minds. . . . [T]he butterfly isn't born yet. But it's definitely fluttering."[154]

NINE

# *A Gutsy Fighter*

## SEX EQUALITY AND JURY SERVICE

> The unfortunate woman plaintiff or defendant is there faced by a male judge, flanked by a male jury, surrounded by male lawyers generally . . . with a male clerk and bailiff, and a mob of male bipeds in the lobby. A woman, especially if she is a timid one, is at a terrible disadvantage in such a place.
>
> CLARA FOLTZ,
> *Describing a woman litigant in 1894*[1]

KENYON HAD ADVOCATED FOR SEX EQUALITY in jury service ever since becoming a lawyer. She was frustrated that the right to participate in this important civic duty varied based on geography, and that state constitutions and statutes exempted women based solely on their sex. She had argued unsuccessfully in *Hoyt v. Florida* that women should be required by states to participate in jury service along the same lines as men. This was a loss she would not forget. A fire was lit within her to convince courts that she was correct that the Fourteenth Amendment required service of women on juries. *White v. Crook* in Alabama would be the case to do just that.

. . .

The first jury that included women was convened in Wyoming Territory in 1870, and the first permanent state statute permitting women to serve was passed in 1898 in Utah.[2] Washington followed in 1911, and California in 1917.[3] With the passage of the Nineteenth Amendment to the US Constitution in 1920, women gained the right to vote in every state. The Nineteenth Amendment caused great debate among legislators and legal scholars about its application, especially regarding the right of women to also sit on juries.[4] In some states, such as Iowa, Michigan, Nevada, and Pennsylvania, statutes that defined juror competency allowed women to automatically be deemed competent once they obtained the right to vote.[5] However, the granting of suffrage did not occasion a universal, automatic removal of the word "male" in state statutes, which raised the question of whether women should, in fact, have the right to serve on juries.[6] The legislation that was enacted to fill that void was mixed. Some laws excluded women from trial juries but not grand juries. Some states made women automatically eligible for jury service, while others did not, based on how those states defined a voter or elector. By 1923, eighteen states and the territory of Alaska permitted women to serve on juries.[7] Some states, however, continued to exclude women wholly, while others passed laws providing that a woman could volunteer to serve on a jury by affirmatively placing her name on the jury list at the court clerk's office.

In March 1929, the *Connecticut New Britain Herald* reported that a measure allowing women to serve on juries had been rejected in the Connecticut senate. The justification, according to the committee that considered the issue, was that there would be "great expense for separate female jury quarters" in the courthouse.[8] Senator Mary Baker Weaver, the only woman member of the Connecticut senate and the one who had introduced the bill, denied that women's jury service was a fad and pointed out that women had served on juries in Babylon in 22 B.C.[9] This statement elicited a snide retort from Senator William Hirschberg: "That was the reason, perhaps, Babylon fell."[10]

There were others in state governments across the country, however, whose beliefs aligned with Senator Weaver. For example, in 1930, New York Lieutenant Governor Herbert H. Lehman went on record supporting compulsory jury service for women as a right of citizenship.[11] And in Ohio, Florence Allen, the country's first woman to sit on a state supreme court, advocated for women on juries because they doubled the chances of "getting good juries."[12] Allen, who was elected to the Ohio Supreme Court in 1922, was a trailblazer for women in the law after she graduated from NYU School of Law in 1913. Upon being appointed to the US Court of Appeals for the Sixth Circuit in 1934, Allen became the first woman to serve as a federal appeals court judge.[13] As an aside, Allen and Kenyon, both graduates of NYU School of Law, were mutual admirers, and Kenyon organized an alumnae dinner in 1948 to celebrate Allen's many accomplishments.[14]

By the early 1930s, activists around the country were proposing legislation to remove male-specific wording from state constitutions and laws. Instead of engaging in a national campaign, activists worked state by state to obtain statutory and constitutional change. The executive secretary of the League of

Women Voters likened the lobbying effort to a "second suffrage campaign—laborious, costly and exasperating."[15]

Legal changes proposed by jury service activists in New York typically died in legislative committee. In 1937 state senator Philip M. Kleinfeld proposed a bill allowing an automatic exemption for women based on their sex. Support for the jury service bill was far from universal, and dozens of county and city bar associations and men's lawyers' organizations filed objections.[16] The bill ultimately passed, however, thirty-four to thirteen, and was signed into law on September 1, 1937. Hundreds of women lined up to register to serve on juries, excited about this new opportunity, with Eleanor Roosevelt being one of the earliest arrivals and most animated participants.[17] The *New York World-Telegram & Sun* reported on the women registering in the Hall of Records and offered its own prediction: women jurors would be harsh in sentencing men who had abused or killed their wives' lovers.[18]

Kenyon's response to the new law that allowed women to affirmatively register for jury service was that it would give "a new lease of life to the jury system."[19] But, disappointed that the bill did not require compulsory service, she also called it "inadequate" and "not amounting to a hill of beans."[20] Although as a lawyer, woman, and public official (at the time she was serving as first deputy commissioner of licenses) Kenyon herself could have claimed the exemption, she wanted to serve and was one of the first to register in New York City.[21] She was sworn in by the acting commissioner of jurors on September 1, 1937.[22] A month later she was seated on a jury, with another woman lawyer serving as the foreperson.[23] At the time, divorce cases were tried in front of a jury, and this high-profile case involved Gladys Kimball, a WPA actress accused of committing adultery. The jury, made up mostly of women, acquitted Kimball. When the judge asked Kenyon whether sympathy for Kimball might have influenced the verdict, she adamantly denied it, saying the case had simply not been proven.[24]

Kenyon was part of a committee to plan "jury schools" where women could learn about courtroom processes. She believed women brought something to jury service that men could not, particularly in criminal cases. Kenyon remarked that "[women] know the social forces that make for crime better than men. They know the effect of home environment, the influence of poverty, the hopelessness of economic insecurity."[25] It is interesting to note that Kenyon was using sex-based stereotypes to support her position.

Public opinion remained mixed on the issue of women's jury service. Some believed that because women helped make and administer laws, and must obey them, they should be eligible to serve.[26] Others argued that women were too easily swayed and that to empanel them could undermine the jury system.[27] Some based their opinion on what judges reported, especially those who said that, in their experience, women jurors were just as able as men to render judgment. Others could not understand why women would want to serve, with one person saying it was "enough to make a man blush" thinking about mixed juries locked in a room together to deliberate a verdict.[28] Another said, "[Jury service] is often trying on the health of men . . . [and] will be worse on the health of women. . . . Many cases tried in court," they went on, "are controversies over questions with which men are generally familiar but which women know little or nothing about. They have no occasion to know about them no matter how high the general intelligence of the women may be."[29]

Opponents argued variously that women belonged in the home, courthouses were not equipped to accommodate women jurors, and "the so-called weaker sex should be protected from the sordidness of criminal trials."[30] A principal at a Texas school, Miss Lida Gibbs, disagreed with those arguments, equating the right to vote with the right to sit on juries. "[S]queamishness should be put aside," she said, "and women take up their duty and right."[31] However, Mrs. H. T. Allard, a Texas housewife, strongly disagreed: "There are too many times in a home when the woman can't leave. Women are too emotional; a good-looking lawyer could sway them too easily."[32]

Women's experiences on juries in Illinois during this period provided evidence to support such claims. Mrs. W. J. Welch, one of the first women jurors in the town of Bloomington, reported not enjoying the experience. "It was a spicy affair and I say no more for me," she complained. "Some women may like that but I don't. It takes you away from home too."[33] Illinois circuit judge Chalmer C. Taylor disagreed that the quality of the work done by juries would suffer if women were allowed on them; after all, he noted, "[N]o one would hold that giving women a right to vote had lowered legislative standards."[34] Years later, however, another Illinois circuit court judge said that all-female juries had brought in "ridiculous verdicts," and he preferred an all-male jury. Speaking to the Men's Club of a United Protestant Church, the judge quipped: "It's amazing to me that [twelve] women could agree on anything."[35]

By 1947, thirteen states still barred women from jury service because of sex.[36] The Arkansas constitution, for one, stated that "women shall not be compelled to serve on juries."[37] In a 1949 ruling by the state supreme court, the reasoning behind this constitutional provision was reiterated: "Criminal court trials often involve testimony of the foulest kind, and they sometimes require consideration of indecent conduct, the use of filthy and loathsome words, references to intimate sex relationships, and other elements that would prove humiliating, embarrassing, and degrading to a lady." The court went on to state that defendants, in order to be successful with a Fourteenth Amendment challenge, needed to provide "something more than continuing failure of jury commissioners to call women for services in a division of the Court where the innate refinement peculiar to women would be assailed with verbal expressions, gestures, conversations and demonstrations from which most would recoil."[38] In Texas, too, women were barred by the state's constitution from serving on juries as well. After being rejected by Texas voters in 1949, an amendment allowing women to serve finally passed five years later.[39]

The Alabama House of Representatives studied a jury duty bill for women in 1955. Representative Albert Brewer expressed his belief that only a few hundred women out of the thousands he represented wanted juries open to them. "Most of those pushing the bill are professional club women," he said. "They don't speak for the average woman who must keep a home and raise a family." Senator Albert Davis, from Aliceville, Alabama, said that women should not be subjected "to the unsavory testimony that sometimes comes up in criminal trials."[40] Another legislator argued that it would be too expensive for counties to provide restrooms and jury rooms for two sexes. These arguments were convincing, and Alabama did not permit women to sit on juries until 1967.[41]

But even as laws changed, attitudes did not keep pace. In Minnesota, one of the states that promptly passed laws allowing women to serve as jurors after the Nineteenth Amendment was ratified, a 1960 *Minneapolis Morning Tribune* story revealed that most men and women still preferred an all-male jury to an all-female one. Vernon Pagel wanted an all-male jury because females are "rattle-brained and let emotions run away with them," but he also said he would like to see his wife on a jury because the "judge wouldn't get a word in edgewise."[42] Donna Bladow wanted to face an all-male jury because "[m]en are more level-headed" and an "all-female jury would take days to reach a decision because they love to argue about anything." Louise McDaniels doubted an all-female jury could understand the judge, as women did not know anything about laws. Fred W. Hall gave a conditional response: "If I still had my hair, I would prefer to face an all-female jury. But under the circumstances, I'd take an all-male jury."[43]

An August 7, 1961, memorandum of the US Department of Labor Women's Bureau included a summary of jury service for women.[44] While the laws of twenty-eight states provided that women were subject to jury service on the same terms and conditions as men, seven of those states permitted women to be excused based on a family responsibility. Sixteen states and the District of Columbia permitted a woman to claim an exemption solely because of her sex. Three states required a woman to indicate her desire to serve before becoming eligible. Alabama, Mississippi, and South Carolina still excluded women from jury service, though women could, and did, serve on federal juries in those states by virtue of the Civil Rights Act of 1957.

• • •

Upon joining the ACLU board in 1965, Pauli Murray was tasked with helping Kenyon write a brief for *White v. Crook*, a case primarily about Alabama's continued exclusion of women and Black men from serving on juries. Their expertise in the cause of women made Kenyon and Murray perfect partners in this challenge, one that began, in a sense, with the end of the Civil War. At this time, although the Reconstruction Amendments ostensibly provided Black males with full citizenship, they still had to fight for those rights and responsibilities.[45] In 1880, for example, in *Strauder v. West Virginia*, the US Supreme Court struck down a West Virginia statute that limited jury service to white adult males, arguing that it violatied the Equal Protection Clause of the Fourteenth Amendment. The denial of the right of a citizen to serve on a jury due to color alone, the majority stated, was "practically a brand upon them affixed by the law, an assertion of their inferiority, and a stimulant to that race prejudice which is an impediment to securing to individuals of the race that equal justice which the law aims to secure to all others."[46] Despite this victory, history proves such exclusionary practices continued, particularly in southern states.

In 1946 in *Ballard v. United States*, the Court confronted the fundamental fairness of women's exclusion from jury service, stating in its decision, "[I]f the shoe were on the other foot, who would claim that a jury was truly representative of the community if all men were intentionally and systematically excluded from the panel?" It was no different, the Court opined, from excluding a certain economic or racial population; indeed, "a flavor, a distinct quality is lost if either sex is excluded." The Court thus concluded that barring women from federal jury service "deprives the jury system of the broad base it was designed by Congress to have in our democratic society."[47]

The case of *Fay v. People of New York* challenged the New York statute that permitted women to serve on juries but allowed them an exemption if they so chose.[48] In its decision, the Court found that merely showing that a class of persons was not represented in a jury was not enough to question its composition; rather, it had to be demonstrated that such exclusion had a discriminatory purpose. Because women could volunteer for jury service, they were ipso facto not excluded. The Court pointed out that "[u]ntil recently, and for nearly a half-century after the Fourteenth Amendment was adopted, it was universal practice in the United States to allow only men to sit on juries."[49]

While *Strauder, Ballard,* and *Fay* undergirded Kenyon's understanding of how the Court had analyzed cases involving jury service laws in the past, by the beginning of the 1960s Kenyon was ready to challenge courts to think differently about the Equal Protection Clause of the Fourteenth Amendment. Her involvement in *Hoyt v. Florida*, which questioned different requirements for men and women to serve on juries, allowed Kenyon to develop her ideas about the US Constitution's take on sex-based discrimination.

Women were first admitted to practice law in Florida in the late 1890s, yet it was not until 1949 that women had an option to serve on a jury.[50] Because of a legislative compromise, the Florida legislature had enacted a statute saying no woman could be considered for jury service unless she registered with the clerk of the circuit court her desire to be placed on the jury list, meaning that Florida women had to make a special effort to participate in jury service. The legal challenge to this statute began when Gwendolyn Hoyt was charged with the murder of her husband after striking him with their son's broken baseball bat.[51] The couple had had a tumultuous relationship—marrying, divorcing, remarrying—with allegations of infidelity and behaviors indicative of what is known today as intimate partner violence.

At Hoyt's criminal trial, only men sat on the jury. Hoyt argued that because the jury was not properly made up of a cross-section of her peers, the Florida statute deprived her of her Fifth, Sixth, and Fourteenth Amendment rights. The trial judge disagreed, and Hoyt was ultimately convicted. The case was appealed to the Florida Supreme Court, which dismissed Hoyt's appeal, relying on the lack of any US Supreme Court decision striking down differential requirements regarding jury service.[52] Hoyt appealed to the US Supreme Court, and Kenyon wrote the amicus brief on behalf of the ACLU, arguing that women were placed in a separate class from men because they had to affirmatively volunteer to be included for jury service. Two distinct rights were thus implicated: the right of a fully enfranchised woman to participate in a public duty without restrictions and the right of all persons accused of a crime to be tried before a jury consisting of an adequate cross-section of their peers.

Kenyon considered the practical impacts on Hoyt herself, lacking as she did the benefit of a female juror perspective. In 1957, Hillsborough County had 114,247 registered voters, 40 percent of them women. Yet only 218 women were registered to serve on juries. Clearly, few women were volunteering for jury service under the current statutory scheme. Moreover, the jury commissioner made it a practice to exclude some of the names of women who had registered. Out of the 218 women potentially able to serve, only ten names were left undrawn from the year before—which meant that only those ten women were available for selection on Hoyt's jury. Kenyon argued that the commissioners and their staff had engaged in "a planned, systematic and arbitrary exclusion of women for all practical purposes from the lists."[53]

Kenyon reminded the Court of when women could not participate in the political system:

> Old habits change slowly; customs survive far beyond the reason for their being; the herd instinct is strong. . . . "Woman's place is in the home," a slogan of ancient origin, has living force and terrific emotional impact even today. It has taken people a long time to realize (and some still do not) that the great revolutionary forces that helped to bring about the advancement and emancipation of women in the last century have changed the patterns of living for women to an astonishing extent and have in effect forced many women to find a new place for themselves in the world outside their homes.[54]

The notion that women needed to be protected from jury service because of their home and family duties, she argued, was misplaced. For evidentiary support, she turned to the US Department of Labor's *Handbook on Women Workers*, which showed that, as of 1958, women made up 33 percent of the total labor force.[55] They were not all staying home.

Kenyon pointed out that a woman's life expectancy was 73.7 years, as compared to men's 67.2 years.[56] Furthermore, only eleven years of the average married woman's adult life was needed for child-rearing. If a woman was to be fully emancipated and enfranchised, Kenyon argued, it was a "genuine humiliation and degradation of her spirit" to deem her ineligible to share this duty of citizenship with her male counterparts. She concluded by posing the following question: "Does it not shock our sense of fair play that, because a few young women with small babies at home might find it inconvenient to come to court . . . [Hoyt] should be deprived of even one single woman on her jury?"[57]

The oral argument before the Supreme Court was held on October 19, 1961. The petitioner, Gwendolyn Hoyt, was represented by Herbert B. Ehrmann, and the respondent, the state of Florida, was represented by that state's assistant attorney general George R. Georgieff.[58] Kenyon was in the gallery listening.[59] Ehrmann went first. Justice Frankfurter asked if one of the arguments for women's suffrage hadn't been that women were more aggressive or more alert than men. Ehrmann said he would argue that men and women were different; however, regarding public service, both groups were "actuated by the same impulses." Frankfurter retorted, "Don't stress the equality of behavior between the men and women too hard. . . . You'd get into trouble." He went on to suggest that if Florida women really wanted to be included in jury service "like men, there'd be no trouble getting that legislation through." Ehrmann could not agree with that, as he was unsure where the power lay in Florida's legislature. He argued, however, that he was not urging the right of all women to serve on juries; rather, he was defending Hoyt specifically, who had been sentenced to thirty years of hard labor and who would, he believed, have benefited from having female members on her jury.[60]

Georgieff stated that Florida's statutes did not exclude women from service, as they could affirmatively volunteer if they wanted to be called for jury duty. This ignored the argument that men did not have an affirmative duty in order to engage in this right of citizenship. Perhaps one of the most patriarchally entrenched statements Georgieff made involved men's and women's separate spheres: "This is unfortunately a man's world and . . . I'm afraid it's going to remain one." He further argued that Hoyt did not have the "right to a woman on this jury. She simply had the right to an impartial jury, no family, no friends, just an impartial jury."[61]

In the end, Ehrmann's arguments failed to move the Court, which found no reason to conclude the statute was unconstitutional. Justice John Marshall Harlan, writing for the majority, declared that "despite the enlightened emancipation of women from the restrictions and protections of bygone years, and their entry into many parts of community life formerly considered to be reserved to men, woman is still regarded as the center of home and family life."[62] According to the Court, states acting in pursuit of the general welfare could pass laws excluding women from jury service because of their special responsibilities.

By identifying women as the center of home and family life, the Court implied that both men and women, and arguably any children, would be harmed by women serving on a jury.[63] It failed to recognize the detrimental sociological impacts that excluding women imposed. The Court also was shortsighted in its unwillingness to understand administrative hardships placed on local and state governments by upholding the exclusion of a large segment of the population. Recycling the same names, and frequently calling the same individuals, required a disproportionate sacrifice of time on the part of those called, with little remuneration from the county for their service.

The Court permitted the volunteer scheme to continue based on the idea that women were home raising children while men worked, without any determination as to whether service would be an actual hardship. The mere fact that there were two sexes was enough for the Supreme Court justices to believe differential treatment of men and women was merited. Chief Justice Earl Warren, along with Justices Black and Douglas, originally wanted to reverse the Florida Supreme Court's decision, arguing that an affirmative obligation requiring women to register with the clerk so they could be included in jury selection limited the number of women on juries and that was essentially the same as excluding them. At the end of the judicial conference, Chief Justice Warren said he would write the formal dissent. Justice Harlan was assigned the majority opinion, and he circulated his draft less than one month later. Justice Douglas drafted a concurrence, which Justice Black joined. Eventually Chief Justice Warren changed his mind regarding writing a dissent and joined the concurrence as well.[64]

The *Washington Post* published an opinion piece on the Supreme Court's decision, saying it was "not likely to be its last word on the subject of women serving on juries." The *Post* opined that because of the Civil Rights Act of 1957, which made women eligible for jury service in federal courts, "most enlightened jurisdictions now make women as welcome in the jury box as they are in the voting booth. The few states that are still holding out against feminine jurors would do well to correct this deficiency in their emancipation statutes before the Supreme Court finds it necessary to reconsider its dictum of four generations ago [referring to *Strauder v. West Virginia*]."[65]

When Ruth Bader Ginsburg began litigating sex discrimination cases on behalf of the ACLU, she believed that overturning *Hoyt* should be a primary goal. At the hearings to confirm her nomination to the US Supreme Court in 1993, Ginsburg said *Hoyt* had had special meaning for her during her time as a lawyer and professor.[66] She believed the opinion "reflected the long-prevailing 'separate-spheres' mentality, the notion that it was man's lot, because of his nature to be the breadwinner, the head of the household, the representative of the family outside the home; and it was woman's lot, because of her nature, to bear and alone to raise children and keep the house in order."[67]

Kenyon would later write that Justice Harlan's opinion in *Hoyt* was a "stupid, insensitive, wicked decision," one she never got over.[68] In 1971, writing to an ACLU colleague, she said his opinion had given her a "clobbering" and that it was "still written in letters of fire in my brain." The Fourteenth Amendment, she went on, "as interpreted by the Supreme Court to date, has in effect said that we are not persons. . . . Without constitutional rights, we are simply pawns in a political bind and as long as men dominate the political machine, we are likely to remain so."[69] *Hoyt* clearly disappointed Kenyon, yet she refused to give up. Instead she focused her attention on convincing the ACLU board members that she was right to use the Equal Protection Clause to eliminate sex-based differentials in the law. The case also spurred her to direct more of her time and energy toward race discrimination cases.

Three years after *Hoyt*, on December 8, 1964, Kenyon traveled to Washington, DC, to watch her friend Constance Baker Motley argue before the Supreme Court in the case of *Swain v. Alabama*. Motley, a lawyer with the NAACP Legal Defense and Educational Fund, had worked on the landmark case *Brown v. Board of Education*. She was the first Black woman to argue a case before the US Supreme Court; the first Black woman elected to the New York state senate, in 1964; the first woman president of the Borough of Manhattan, in 1965; and the first Black woman to serve as a federal judge, appointed in 1966.[70] She would be promoted to chief judge in 1980.[71]

Robert Swain had been convicted of raping a white woman in Talladega County, Alabama, and sentenced to death by an all-white, all-male jury. In that county, Black citizens had been historically excluded from serving on both criminal and civil juries. Motley was therefore arguing that Swain's due process and equal protection rights had been violated. Kenyon thought that Motley's argument should have been specifically that *women* had been excluded from jury service, but because it had not been used in the lower court, Motley was prohibited from arguing it.[72] Still, Kenyon believed that Motley had presented a strong case and thought the Court would decide in her favor.[73]

In the end, that did not happen. The Court issued its 6–3 opinion in *Swain* on March 8, 1965, holding that the exclusion of Black jurors had not been demonstrated to amount to discrimination as outlined by the Fourteenth Amendment. Kenyon wrote Motley a month later saying how much she had enjoyed watching her argue before the Supreme Court, only to end up furiously gritting her teeth upon reading the opinion. "It's one of those odd swings of the pendulum in civil rights cases which the Supreme Court indulges in every now and then," Kenyon wrote, "like a dance that takes two steps forward for every one back. But I hate that it should have happened to *you* with your wonderful record of victories."[74]

Kenyon went on to say she wished the case could have been argued on the basis of unconstitutionality due to the statute's "total exclusion of women from jury service." At this point, Kenyon worried about using the exclusion theory in jury service cases and wondered if they should develop a new approach. Because the Fourteenth Amendment granted affirmative rights to Black citizens, she argued, government officials had a duty to choose jury members "fairly and equitably among the various distinctive groupings in the community," which meant they could "no longer take shelter in the smug remark (almost always untrue) that they have no idea who is on the list" and whether they were Black or white.[75] Kenyon wanted an end to the practice of commissioners cherry-picking white men for juries.

Because of the assigned role of women in society, which caused legislatures and courts to treat them paternalistically, all previous attempts to challenge sex-based discrimination using the Fourteenth Amendment had failed. The Alabama case *White v. Crook* would successfully link the civil rights and women's rights movements through the talents and intellectual prowess of Kenyon and Pauli Murray.

. . .

Lowndes County, Alabama, known locally as "Bloody Lowndes," was historically a violent community.[76] No Black citizen had voted or served on a jury in the county for over fifty years.[77] A saying among white citizens was that any Black person who tried to register to vote "would be dead by nightfall."[78] The county was described as the very "symbol of segregated or all-white justice in the nation."[79]

In 1965, civil rights workers were focusing their attention on Lowndes County. On March 1 of that year, thirty-seven Black citizens, encouraged by volunteers with the Southern Christian Leadership Conference and the Student Nonviolent Coordinating Committee, tried to register to vote but were turned away.[80] Two weeks later, seventeen Black citizens succeeded in completing the voter registration form and taking the literacy test; of these, two passed and became registered to vote—John C. Lawson and John Hulett.[81] Additionally, the school board, so as not to lose federal funding, had submitted a high school desegregation plan in compliance with the *Brown v. Board of Education* decision of 1954.[82] Tensions were high because of these changes in the status quo.

The Voting Rights Act was signed into law on August 6, 1965, outlawing literacy tests as a barrier to voter registration. The US Attorney General sent federal examiners four days later to Lowndes County to facilitate voter registration drives, since only 3.8 percent of Black citizens of voting age were registered, all of them since March 1, 1965.[83] The white citizens of the county reacted to the arrival of federal examiners with hostility.

Jonathan M. Daniels, a twenty-five-year-old white seminarian from New Hampshire and graduate of the Virginia Military Institute, was doing civil rights work in Alabama for the Episcopal Society for Racial and Cultural Unity.[84] After participating in the historic Selma march, he went to Lowndes County to continue his work.[85] On August 14, 1965, Daniels, together with a Catholic priest, Father Richard Morrisroe, was demonstrating against whites-only local businesses in the town of Fort Deposit.[86] They were joined by other protesters, including Ruby Sales, a seventeen-year-old Tuskegee University student and volunteer with the Student Nonviolent Coordinating Committee, and Joyce Bailey, a local nineteen-year-old.[87]

The demonstration had barely begun when they were met by a mob of white men with weapons. The protesters were promptly taken into custody for "resisting arrest and picketing to cause blood" and brought to the Hayneville jail, some twenty miles away, in a flatbed truck used to collect garbage.[88] They were incarcerated for days in horrific conditions: the toilets overflowed, leaving raw sewage on the floor of the cells; the jailers threatened to only supply drinking water from the toilets; no showering was permitted; and there was no air conditioning, or even fans, to combat the Alabama heat.[89] While the protesters were incarcerated, Peter Hall, a Black civil rights lawyer, filed a petition to transfer the state charges to federal court. Worried about the implications of a federal lawsuit, the mayor contacted the jailer and demanded the protestors be freed.[90]

Upon their release from jail on August 20, six days after their arrest, Daniels, Morrisroe, Sales, and Bailey went to the local convenience store, Varner's Cash Store, for cold soft drinks. There they encountered Tom L.

Coleman, a fifty-four-year-old white resident of Lowndes County who served as a deputy sheriff when needed.[91] Coleman, armed with a twelve-gauge shotgun, shouted at them to get out or he would blow their heads off. Daniels asked if Coleman was threatening them, to which Coleman replied, "You damn right I am!"[92] Daniels grabbed the back of Sales's blouse and pulled her to the ground.[93] Coleman then fired the shotgun, killing Daniels instantly. Morrisroe grabbed Bailey's hand and turned to run, but Coleman shot him in the back, causing him to fall to the ground.[94] Bailey ran for cover near an abandoned car.[95] Morrisroe was taken by ambulance to a local hospital, where he underwent a lengthy surgery that led to the removal of his spleen and part of his lung.[96] He remained in critical condition for several days.[97]

Initially, police charged Coleman with murder, but a grand jury returned a first-degree manslaughter charge, punishable by one to ten years in prison.[98] The grand jury also returned an assault and battery charge for the shooting of Morrisroe, a misdemeanor punishable by up to one year in jail.[99] The office of Alabama attorney general Richmond Flowers, who said he was shocked the grand jury did not return a first-degree murder charge, eventually took over prosecution of the case.[100] The trial was quickly set for September 28, 1965.

Charles Morgan Jr., an attorney working for the ACLU, saw the Coleman trial as an opportunity to challenge jury service exclusion in Alabama. He wanted to file a concurrent suit in federal court in an effort to halt Coleman's criminal trial until it could be determined that women and Black men could serve on the jury. Morgan recruited Gardenia White, a Black woman from Lowndes County who was excluded by state law from serving on the jury because of her sex, to serve as the primary plaintiff in a suit against the jury commissioner, Bruce Crook, who was white.[101] White's fellow plaintiffs in the federal lawsuit included both women and men—one of whom was John Hulett.[102] Morgan sought an injunction of all Lowndes County jury trials until the federal court had adjudicated on the question of jury discrimination. He lost that motion, so Coleman's criminal trial continued. The federal lawsuit would also continue.

The trial, set in the whitewashed, slave-built county courthouse, was full of irregularities, all of which appeared to work in Coleman's favor.[103] Coleman's name appeared on the list of jurors summoned for his own trial, and no Black men were called to serve as jurors.[104] At trial, the assistant prosecutor, Joe Breck Gantt, informed the court that his primary witness, Father Morrisroe, was still hospitalized and unavailable to testify. He then stated that he wanted to dismiss the manslaughter indictment so he could seek murder charges in the future against Coleman. When the judge ordered Gantt to proceed with the prosecution, Gantt responded that he could not do so without Morrisroe. Judge Thagard threatened Gantt with contempt if he did not move forward, and again Gantt refused. Instead of citing Gantt with contempt, the judge removed him from the case, reinstated the local prosecutor, and opened the trial.[105]

At trial, the defense witnesses testified that Daniels had a knife and Morrisroe had a pistol, though neither weapon was ever found.[106] A defense witness said that Coleman had gone to the store to protect it from civil rights demonstrators.[107] But the prosecution's witnesses stood firm. Ruby Sales testified that Daniels pushed her to the ground and that Morrisroe was shot in the back while trying to run from Coleman.[108] Joyce Bailey testified that Coleman threatened them with the shotgun before shooting Daniels and Morrisroe. A written statement by Morrisroe was read to the jury, reporting that they had approached the store to purchase soft drinks. "When Daniels was shot," the statement read, "I turned to leave. I did not want to play hero. Another shot was fired, and I was struck by that shot in my lower spine, and I fell to the ground." As to any weapons the victims were alleged to have had, Morrisroe stated: "To my knowledge, at the time of the threat and the first shot, Daniels did not have a knife, gun, stick, or other weapon in his hand. The only thing I had in mine was a dime."[109]

Coleman did not testify at the trial, but during his closing argument Coleman's defense attorney called the victims "false prophets in sheep's clothing."[110] Despite the evidence suggesting otherwise, the defense attorney reiterated that Daniels and Morrisroe were armed and that they were were hiding "their evil motives behind the cloth of the church. These were not men of God as we know the term here in Alabama."[111] The jury, after deliberating for one hour and twenty-nine minutes, found Tom Coleman not guilty of manslaughter in the death of Jonathan Daniels.[112] Given everything, including the fact that during an adjournment one of the jurors turned and winked at Coleman, this outcome was not a surprise. Coleman was never prosecuted for shooting Father Morrisroe, and the charges were dismissed.[113]

The misdemeanor charges against the protesters in Fort Deposit were dismissed by the federal court on September 30, 1965.[114] The court held they had been exercising their First Amendment rights to free speech and peaceful assembly and should not have been arrested and incarcerated.

Attorney General Flowers denounced the not-guilty verdict, stating, "Now those who feel they have a license to kill, maim, and destroy have been issued that license."[115] After the trial, Judge Thagard called a lawyer from the Department of Justice (DOJ), James Turner, into his chambers to pass along a message to the DOJ. The judge told Turner that he had ruled for Coleman to have a speedy trial in compliance with Alabama law. He also said he was unwilling to postpone the trial on the hope of "some far-off witness recovering from a serious wound [who] was not subject to the court's subpoena power and might never agree to come to Alabama to testify."[116] He was referencing Father Morrisroe, who was still hospitalized for his injuries at the time of Coleman's trial. Judge Thagard, who was being lambasted by members of the national press for his handling of the Coleman trial, seemed to care only about public perception, not Coleman's victims. Turner passed along the judge's message to the DOJ.

Coleman told reporters the next year that he would not have changed his actions even if he could: "If the same thing happens in the morning that happened that day, I would shoot them both tomorrow."[117] Ruby Sales would go on to become a human rights activist, theologian, and founder of the SpiritHouse Project, an organization working for racial justice.[118] After processing the shooting, Sales realized that Daniels had saved her life. She later said that she was "traumatized and paralyzed" by the event, and remarked that she "saw both love and hate coming from two very different white men that represented the best and worst of white America."[119]

Morrisroe spent six months in the hospital recuperating from his injury. He was honorably discharged as a Roman Catholic priest and went on to obtain his law degree.[120] He had a son, whom he named Richard Jonathan in honor of Daniels.[121]

In 1991, the Episcopal Church placed Jonathan Daniels on its roster of Christian martyrs. The church celebrates his life on August 14, the day of his arrest with his fellow protesters. On the second Saturday in August, people remember Daniels through a pilgrimage to Hayneville in Lowndes County. The pilgrimage begins at the courthouse where Coleman was acquitted, moves to the former location of the convenience store where Daniels was shot and killed, and ends at the courthouse, where bread and wine are consecrated.[122]

Following the criminal trial, *White v. Crook* went forward in federal court. Kenyon and Murray had been looking for a case that would involve a set of facts that could squarely "come face to face . . . with the constitutional issue" that Kenyon had argued in *Hoyt v. Florida*.[123] This was that case. Murray described their team effort as "a double-barreled challenge of the constitutionality of all-white, all-male juries."[124] The brief argued that the jury selection system as administrated in Lowndes County, which featured the systematic exclusion of Black citizens from juries, violated the Fifth, Sixth, and Seventh Amendments.[125] They also argued that this jury selection system, along with the Alabama statute that excluded women from jury service, was a violation of the Fourteenth Amendment's Equal Protection Clause. Finally, they argued that the willingness of the Supreme Court to apply the Equal Protection Clause to racial discrimination but not sex discrimination was a mistake. Alabama, Mississippi, and South Carolina were the remaining states that prohibited women from serving on trial and grand juries, yet thirty other states still allowed some type of jury restriction based on sex.[126]

The DOJ intervened in the lawsuit, and its brief linked jury service with the right to vote, which they called a person's "most direct opportunity to participate in the operation of government."[127] The DOJ asked the court to find Alabama's wholesale statutory ban unconstitutional and to provide prospective relief. The argument to ban women from jury service because "a woman's place is properly in the home," the DOJ argued, was overly broad, for it did not consider single women, women whose children were grown, or women who could discharge their homemaking responsibilities while serving.[128] The DOJ endorsed the argument that Alabama's exclusion of women was a violation of the Equal Protection Clause of the Fourteenth Amendment; however, it did not go so far as to say that the statutory exclusion of women from jury service rendered trials unfair. That standard remained restricted to race.

The federal trial court in the Middle District of Alabama held a hearing on November 26, 1965, and Kenyon flew to Montgomery to make her argument. Judge Thagard, the presiding judge in Tom Coleman's trial, was questioned by the three-judge panel. He testified that he could not recall a Black man serving on a Lowndes County trial jury in the prior thirteen years, even though Black citizens made up about 80 percent of the county's population. The DOJ presented six names of Black men in Lowndes County who were qualified to serve but had never been called. The DOJ attorneys asked the court to enjoin Lowndes County from discriminating against Black citizens by failing to call them for jury service. The DOJ, however, described the exclusion of women jurors as a "side issue" in the suit. When Kenyon rose to make her oral argument that the exclusion of women was unconstitutional and equally injurious as race discrimination, the panel stopped her and called instead for submission only in written briefs. When Kenyon insisted on making her argument, one of the judges addressed her sharply.[129] Nevertheless, she managed to argue briefly against the law denying women the right to serve on juries, eliciting a remark from Judge Rives that he was concerned about that part of the case, describing it as "a serious constitutional question."[130] Kenyon felt her chastisement was worth it because Judge Rives repeated her point that the exclusion of women from juries was a constitutional issue that needed consideration.[131]

The brief was due on December 10, 1965. In it, Kenyon and Murray argued that there were many women, Black and white, who desired to serve on juries and were qualified to do so, but they were barred by statute. The exclusion of both women and Black men from juries "seriously hampered the efforts of those seeking to exercise constitutionally guaranteed rights there."[132] In the case under deliberation, all persons employed in the administration of justice, along with the jury commissioners, were white. Lowndes County counted 738 white men between the ages of twenty-one and sixty-four, making up 13.2 percent of the population. Black men made up 32.1 percent; Black women, 34.8 percent; and white women, 19.9 percent. Because only white males in the applicable age group were allowed to serve, 86.8 percent of the county's total population was excluded from sitting on a jury.[133] They attached the article that Murray and Mary Eastwood had published in the *George Washington Law Review*, "Jane Crow and the Law: Sex Discrimination and Title VII," to the brief as an appendix.

Kenyon and Murray also pointed out that the presiding judge of the Alabama State Court of Appeals was a woman—Judge Annie Lola Price. Astonishingly, Judge Price could reverse a jury verdict, or if she were to resign her post and return to practice, she could argue cases before a jury; but she could not serve on one, solely because of her sex.[134] The US Supreme Court had recognized that jury exclusion based on race was unconstitutional and inconsistent with democratic concepts; Kenyon and Murray now argued that sex was no different. It was a matter, they argued, of the "mandatory exclusion of an entire class based solely upon the biological fact of being female."[135] When considering the inferior status of both women and Black individuals, scholars recognized the "similarity of the myths used to sustain discrimination against both groups."[136] Kenyon and Murray urged the district court to rectify this wrong.

Once the brief was submitted, the hardest part was to wait for the ruling. Kenyon wrote to Murray thanking her for her friendship, and reminded her of the important work they had accomplished as a team on behalf of the

ACLU. But their work was not done. "We've got to pull the Board together. For me it's onward and upward fast now."[137] Describing her work on civil rights cases in the South as "Operation Southern Justice," she felt optimistic that their work would eventually lead to victory. She wrote to another friend about her efforts in Alabama, remarking that they were "sure to win."[138] In an article for the ACLU's *Civil Liberties* magazine, Kenyon remarked on the revolutionary case that they were awaiting a ruling on:

> Supreme Court decisions in this area are clear. Systematic exclusion of Negroes from jury service is repugnant to the Fourteenth Amendment. The other half of the case is more novel. Perhaps it would be the part of wisdom (and modesty on the part of the writer) not to prognosticate the result at this time. But the combination of total Negro exclusion (of both Negro and white women), with women in the majority in both categories, shows how greatly the true cross-section of the community, which a jury is supposed to exemplify if it is to be truly "impartial," is out of balance—and how far the system of justice in a democracy is askew. Let women and Negroes, we say, Jane Doe, Jane Crow, and Jim Crow, all have a fair chance to serve—and justice, instead of guns, may return even to Lowndes County.[139]

On February 7, 1966, the three-judge panel ruled unanimously in favor of Gardenia White and her fellow plaintiffs. It was an extraordinary victory, the first time a federal court applied the Fourteenth Amendment's guarantee of equal protection to sex as well as race. The court considered it significant that the all-white jury commissioners relied almost entirely on the qualified voter lists, which prior to March 1, 1965, contained no names of Black citizens. The panel ordered Lowndes County to add registered Black male voters to the jury lists.

The court also found the statute prohibiting women from serving on juries to be unconstitutional. Jury service, the court noted, was an important process of government that should be shared by all citizens; hence, "the Alabama statute that denies women the right to serve on juries in the State of Alabama therefore violates the provision of the Fourteenth Amendment." As the court explained, this constitutional provision is intended to prohibit prejudicial disparities before the law for all citizens—including women.[140]

The court reminded Alabama that the Constitution "must be read as embodying general principles meant to govern society and the institutions of government as they evolve through time."[141] When the court applied the Fourteenth Amendment to the facts in *White*, the complete exclusion of women from jury service, as Alabama did, was found to be arbitrary.

Accordingly, the court struck down the Alabama law, although it did delay the ruling until 1967 to give the state legislature time to decide whether jury service for women should be mandatory or voluntary.

Kenyon and Murray were thrilled with the opinion. Everyone involved hoped that this decision would impact jury service laws well beyond Alabama. Murray and Mary Eastwood were excited to see the ruling adopt the same position they had argued for in their law review article.[142] Eastwood wrote that the ruling was "far better than I had dared hope for. It's the most important thing to happen to women since the Nineteenth Amendment. (At least.)"[143] Kenyon, too, dared to dream expansively, believing that the decision might open other "fascinating possibilities of even greater import to women."[144]

The ACLU issued a press release hailing *White v. Crook* as "a major civil rights victory" and "a triumph for the ACLU's long held position that the Fourteenth Amendment's 'equal protection of the laws' applies to women."[145] The case had been filed by the ACLU as part of its campaign to end "all forms of segregated justice" and was dubbed "Operation Southern Justice." Other groups understood the importance of the decision. Margaret Hickey, chairwoman of the Citizens' Advisory Council of the President's CSW, prepared a memo on behalf of the council informing interested groups about the decision. "I believe that you will be as pleased as we are," Hickey wrote, "that a Federal court has held for the first time that women are protected by the Equal Protection Clause of the Fourteenth Amendment." The decision could, she said, be used as a basis for litigation that attacked sex-based discrimination in public education, public employment, and property rights of married women, as well as in advancing equal jury service in the states. She applauded the work of Kenyon and Murray and noted that the ACLU "takes the position that the equal rights of women are an integral part of the whole movement to protect the civil rights and civil liberties of all individuals."[146]

Kenyon wrote to a colleague, Esther Peterson, a former director of the Women's Bureau and now special assistant for consumer affairs under President Johnson, saying she was claiming victory for the ACLU. "I have fought for the application of the XIV Amendment to women's rights for years as you know," Kenyon wrote, "and considered it the clinching argument against those who wanted a separate amendment for women. Nobody is ever going to give me any credit, of course, now that we have won. And the separate amendment gals will always say that I was against equal rights."[147] In a second letter to Peterson, Kenyon reiterated that the work was far from over.

"We are all workers in the same vineyard and there is so much more work to be done before women are truly 'free.' And men too for that matter."[148]

Of all the lawyers who had worked on the case, Murray wrote, it was Kenyon who had been "a stalwart survivor of the earlier women's movement" and "devoted to the 'Cause of Women' since her youth." Throughout her long career, Kenyon had battled to become a lawyer "in a male-dominated profession, disarming her male colleagues with amusing witticisms to win their support of her point of view when her brilliant logic failed."[149] Although Kenyon had advocated for women's social, economic, and political rights since the 1920s, *White* was the first time she had been able to successfully persuade a court that the Equal Protection Clause of the Fourteenth Amendment should be applied to cases of sex-based discrimination. As Kenyon herself put it, *White* was "a victory for women which has pleased the American Civil Liberties Union and me [to] no end."[150]

In a March 23, 1966, letter, Kenyon wrote: "Other victories will follow. But this one turned the key in the lock. Like the Civil Rights boys when the *Brown* decision was handed down in 1954, 'I could cry.'"[151] Kenyon was not the only one to make this comparison. Murray, too, believed that *White* was the *Brown v. Board of Education* for women, saying that if a comparable case came before the Supreme Court, it would rule similarly to the Alabama federal district court.[152] Murray also believed the deeper significance of the case would be its impact on southern juries, stating that women on juries increased the chances for impartial trials.[153]

Alabama did not appeal the decision. Although this meant the ACLU would have to wait to argue sex discrimination before the Supreme Court, *White* was still cause for celebration. The associate dean of faculties at the University of Oregon wrote Kenyon to say that the ruling would lead to change in the South, praising her for moving progress forward.[154] In her reply, Kenyon wrote that she had been "anticipating a great earthquake of some sort in the South and hoping it would come soon. Maybe Jane Does and Jane Crows side by side will be the catalysts. After all, as Mary Beard once said, while men were out huntin', fishin' and feudin', women were busy creating civilization. Maybe in Lowndes County they'll do just that."[155]

After the *White* opinion, the Alabama legislature amended its statute to allow women to serve on juries. But the fight over equal jury service opportunities for women would persist, particularly in the southern states. In 1966, for example, the supreme court of Mississippi issued an opinion in *State v. Hall*, a case which argued that the exclusion of women from jury service denied equal protection guarantees to female defendants. The court, however, did not consider itself to be bound by *White* and denied the defendant, Virginia Hall, relief, saying that determining eligibility qualifications for jurors was a legislative matter, and that classification by sex was reasonable. The court wrote it held the firm conviction that women could be excluded "so they may continue their service as mothers, wives, and homemakers, and also to protect them (in some areas, they are still upon a pedestal) from the filth, obscenity, and noxious atmosphere that so often pervades a courtroom during a jury trial."[156]

The *White* victory did not signal the end of Kenyon and Murray's work for sex equality in jury service. In May 1966, they drafted a fifty-nine-page document for the ACLU titled "The Case for Equality in State Jury Service." This document outlined the ACLU's proposal to amend the Civil Rights Protection Act of 1966 to address the exclusion of women on state juries and provided a comprehensive analysis of jury litigation cases and state statutes excluding women. They argued that the Fourteenth Amendment was not limited to racial discrimination and that "extensive litigation will continue to be required before equality of jury service can be achieved in all states." Additionally, they urged Congress to enact remedial legislation to clarify that justice is a shared obligation on the part of all citizens, regardless of race, color, or sex. The hope, as they explained it, was that broad reforms would be effected to insure equal jury representation in both federal and state courts, thus "right[ing] an ancient injustice in which a large body of citizens—women—have suffered the humiliation of an inferior, then ambiguous, constitutional status."[157]

After Kenyon's death in 1972, her work regarding jury service continued on. In 1975 in *Taylor v. Louisiana*, the US Supreme Court held that systematic exclusion of women from juries violated the requirement that a jury be drawn from a fair cross-section of community members. Although women were not strictly excluded from serving in Louisiana, they, unlike men, had to make known to the jury commissioner their desire to serve, as in the *Hoyt* case. The effect was to exclude women from serving. The Court found it untenable "to hold that women as a class may be excluded or given automatic exemptions based solely on sex if the consequence is that criminal jury venires are almost totally male." As such, it could no longer "follow the contrary implications of the prior cases, including *Hoyt v. Florida*." The Court wrote, "If it was ever the case that women were unqualified to sit on juries or were so situated that none of them should be required to perform jury service, that time has long since passed. If at one time it could be held that Sixth Amendment juries must be drawn from a fair cross section of the community but that this requirement permitted the almost total exclusion of women, this is not the case today."[158]

In examining the history of women and jury service, one can see that Kenyon and Murray were on a quest for equality. Their litigation strategy prevailed in *White v. Crook*, and led directly to the success of *Taylor v. Louisiana*. But their aspirations were not restricted to jury service. In 1971 in *Reed v. Reed*, their strategy persuaded the Court to apply the Equal Protection Clause of the Fourteenth Amendment to sex-based differentials more broadly. These efforts began within committee meeting rooms of the ACLU and ended with successful decisions at the US Supreme Court. It was quite a feat. As she aged, Kenyon considered the legacy she would leave behind.

TEN

# *Life Is Sweet and Life Is Sour*

## THE LATER YEARS

> This storm is our storm, the storm of human beings crying for fair play everywhere, and we cannot stand aside. We must move with the wind.
>
> DOROTHY KENYON

WHEN SHE WAS IN HER SEVENTIES, Kenyon transitioned her law practice from her downtown office at 50 Broadway to her apartment in Chelsea. She was adamant, however, that she had no intention of discontinuing her practice. It was simply easier and more efficient for her and her secretary to work out of the apartment, which she called her midtown office. The apartment was painted in bold colors and furnished with outdated furniture, most of which Kenyon had inherited. Kenyon wrote to a friend saying she was hoping never to retire.[1] Her sister-in-law Mildred said Kenyon "steadfastly refused to be a senior citizen. She hated the term."[2] Indeed, old age was a difficult concept for Kenyon to embrace. She felt there was still more to do and learn. Always on the go, she began learning Spanish in her eightieth year of life.[3] Her trademark hat, large with a wide brim, was regularly spotted throughout Chelsea, often as she waited impatiently for the city bus.[4]

Kenyon was protective of Chelsea and worked hard to benefit her community. At a congressional subcommittee hearing on potential construction, she spoke of her affection for her neighborhood, emphasizing that she had lived her entire life in Manhattan and that she was prepared to fight to preserve it. She presciently argued, "There's great danger . . . that we may be overwhelmed by the people who want to come in and build the glass palaces in which the beautiful people live and waste their lives."[5] She advocated for rehabilitating the deteriorating housing in Chelsea, or demolishing it and rebuilding, but always with a goal of supplying decent housing at a low cost to members of the community so they would not be driven out. Kenyon recognized that the value of her own apartment building was rapidly diminishing, and that the only thing of value was the land on which the building stood. In a letter to her neighbors, Kenyon wrote of the building's declining conditions—cockroaches, dirty floors, trash overflowing from the trash chute.[6] The building cooperative and tenant-ownership would eventually be replaced by a commercial company that charged rent. In 1968 she would write of Chelsea going through a type of rebirth, away from its decaying brownstones.[7]

Kenyon was active in the Community Corporation of the Lower West Side; Mobilization for Youth, where she donated her legal services; and the board of Project FIND (Friend, Isolated, Needy, Disabled). These were some of President Lyndon Johnson's Great Society programs, aimed at boosting education, renewing urban areas, and fighting poverty. Kenyon's service with these groups was a continuation of her work during the Progressive and New Deal eras. She chaired an advisory committee to create the publicly funded Project FIND coffee house, a free place where senior citizens could meet and talk. As chair, she drafted the papers of incorporation, but, as Mildred Adams Kenyon wrote, she felt the project "smacked too much of paternalism and old fashioned social service to enlist her enthusiastic cooperation."[8]

Kenyon loved living in New York City, even though Chelsea was not always a safe place at the time. Once while riding the bus she was pickpocketed and lost thirty dollars, a substantial sum for her. Following the incident, she wrote to the transit authority to demand that they install signs on their buses warning people to "Beware of Pick Pockets."[9] The transit authority declined. Not one to let things go, Kenyon wrote again, saying that she disagreed with their decision and that passengers were owed a warning.[10]

She was assaulted three times in Chelsea by muggers. The first time it happened, she was seventy-nine years old. In broad daylight, the mugger tried to overtake her from behind. When she felt the tug on her handbag, she began to yell, holding onto the bag, until the mugger ran away. The second incident occurred outside her apartment building in the evening. A boy ripped the purse from her and knocked her to the ground. Her purse was later found thrown into the gutter.[11]

The third time, she was walking back to her apartment at around 11 in the morning when she saw a man swinging an antenna. She crossed the street to avoid him, but he followed, hitting her hard on the back.[12] He hit her four times as she ran, calling for help.[13] As blood spurted from her hand, the man fled. A taxi took her to the Beekman Downtown Hospital where she received eight stitches.[14] Her brother Houston rushed to her side while she was waiting for X-rays. In true lawyer style, Houston dictated notes about the incident to be typed up later. He subsequently reported that although Kenyon said she did not have any pain or discomfort, the incident had clearly left her in shock.[15]

The attacker, Paul Kaplan, was arrested and taken to Bellevue Hospital. The arresting officer said he had been tempted to shoot the suspect but decided against it and wrestled the antenna from him instead. Kenyon, who was subpoenaed to court to identify Kaplan, was grateful that the officer had not resorted to his gun, as it was obvious the man was "a mentally sick person, and not a criminal."[16] In a letter to a friend about the incident, she wrote that she "had no intention of suing a crazy man, only a desire to see him committed and taken care of."[17] Kenyon was so in favor of rehabilitation that she testified in Kaplan's favor. Her grandnephew John Fisher later said this showed both Kenyon's strength and her compassion.[18]

On Kenyon's recommendation, Kaplan, whom she described as the "poor psychotic who beat me up," was sentenced to probation. She truly believed that a criminal conviction and prison term would only have destroyed him.[19] Upon the recommendation of the probation officer at trial, the court ordered Kaplan to work with Vera, an organization that helped indigent defendants.[20] Kenyon was in favor of the recommendation and hoped the program would give Kaplan a chance.

Kenyon actively followed up with everyone involved. Once she had recovered, she decided to throw a party at her apartment, inviting Kaplan, the taxi driver, the patrolman, and a young boy who had come to her aid during the attack.[21] As a final gesture, she also wrote the police commissioner, commending the police officer who had responded to the attack.[22] She later checked up on Kaplan's progress. His attorney wrote that Kaplan had presented himself with very serious emotional problems and initially was resistant to counseling. However, through both group and individual counseling, he had started showing more self-control and expressing a healthier self-image.[23] It appears that Kenyon's commitment to supporting Kaplan made a difference.

• • •

In keeping with her lifelong sympathy for underdogs and her affinity for 1960s anti-poverty programs, Kenyon worked with others to set up the first free legal services division for the poor on New York City's Lower West Side. She started laying the groundwork for the office in 1965. It was to be a private nonprofit, a committee of lawyers who would provide voluntary legal counsel, primarily regarding civil matters, in an area of Manhattan with "extensive pockets of poverty."[24] Kenyon understood, especially from her time on the bench, that far too often justice was beyond the reach of the poor.

This imbalance had been brought to the bar's attention by Reginald Heber Smith in his 1919 book *Justice and the Poor*, which analyzed legal aid programs and concluded that poor populations were routinely denied access to the courts. Smith linked these "defects in the administration of the law" specifically to case delays, the expense of fees, and the cost of hiring counsel.[25] It was up to the bar association, he said, to remedy the situation.[26]

Kenyon essentially built on Smith's arguments. Indeed, her advocacy for this type of law office was timely. The US Supreme Court had recently ruled in *Gideon v. Wainwright* that the Sixth Amendment's right to counsel required free legal representation in serious criminal cases be provided to those who were indigent.[27] Kenyon realized that poor populations not only deserved this, but they were entitled to it—and not just in criminal cases. Providing this type of service, she argued, was not "a charitable handout from the rich," but a necessity to ensure the dignity of the city's poorest residents.[28] Citing Marvin Frankel of Columbia Law School, Kenyon said, "It is no new discovery that the promise of equal justice is a hollow one for people too poor to retain counsel."[29] It was thus critical that her law office be located where the poor themselves lived, making access to services easy for them, especially in the areas of tenant and consumer protection. She envisioned a small, intimate office that belonged to the community.

Kenyon's concept faced both judicial and political opposition in its development, however.[30] In 1966, the Appellate Division of the New York Supreme Court turned down her original application, concerned that the project was too complex and ambitious to work effectively. In a letter to the editor of the *New York Times*, Kenyon wrote of her displeasure with this decision, lamenting that "while lawyers resolve their differences, the poor, as usual, must wait."[31] She believed law offices of, by, and for the poor should be publicly funded, and now that the federal government was making money available to expand access to lawyers for those living in poverty, Kenyon wanted to take advantage of that resource.[32]

In 1968, the Law Office for the Poor of the West Side finally opened in a three-story building at 51st Street and Tenth Avenue, with plans for additional offices in two other locations.[33] Those with housing disputes, welfare issues, and other legal problems could now access help from lawyers, law clerks, volunteer workers, and social service workers. The New Chelsea

Reform Democratic Club established a scholarship fund in Kenyon's honor to be awarded to a third-year law student who volunteered at the West Side office. Every cent brought into the clinic went directly toward client services. As resident counsel, Kenyon took on a criminal case where she defended several young mothers who had blocked 26th Street after a neighborhood child was killed by a speeding automobile.[34] The mothers were arrested when they refused to leave during their protest of unsafe streets. Kenyon convinced the district attorney not to prosecute them, and the case was dismissed.[35]

As she was fighting poverty and providing legal services, Kenyon was still concerned with how women were being accepted (or not) within the legal profession. An article in the *New York Times* left Kenyon momentarily speechless (something that was hard to do). The piece, titled "The New Portia: Brainy, Idealistic but, Above All, Just a Girl," described female law students as "brainy," "doll-like," and "fetching." Approximately 3.5 percent of the nation's lawyers were women, and the number was rising as more women attended law school. Yet women were still "being ribbed for husband-hunting and usurping male prerogatives" by their male classmates and male faculty members. The article noted how women law graduates were traditionally accused of wasting their education because of their obligations related to motherhood, while also asserting that "the average woman is not yet the equal of the mediocre man" when it came to job placement. One of the women graduates interviewed for the article stated, "The type of woman who goes into law has changed. She used to be a four-eyes, overly studious type. Now she's just a girl."[36]

Kenyon responded in usual fashion by writing a letter to the editor. "I myself have never had more than two eyes but, since I am still able to read the *New York Times* without glasses at eighty, I suppose it might be said that I qualify for the type. Though studiousness has always seemed to me fairly common—even among males. But the young girls are 'fetching' to boot! How cute!" She wondered why women's appearances mattered when men's looks were rarely mentioned. "Why this over preoccupation with sex in places where it surely doesn't belong and subtly patronizes and denigrates the woman in the doing?"[37]

Even as she was seeing discrimination in print, she was also experiencing it within the law office she helped create. In one incident, Kenyon encountered New York state senator Manfred Ohrenstein holding a paper brought by a law clerk, and when she asked the senator about it, he responded rudely, dismissing her. Not surprisingly, Kenyon, at age eighty-one and still a practicing lawyer, did not appreciate this. She wrote him a letter expressing her frustrations:

> Because I like you very much, and not to give too much importance to what appeared to you to be a trifle but to me is basic, let me give you a bit of my philosophy. As you know, I have spent a large part of my life fighting all sorts of unfair discriminations; one of them being economic discrimination against women. In the field of law I have called myself a lawyer (as you are) and a judge (as you are not), *never* a *woman* lawyer or *woman* judge. I don't recognize such an animal. I am a lawyer and judge, good, bad or indifferent as the case may be; but never of that strange and alienated grouping called *women*. . . . So it was a shock to hear you say, in a case of mine featuring my single-handed creation . . . , "Everything's all right. Don't worry. Just go and sit down." Those words were patronizing to *me, as a woman*, insulting to *me, as a judge*. You would *never* had said that to a *male* judge of my age, experience or reputation. Your behavior was that of the average stereotype white male.[38]

After practicing for more than fifty years, Kenyon was exasperated that she still had to demand respect from others.

. . .

Expanding her passion for fighting on behalf of disadvantaged populations, Kenyon sought to work on more civil rights cases. To that end, she joined the Chelsea Civil Rights Council as a director. This organization was an action committee serving the civil rights needs of New Yorkers residing in Chelsea.[39] Among the events the council coordinated was a march in support of the civil rights protests in Selma, Alabama, in which over one hundred people, including Kenyon, walked the five miles from Chelsea along Central Park West to 125th Street with a police escort.[40] After Dr. Martin Luther King Jr. was assassinated, Kenyon went to Memphis to walk in a memorial march there. She felt sure his spirit was walking with them, and described his death as a "hero's death" that would change the course of history.[41]

In a 1964 letter to Constance Baker Motley, Kenyon, age seventy-six at the time, said she was "becoming obsessed with the idea of trying to get on your staff" at the NAACP Legal Defense and Educational Fund. She offered to work as a paid part-time lawyer, since she needed to maintain her own private practice. "I'm a hard, persistent worker who loves to work and am also quite teachable, especially when deeply interested[,] as I am in this field of law. The best things I do are talking and writing and I'm sometimes not bad on ideas either, although you've probably already got more than you need of such qualities on your staff. Anyhow I wish you'd give me a try and the worst I can do is to fall flat on my face?"[42]

When Motley was nominated for a federal judgeship, Kenyon wrote to share her dream that Motley would be on the Supreme Court bench one day, with Kenyon arguing a case before her.[43] Motley thanked her for the faith that she could not place in herself, remarking: "Having just reached the District Court I cannot foresee the day—as you can—when I will become a Justice of the United States Supreme Court!"[44] The next year, Thurgood Marshall, Motley's former supervisor at the NAACP Legal Defense and Educational Fund, would be appointed to the US Supreme Court, the first Black justice to be so honored.

When Kenyon was asked what the major cause of American liberalism would be in the next decade, she said: the "removal of [the] habit of white supremacy from the land, conscious in the South, largely unconscious in the North. Quite a job."[45] Kenyon began working on a chapter for the co-authored book *Equality*, intended to bring attention to the systemic racism experienced by Black citizens. She described the book as a manual on "how to combat the bad habit of 'white supremacy' in favor of something more brotherly as a constitutional lawyer sees it."[46] Kenyon specifically argued for legislative action along with compensatory measures in the South and encouraged the nation as a whole to join the fight for civil liberties.

She enjoyed writing immensely, wishing she could "make a career out of books," as she had grown tired with the "drudgery of the law."[47] In 1970, she wrote her sister-in-law Mildred about her love of writing:

> Born in a library, a bookworm from birth, given a name that Father thought was lovely for a writer (as he firmly expected me to be—he'd wanted to be one himself), I was destined by the school of hard knocks to an activist life of pot-boiling law work, grabbed wherever I could find it, with no time for research or thought that amounted to a hill of beans. Quick, superficial, grab the dough, if any, that's true of a large majority of lawyers. It leaves no time for real writing. I had always preached that lawyers were the social engineers of our habits and customs (law), that they not only interpreted the law, but also were in a position to make improvements, new and better ways of doing things, and that they could and should be creative for the common good. Everybody agreed that it was a lovely thought but not often rewarding in money. I'm therefore deeply interested in the change of mood that seems to have come over the youngest generation of lawyers as a result of all these Law Offices for the Poor of one of which I am the happy mother. I hope the mood ripens and takes hold.[48]

There was always tension between doing what she wanted and earning a paycheck. Although Kenyon knew she had earned something of a reputation as a lawyer, she never saw much money from the endeavor. She called herself a pioneer and, like her father, expected to work all her life and "die in harness."[49]

At one point, steeped in exhaustion, Kenyon wrote to her brother Theodore saying that she was considering her future and wanting to find less tiring work.[50] Her brothers were glad to hear she was "aiming at some relaxation," and each of them sent her a check for $150 to help relieve "immediate pressure and to ease the period of readjustment."[51] If she needed more, she should let them know. Kenyon wrote back, appreciative but somewhat embarrassed. "At the moment I'm swamped with arrears of law work with no money to speak of in sight for quite a while. That's natural, of course, and I *hope* to see the pace quicken."[52] The checks continued, and Kenyon gratefully accepted them.

As her need for money grew, however, her ability to work long hours lessened. In her seventies, Kenyon began to experience bouts of serious illness. In 1967, she underwent a stomach surgery for ulcers and was hospitalized for almost all of August.[53] Kenyon was also dealing with vertigo and extensive dental issues, needing further help with bills from her brothers.[54] Kenyon wrote Theodore a note expressing gratitude for his monetary gifts and for the support of her family:

> You've been wonderfully kind to me, kind and tender and patient and generous and understanding almost beyond imagining. I've felt so safe, so protected in your love. . . . It seemed like a rejuvenation in friendship and family affection after many years of going our own ways. We mustn't spoil any of that now. You must remember that I'm holding my head very high these days and putting on an act of good health that I don't always feel. Tension sometimes shows through as it did this morning when I found my leg failing me for the second time in two months and I didn't know how to hide it from you. . . . I must be more careful and less cocky.[55]

Her advancing age also brought greater public recognition of her achievements. The New Chelsea Reform Democratic Club, of which Kenyon was a founding member, sponsored a testimonial dinner at Tavern on the Green in New York City on February 22, 1968, to celebrate her eightieth birthday. The program included "Quotes for a Lady," expressions of gratitude for Kenyon's years of service in the legal profession and in political circles.[56]

More than two hundred sponsors and three hundred fifty guests attended the dinner, among them numerous legal and political heavyweights. Senator Robert F. Kennedy shared the following in the testimonial program that "Dorothy Kenyon has earned the gratitude and admiration of all of us for her pioneering effort in almost every legal and social reform movement of consequence."[57] ACLU executive director John de J. Pemberton noted that her colleagues at the ACLU, even when they disagreed with her, which was less often than Kenyon thought, retained a high loyalty to her. "Her unique combination of personal courage, wit, and incisive analysis are responsible for the intensity of this loyalty she produces in her friends."[58]

In his introductory remarks, the dinner's chairman, Justin N. Feldman, was affectionate and teasing:

> One might think that a testimonial dinner would not suit Dorothy Kenyon. It is in a way so traditional. Many adjectives have been used for her but *never* "traditional." Traditions represent the past. Dorothy has always been relevant to her times—always in the forefront of every significant effort to test, to probe and to stretch social frontiers. In her 50 years as a lawyer, they have been the frontiers of equality and the frontiers of justice.

Feldman asked the attendees to think in color—a sweeping red cape, a bluestocking, the colors of roses. "Think in any color, so long as it is the color of a flamboyant hat. If you can do that, you have caught the spirit of Dorothy Kenyon."[59]

The guest of honor, true to form as a lover of color, entered the room in a long, purple gown. She was toasted with speeches, which were interspersed with various audio greetings and recordings about her life. Songs from the Roundabout Theatre Players filled the space.[60] Kenyon reveled with the guests, drinking manhattans and addressing her friends and colleagues: "I despair a thousand times for the human race," she said, "and then, like a fool, I refuse to lose confidence."[61] The profit from the dinner for the club was $3,085, equivalent to $29,786.76 in 2026 dollars.[62]

The party overwhelmed Kenyon. She found it shocking that she had so many friends and people who had such nice words for her, joking that she was "much more accustomed to brickbats."[63] After the event, however, Kenyon had a hard time finding clients. She felt the party was partly to blame, telling Theodore that the advertisement of her age of eighty was not good for her legal practice. She could only hope her legal work picked back up.[64]

• • •

In the summer of 1969, Kenyon traveled with Theodore and eighteen members of the Kenyon family, ages eight to eighty, in a Pullman train across

Canada. Theodore's teenage grandson (and Kenyon's grandnephew) David S. Kenyon was one of those in attendance, and he later remarked that Kenyon had been the "queen of the trip."[65] Although David was supposed to be at the Woodstock music festival that summer, and was a bit annoyed at having to go on a family trip instead, in hindsight he was happy to have had the experience. He recalled that they played chess as they crossed Canada, and that Kenyon had kilts sewn for the entire family to celebrate their Scottish heritage.[66] The train pulled into an oil town in Canada where they had reserved a private room in a bar by the train station for Theodore's birthday party. The entire Kenyon group, in kilts, walked through the rough-and-tumble locale together, surely a spectacle for the oil workers' eyes. Kenyon and Houston were beaming, having the greatest time.[67]

Kenyon later wrote to express her feelings about the trip to Theodore: "[F]or the first time since mother's death, [the trip] gave me the feeling that, proud wanderer, loner and adventurer that I had been and still am, I really and truly had a *real* family. I never could thank you for that trip, darling, and . . . it touched me very, very deeply."[68]

Regardless of how much Kenyon and her brothers appreciated one another, they were still siblings, and as such they suffered from differences of opinion and the occasional quarrel. Still, there was always love between them.[69] In one letter to Theodore, whom she called TO, Kenyon wrote: "I do love you, my sweet brother, and I wish we didn't get so often on one another's nerves. Time is too short to waste."[70] In another, she commented on how kind and selfless he was in his treatment of her—except when he was "trying to *run me*!" In that same letter, she observed how different she and TO were when it came to talking about feelings. Likening him to a "crystal clear mountain stream," she said she was more of an introvert who tended to lock her deepest feelings away, to the point of choking on them. "When mother died," she wrote, "I remember you wept with father but I stood like a frozen image. I couldn't cry. I was numb. It's those kinds of feelings I have about you, TO, and I never can convey them to you."[71] Kenyon may have been too hard on herself. Although she said it was difficult to open up to her family, her correspondence with them through the years reveals a loving and trusting relationship. Still, as one friend, Dorothy Dunbar Bromley, observed, Kenyon tended to keep her brothers at arm's length: "With them . . . her guard was always up—ever the feminist, defending her turf."[72] Bromley also questioned whether Dorothy ever expressed proper gratitude for Theodore and Houston's support.

PLATE 1. Minnie Kenyon reads with her daughter, Dorothy, and her son Theodore in the late 1800s. Minnie passed away when Dorothy was a teenager. Courtesy of Smith College Special Collections, Dorothy Kenyon Papers.

PLATE 2. Dorothy, age 13, in New York City. Kenyon and her family lived near Riverside Park in Manhattan. Courtesy of Smith College Special Collections, Dorothy Kenyon Papers.

PLATE 3. Dorothy and her father, Will Kenyon, walking on the campus of Smith College in Northampton, Massachusetts. Both Will and Minnie supported Dorothy's pursuit of higher education, and Smith College was chosen for her. Dorothy was a student at Smith from 1904 through 1908. Courtesy of Smith College Special Collections, Dorothy Kenyon Papers.

PLATE 4. An aerial photo of Barn House on Martha's Vineyard. Kenyon and her friends started a cooperative enterprise in 1919 called Chilmark Associates, which continues today. Members of the cooperative share in the upkeep of the property through various chores. Kenyon visited Barn House every summer from 1919 through 1971, often bringing family members with her. Courtesy of Chilmark Associates.

PLATE 5. The DK Coop, named after Kenyon, is still in use. When she built the coop at Barn House, she chose a pink floor. The interior is spartan, with a bed, desk, and chair. Courtesy of Chilmark Associates.

PLATE 6. Wolcott "Patsy" Pitkin, an attorney, was a founding member at Barn House. Not only was Pitkin Kenyon's boss at his law firm in Manhattan, but he was also in a romantic relationship with her for years. Courtesy of Chilmark Associates.

PLATE 7. Kenyon on an apartment terrace in Manhattan, with the signature bob hairstyle she wore her entire adult life. Courtesy of Smith College Special Collections, Dorothy Kenyon Papers.

PLATE 8. Mayor Fiorello La Guardia hosted the women serving in his administration at the Hotel Brevoort on December 6, 1937. Kenyon sits in the front lower right. Mayor La Guardia is in the back center. At the time, Kenyon served as first deputy commissioner of licenses in New York City. She would ultimately resign from the position over differences of opinion with Mayor La Guardia regarding censorship. Courtesy of the La Guardia and Wagner Archives, La Guardia Community College/The City University of New York.

PLATE 9. Kenyon being sworn in by Mayor Fiorello La Guardia as a municipal court judge. She was appointed to the position by Mayor La Guardia on January 21, 1939. She loved hats and was often photographed wearing them. Courtesy of Bettmann/Bettmann Collection via Getty Images.

PLATE 10. Kenyon in her judicial robe, serving on the bench as municipal court judge in New York City. She lost the election to retain her seat in November 1939. Courtesy of Bettmann/Bettmann Collection via Getty Images.

PLATE 11. Kenyon and her brother Theodore in Washington, DC, on March 14, 1950. Theodore is reviewing the remarks Kenyon gave before the United States Senate that day. Her brothers, also lawyers, were supportive of her career and were strong defenders of hers when she was accused by Senator Joseph McCarthy of being a communist—a claim she vehemently denied. Courtesy of AP Images.

PLATE 12. Herbert Block's political cartoon that ran in the *Washington Post* after Kenyon's testimony before the United States Senate. Kenyon received a framed copy and hung it in her office. A 1950 Herblock Cartoon, © The Herb Block Foundation.

PLATE 13. Mildred Adams Kenyon, Houston Kenyon, and Dorothy Kenyon sitting together on a bench at Barn House. Courtesy of Chilmark Associates.

PLATE 14. Kenyon holding a drink and enjoying the sunset at Barn House. She celebrated her fiftieth summer there in 1969. Kenyon was described as the Mother Protectress of Barn House. Courtesy of Chilmark Associates.

PLATE 15. Kenyon photographed by portrait photographer Rhoda Nathans at Kenyon's apartment in Chelsea. Nathans sent the photo to Mildred Adams Kenyon and Houston Kenyon following Kenyon's death. In her letter to Mildred and Houston, Nathans said she had used the photo in her exhibitions. She called Kenyon an extraordinary human being and wanted Mildred and Houston to have a copy, free of charge, as it had been a source of joy for her. This is probably the last portrait Kenyon sat for prior to her death from cancer in 1972. Courtesy of Smith College Special Collections, Dorothy Kenyon Papers, and the family of Rhoda Nathans.

In the end, the fact that her brothers accepted her choices meant a great deal to Kenyon. She had lost her mother, Minnie, at a young age, and her father, Will, although he clearly loved her, had expressed disappointment in her decision not to marry and have children. She accepted that disappointment as gracefully as possible, knowing that he was in fact proud of all his children, but his words stung.[73] Houston did not have children either, yet it was Kenyon who was perceived as deficient because of her single and childless status. On her thirtieth birthday, Will wrote to her saying he had no greater hope for her than that she marry and have children.[74] When she was forty-two, Will wrote saying that he sometimes pondered how different her life was from Minnie's, especially when Theodore discussed problems he and his wife were having in bringing up their daughter, Madge. Will recalled that Minnie had had to face and solve "similar problems . . . with you." As he put it, Minnie's handling of Kenyon as a child had required "a good piece of work. Pity you haven't the opportunity to duplicate it. Your problems seem to be utterly different. But we all love you."[75]

Theodore married three times. He and his first wife, Martha Tipton, had three children, Stanwood, Madge, and Edward. Martha passed away in 1935.[76] Theodore's second wife, Helen Ward, died on November 14, 1963. Helen had been ill for several years and did not want anyone to know, which put a strain on Theodore. Kenyon did not agree with that decision, saying it was unnatural for him to have to hide his feelings—yet she would hide her own diagnosis when illness came upon her in later years. Kenyon wrote to Theodore a few months after Helen's death to express her condolences, inviting him to come stay with her. "The latch string is out, whenever you want to come to 433, and a key is yours for the asking. Only one gentle cat around and she won't bother you. I love you."[77] He wrote back that he would accept her invitation to stay the night, as long as there was "only ONE cat."[78] She responded, "Cross my heart and hope to die, ONE CAT."[79] Eventually Theodore married his third wife, Sarah Whitney.[80]

Kenyon loved animals, particularly cats, and was said to have had a weakness for them that sometimes distracted her from her work.[81] She wrapped the terrace of her eleventh-floor apartment in chicken wire so the cats would not fall while they were outside.[82] In particular, Kenyon adored her Siamese cat, Rita. Later in life, Kenyon shared her home with another cat, Missy, for more than fourteen years. Kenyon believed there was a "special gap when you love an animal with whom by rare luck you have established a genuine communication, a special kind of private grief that is like no other. It is as though a miracle had passed leaving only memories."[83] After Kenyon's passing, her relatives discovered boxes of her cats' cremated remains in her apartment closet. A grandnephew took the ashes to their hometown of Summit, New Jersey, for burial.[84]

Over the years, Kenyon's initial animosity toward her stepmother, Lestra, softened and they grew closer. In 1936, after Kenyon's father passed, Lestra moved back to her hometown of Xenia, Ohio.[85] In 1965, Kenyon wrote to Lestra to tell her that, as the years had passed, her feelings for her had deepened. "We were so apart once. A shy seventeen-year-old girl can never forget her mother and I'm sure you wouldn't have wanted me to. I still do remember her, passionately. But I love you too and I now find it right and what I want to do. There are merits in growing old, aren't there, dear? Barriers come down and we can see one another more fairly and as we really are."[86] Lestra was touched by Kenyon's words and wrote back with compassion and understanding:

> I have always understood just how you felt about your father's marriage. At twenty, had I been put to the test, I feel that I would have seen things just as you did . . . for I too was a passionate young girl once with an idealistic view of life. You must not reproach yourself for actions which you could not help. You were too sincere to hide your feelings, I knew that. I also knew that you had no ill will toward me, that your rebellion was against the circumstances. I am glad that I showed you that I wanted to love you and I am glad that you wanted to love me in spite of yourself. . . . Any barriers between us have been superficial ones and even those have now been broken down. . . . I feel a fine friendship growing up between us. We are both a little reserved and shy about letting anyone see just how deep our feelings are; but we both know. I shall count on your love and loyalty and you may count on mine. I am very lonely and need the love of which I am receiving in such rich measure. You, too, will always be lonely with something so fine gone from you. I would like to make up to you a little bit for that. I'll try.[87]

Lestra passed away not long after sending that letter to Kenyon, at age ninety-nine.[88]

According to Kenyon, Will had told her that since she was the only daughter of his marriage with Kenyon's mother, Minnie, and because Kenyon had not married, she should have what she wanted of her mother's property.[89] In response, Kenyon promised her father that Lestra could keep the furniture through her life, since it was her home, too. Upon Lestra's death, Kenyon received $2,500, Theodore and Houston received $500 each, and the remaining personal property, along with the house, went to Lestra's sister, Clara.[90] This decision did not sit well with Kenyon, who wrote to Theodore describing her frustration: " [T]he old furniture I remember just as [it] stood in Mother's lovely pale green parlor with the big mahogany pieces in the dining room beyond and the darling Lakeville house.... I can see Mother in ... them. They are all I have left of ... happy childhood recollections." Kenyon wrote that she wanted "a little spot in my home where Mother can come alive once more."[91] Ultimately, Clara begrudgingly agreed to part with some of their mother's items; Kenyon's sister-in-law Mildred took possession of them and brought them back to New York.[92]

Theodore's son Stanwood was close to Kenyon. They had a lot in common. Neither married, neither had children, and they were both tenacious spirits.[93] With Stanwood, she felt she could also improve her relationship with Theodore. Her letters to Stanwood often referenced the benefits of their close relationship: "I think sometimes I'm beginning to get the hang of TO and that perhaps you and I between us can understand him and handle him a little better than I ever could do a few years ago. He's so good and generous and kind and even very perceptive sometimes. And he's had so much hard luck—well—I love him. You, too."[94] Kenyon described Stanwood as "quite complex, cool where I am passionate; and withdrawn yet very warm and friendly and wonderfully observant and thoughtful of others; totally unambitious in a family of competing hot heads, me probably the worst."[95]

Kenyon would often attend meals with Theodore's other son, Edward, and his family at their home in Summit, New Jersey. She responded in writing to one invitation to share Thanksgiving asking not only what time they would eat, but also when they would "perhaps begin to drink?"[96] Although she was typically hyperfocused on her work, Kenyon still enjoyed moments of light socialization with friends and family.

Conversations at Edward's dinner table would often turn to politics and current events. Edward described Kenyon as "totally intolerant" of Republicans, though she once remarked to a reporter that she was "the original non-partisan voter," choosing candidates not by party but by who stands for good government.[97] In a 1928 letter to the editor of the *New York Times*, Kenyon demanded a correction where the paper had referred to her as a "Republican lawyer." "Lawyer I am," she wrote, "but Republican never."[98] Her father, Will, had been active within the Republican party, and her brother Theodore was a Republican.[99] Edward described his uncle, Houston, as "sometimes Democrat, sometimes Republican, but mostly a Democrat....

[H]e liked to talk about it but he never wanted to dirty his hands."[100] These political differences would cause some unpleasant arguments over the years. Kenyon's grandnephew David remembers learning how to debate at their dinner table gatherings. He described it as feeling "like a courtroom," with arguments made in "respectful but vehement" ways.[101] Kenyon was the liberal and the champion of the weak, exhibiting a humanitarian streak.[102]

Even if dinnertime arguments got heated at times, David remembers them as enjoyable. Whenever he and his father would argue about current events like the Vietnam War, Kenyon encouraged David to "stick by your guns" and "stand up for what you really believe."[103] In the end, David believed Kenyon had a big influence on him, shaping his ways of thinking. She wrote of her admiration for her nephew Edward's children and was especially diligent about keeping in touch with David, saying, "I like to keep up with my young ones."[104] David, for his part, remembers Kenyon as "the life of the party" and someone who "carried herself like a young person." At one holiday dinner when David was ten or eleven, he remembers Kenyon disappearing under the dining table and, to the delight of all the kids, grabbing their legs. Although she must have been about seventy-five years old at the time, she still enjoyed goofing off.[105]

David described Kenyon as unique, observing that "she didn't really share the family's politics. . . . [F]rom an early age she was a rebel, she was doing different things." Then again, he acknowledged, one had to "be a big personality to survive in New York." Kenyon often talked about possessing a survival instinct, a necessary trait for a female lawyer at the time. She was "unafraid to go out there and make noise."[106]

According to Edward, Kenyon was generally late for social engagements due to her busy schedule. He remembered a family gathering at her brother Houston's apartment one snowy winter night. Everyone was there to celebrate Kenyon's birthday. She arrived an hour and a half late, "soaking wet . . . to the skin, cold." When they asked where she had been, she said she had been picketing Governor Nelson Rockefeller's office because his administration was attempting to evict and relocate a group of senior citizens. As Edward explained it, "She lived on picket lines . . . Dorothy really loved to work. She loved to express herself by action. She was a true activist. She wasn't just a talker."[107]

Her grandnephew John Fisher describes Kenyon as "flamboyant, outspoken, colorful, and resilient." As a lawyer, he appreciates the legacy she left behind. John and his sister, Ellen Fisher Gager, were able to see their great aunt's influence firsthand when, along with their spouses, they met with Associate Justice Ruth Bader Ginsburg in her chambers at the Supreme Court. They appreciated that Ginsburg was "the successor to Kenyon's way of thinking and doing things."[108] In preparation for their visit, Ellen emailed and asked Ginsburg what she was hopeful for in the future. Ginsburg emailed back, writing that when she was younger "lynchings were still occurring, many occupations were closed to women, and Joe McCarthy was terrorizing people."[109] Ginsburg could appreciate how positive changes had been made during her life and predicted they would see light emerging again. This was very similar to Kenyon's belief that fair play and equality would ultimately prevail, as long as people kept fighting to achieve it.

. . .

In 1971, Jacqueline Van Voris wrote to Kenyon about participating in an oral history project to mark Smith College's upcoming centennial, saying that Kenyon's name was one of the first to be suggested.[110] Kenyon responded with an emphatic yes, giving a warning, "I am known, as I suspect you know already, for my frankness. But don't be alarmed, I am also kind."[111] She expressed her thrill that Smith students "are at last interested in law as a career and that fills me with joy."[112]

During the ensuing interview, Kenyon remarked that as she had aged, she had shifted her attention to listening to the concerns of the youth. "I'm going to find out what the young people are saying. I'm going to try to understand it. . . . I think we should give more time and care and respect to the views that the young people are expressing." She was interested in the cause of women as a deprived group, while mindful to focus on other populations, remarking, "I'm interested in all kinds of people who are in one way or another disadvantaged. That covers disadvantages regarding race, national origin . . . sex, religion, age, all the rest of it. I'm a little bit, let us say, on the side of the underdog." She found hope in the idea of disadvantaged groups "beginning to feel in themselves a sense of identity, of their personality as something which is entitled to respect and to fair play."[113]

Kenyon remained optimistic about the future and had faith that great problems could be addressed. Unfortunately, her time was running short.

ELEVEN

# *Saying Goodbye*

## A LIFE RICHLY LIVED

Life is full of fighting things and I am still hard at work fighting.

DOROTHY KENYON

PRIOR TO THE FAMILY'S SUMMER VACATION to Canada in 1969, Kenyon thought she had experienced a twenty-four-hour flu. By September, she had lost thirty pounds. Once she finally sought medical care, doctors immediately hospitalized her. The diagnosis was cancer. Doctors quickly performed an operation, removing her entire stomach.[1]

Instead of being forthcoming about the cancer diagnosis, she told most people that she had undergone another ulcer surgery.[2] She spent months in Columbia Presbyterian Medical Center, finally returning home in December. Alan Reitman, the ACLU's associate director, wrote her while she was in the hospital, wishing her a speedy recovery and saying her indomitable spirit would see her back fighting legal battles soon.[3] Pauli Murray also wrote to Kenyon in the hospital, and tellingly, she, too, cited her indomitability, which had so often served as an inspiration to others.[4]

Kenyon blamed herself for her health troubles but reported that her doctors called her "practically indestructible"—though of course, she joked, she knew that already. In a letter to Eleanor Holmes Norton, Kenyon wrote: "This latest illness was caused entirely by my own ignorance and cock sureness and contempt for doctors generally. . . . I allowed myself to bleed internally without even knowing it for months and months. Thus it takes longer for me to come back than if I had had a little more sense. But the timbers of this ship are as tough as ever."[5]

Her correspondence suggests that she was becoming increasingly aware of her mortality. Impatient to return to work, she wrote to one friend that she was "crazy to get back full-tilt, but it seems I can never get fat enough to please my doctor who is a tyrant. He says it takes time and I haven't any time to waste."[6] She was down to 110 pounds, but not from a lack of trying. Her cook, Maria, made her delicious food, which made her feel a bit stronger. "If trying could do it," she remarked, "I ought to be a butter ball. But I ain't."[7] Although she felt weak, she had hope.

In August 1971, at the age of eighty-three, Kenyon was working on a case involving a mother in New York who was surrendering her child to adoptive parents residing in Kentucky.[8] She was also working on a law review article for the *Hastings Law Journal* about women and the Fourteenth Amendment.[9] As she wrote to a friend, she was intent on meeting the deadline, "burning my candle at both ends—but it's hardly a 'lovely light.'"[10] Later that month Kenyon wrote her last letter to the editor of the *New York Times*. The topic was sex bias in colleges. In it, she argued that a student's educational needs should not be determined by their sex; rather, "[o]ne of the most important precepts of the movement for women's rights is that the aspirations of women are bounded only by their talents, abilities and potentialities as individual human beings."[11]

This frenetic pace of life could not continue.

She wrote her doctor in November seeking guidance, saying her lack of a stomach was "raising lots of hell which sap[s] my energies."[12] Kenyon was having a hard time gaining weight, and keeping it on even if she was able to add a pound or two. The lack of energy concerned her the most, for it made her reluctant to work, something she had never experienced before. She expressed continued frustration and impatience with her difficulty in eating. Foods she used to enjoy, prior to her surgery a few years before, no longer satisfied her. Ultimately, Kenyon realized that she might not be able to gain weight—but she still hoped to return to her law practice, thinking that would lift her spirits.

About a week later, because of her inability to keep on weight, Kenyon was going to be hospitalized for tests, and she wrote to her doctor again. This time, though, she was not seeking his advice. After her operation, she reminded him, he had told her he removed her entire stomach "because it was imbedded in a cancerous mass"; had he not done so, he said, she would have died within a matter of hours.[13] His words, Kenyon told him, were emblazoned on her mind. He had also told her that her type of stomach cancer was not metastatic and would not return, which she took to mean that she should no longer fear cancer. However, unbeknownst to Kenyon at the time, the surgeon told her brothers that even if the surgery was successful, her life expectancy would be only two to three months. It seems the surgeon had treated her paternalistically, instead of being wholly forthcoming about the seriousness of her condition and what it might mean for her mortality.

She wrote that she had accepted his words as the whole truth, which was all she wanted from him—the truth, which she would convey to those she chose to tell. The letter then reveals her discovery that he had conveyed an entirely different story to her brothers. She said she found it difficult to even write about how this made her feel, telling him that it went "too deep for any words and could only wound, futilely. I go my own way as always."[14]

Although she did not specifically state what the surgeon had told her brothers, a letter written by Houston following her passing sheds light:

> Dorothy will also occupy a place in history as a minor medical marvel. Following total removal of her stomach in November 1969, the surgeon told me that it was a bad case of cancer and that, while it would be possible for her to live without a stomach, the end would probably come within six weeks to three or four months. The fact that she "made it" in reasonably good health until the summer of 1971 indicates how she fooled the surgeon by her stamina and dedication.[15]

She reported to the hospital for tests on November 13, 1971, and would remain there through December. She told colleagues that she had phlebitis and would be back at meetings soon, "with bells on."[16] In reality, the cancer had returned, with no treatment options available.

Kenyon wrote to Houston from the hospital, saying that she loved him very much and was deeply grateful to both her brothers for their generosity. She proudly noted that although they had helped pay some of her bills, the bulk of her monthly expenses—her rent, employee salaries, weekly B12 injections, dental bills, and other miscellaneous law office bills—were paid out of her own modest earnings. She made it clear that she wanted to try to pay her share as long as possible.[17]

In late December Kenyon returned to her apartment, where day and night nurses cared for her. Pauli Murray visited on Christmas Day. They discussed politics and clothing, and Kenyon's sense of humor was on full display. Murray said that although Kenyon was "probably aware that she was in the closing chapter of her life, she had the same quality of ongoingness in the face of affliction which I have seen her display in many of our struggles together."[18]

In January 1972, Kenyon received the Vanderbilt Associates Gold Medal from NYU School of Law, recognizing her contributions to her community and the legal profession.[19] Houston accepted the award on her behalf at the ceremony.[20] Later that month, Houston updated Murray and members of Kenyon's family about her condition. She had, he said, been confined to her apartment for the last month, and the doctors did not express hope for her recovery. Houston wrote that in the tests the previous fall the doctors had found malignant tumors.[21] One made it difficult for Kenyon to swallow, and a suspected brain tumor had taken her power of speech. Houston stated that Kenyon's greatest cross to bear was not pain, but her inability to communicate.[22] Nevertheless, Houston described his sister as appearing a bit stronger, with a healthier appetite, while also acknowledging that she was very weak and spent most of her time in bed. Since Kenyon knew where she was and took comfort in being at home, they were keeping her in the apartment instead of transferring her to a nursing facility. Houston warned it would not be long before the end of her life.

Soon, Kenyon no longer recognized her family. Murray and Houston kept in touch by telephone during her final days, and Houston followed up one of their conversations with a letter in which he asked Murray if she would deliver Kenyon's eulogy. He desired a simple service for his sister, he said. In this letter, he also waxed nostalgic:

> As I came down Ninth Avenue I realized that she had been born in one of the first apartment houses as high as eight floors which still stands, now old and dingy, on the west side of Ninth Avenue at 78th Street; and that she now lies dying in an apartment house which is just a few doors off Ninth Avenue at 21st Street. Except for a brief period of about two or three years when she lived in a little house overhanging the East River (just north of where the U.N. now is) she has lived on the West Side of New York all her life, most of the time directly on or within a few yards of Ninth Avenue. . . . Dorothy has seen Ninth Avenue through almost every phase of its existence to date.[23]

Kenyon died on February 11, 1972. Houston described her passing as peaceful. She was sedated, which was only necessary near the very end, and it calmed her in such a way that "practically without warning, she simply stopped breathing."[24] Her passing was "like the going out of a candle."[25] The night nurse reported her death at about fifteen minutes before midnight. However, Houston and his wife, Mildred, were unable to get a doctor to certify the death until around 3 a.m., which created confusion that she had passed away on February 12.[26] Houston believed Kenyon had faced the fact that her life was ending and had made peace with herself and the world.[27] He also believed that with a lengthened perspective historians would "give her a place, perhaps of some importance, in the history of the twentieth century democracy in this country."[28]

Kenyon had been raised Episcopalian (though her Smith transcripts indicate her denominational preference as Unitarian), but she was not particularly religious and did not have a home church. Because she had grown up on the West Side, in Chelsea, it was only fitting to celebrate her life there. Houston chose St. Peter's Episcopal Church of New York, also known as St. Peter's Chelsea, for the memorial service because it was only a five-minute walk from her home, was big enough to hold the large crowd he anticipated, and had a history of supporting social justice movements.[29] During the 1960s, St. Peter's housed civil rights and unionizing organizations, including the national offices of the Student Nonviolent Coordinating Committee and Black Women's Liberation.[30]

On a cold afternoon, hundreds of friends, colleagues, and family members walked the snow-crusted sidewalks to the gray stone church, which was brightened by large red doors. The two nineteenth-century pipe organs rang out as they gathered to celebrate Kenyon's life. It was February 17, 1972, what would have been her eighty-fourth birthday. Inside, as sunlight streamed through stained glass windows, the dark wood pews filled. The pulpit gleamed golden in the light. By Houston's estimate, almost six hundred people attended the service.[31]

The memorial began with a reading from the Book of Common Prayer. Houston wanted a portion of Beethoven's Ninth Symphony to be played, but the organist said the hundred-fifty-year-old organ could not handle it.[32] Instead, the organist played Bach's Fantasia in G. Hymns, chosen by Houston, were sung—"Abide with Me" and "O God, Our Help in Ages Past"—both of which Kenyon had known in her youth.[33]

Pauli Murray crossed the tile floor to the pulpit, the crowd waiting expectantly. Her southern voice filled the room as she began, sharing Kenyon's story:

> Dorothy Kenyon's presence sparkled in every group in which she took part, and the removal of that sprightly presence leaves us with a sense of being diminished, of a loss which cannot be replaced in our time. Yet, the central lesson of her high-hearted spirit impels us not to mourn but to rejoice in the triumph of a life richly lived, valiantly fought, dedicated to service on behalf of human rights for all, creative and productive almost to the very end. Our legacy is the fire of that dauntless independent spirit, forever in rebellion against injustice and inequality, and having the capacity to endure and overcome many defeats until her ideals became accepted principles. . . . And it was through our seven years of working closely together on the ACLU Board and our mutual concern for women's rights that I got to know Dorothy as a

> colleague and to share a sisterhood with her which has inspired me in my own life. I grew to appreciate more fully the debt of gratitude women in the United States owe to her unflagging efforts to make the issue of women's rights an integral part of the work of one of the most vigorous civil liberties organizations in the country. . . . It is the vindication of a lifetime of patient effort that she lived to be one of the attorneys who persuaded the Supreme Court in November 1971 to adopt the view that the Fourteenth Amendment applies to discrimination on grounds of sex, and that today the ACLU has adopted a comprehensive program to implement its policies on women's rights as a priority in 1972. . . . I think when future historians assess the important issues of the twentieth century they may well conclude that Judge Dorothy Kenyon was one of the giants who stood in bold relief against the American sky.[34]

Algernon Black, the leader of the New York Society for Ethical Culture, attended the memorial service and wrote Murray an appreciative note afterward about her eulogy, remarking on the integrity and courage that Kenyon personified.[35] Murray wrote him back and said giving the eulogy had been incredibly difficult.[36] Afterward Murray created a handwritten chart titled "Leaders for Women's Rights and Reforms (U.S.A.)."[37] On it she listed individuals, no longer living, whom she considered leaders in the women's rights movement. The first name she included was Anne Hutchinson, a seventeenth-century spiritual leader known for challenging Puritan elders in the church to let her speak on religious doctrine and who is now considered one of the earliest American feminists.[38] The last name on the list was Dorothy Kenyon. Although Kenyon was first on many lists, including, to her deep chagrin, that of Senator Joseph McCarthy, Murray was sure to name Kenyon last on her list of trailblazing women.

Tributes poured in following Kenyon's death. US representative William F. Ryan's remarks, published in the *Congressional Record*, expressed his sorrow that Kenyon had passed away. He had worked with her in the New York Democratic Party and held her in high esteem. Ryan said that Kenyon "strove to make this Nation live up to its promise of equality for all" and called on individuals to rededicate themselves to her quest.[39]

Organizations to which Kenyon dedicated her life wrote announcements and resolutions, bringing attention to a life dedicated to the pursuit and protection of individual liberties. Roger Baldwin, who worked closely with Kenyon for decades through the ACLU, recognized her staunch defense of women's rights. "She carried the ACLU board on all women's rights matters; she was our one-woman expert," he said. "Nobody was more faithful in attending board meetings and taking an active part. She loved meetings anyway . . . they were a form of social life. Her best friends were those she worked with. She was popular in the ACLU circles in the warmly personal way she had, and she was always listened to unless she talked too long, as happened."[40]

The New York City Bar Association memorialized Kenyon's fighting spirit, describing her as attacking injustice "with a warm smile" while disarming those who disagreed with her by "using reason and patience to make converts to her point of view."

> She enhanced the state of women lawyers by demonstrating that they were as competent as men to carry professional burdens and that they did not depend on mere gallantry for their success. Those who disagreed with her violently nevertheless remained her friends. She was never a slave to achieving mere consensus; the result had to involve no basic sacrifice of principles. She knew that the truth and right were to be found on the high peaks and that ascent was hard and dangerous and, in her friend Arthur Vanderbilt's phrase about judicial reform, "not for the short-winded."[41]

The *Chelsea-Clinton News* gave credit to Kenyon's long fight during a turbulent time in history, saying she was involved in "all of the important human rights movements of the century . . . invariably on the side of the underdog."[42] An editorial noted that many present freedoms enjoyed by individuals were owed to Kenyon. It praised her accomplishments while recognizing her humanity. "Dorothy was far from sainthood. She was capable of enormous rages and stomped out of many a meeting. She kept grudges and hates going for years. But her incredible wit and her ability to laugh at a situation were saving graces in what otherwise could be a truly miserable situation." The editorial went on to explain how knowing Kenyon could connect someone to past generations. "It made you feel part of some glorious struggle for human rights and human dignity which was still going on. A struggle that Dorothy never stopped fighting. We were all richer for having known her."[43] A neighbor described seeing Kenyon going from meeting to meeting and hearing her typewriter constantly clacking. She was, he said, "a tough, shrewd, and courageous woman. But rarest of all, she was a genuinely involved person. She contributed to her world. She was truly committed to living right up to the end of her life."[44]

It was a fact within Kenyon's family that her friends held first place in her life, and those friends remained loyal to her even after her passing. Years later, Pauli Murray would continue to advocate for her. For example, when the

ACLU published a volume titled *The Rights of Women* by Susan C. Ross, Murray wrote a chastising letter to Aryeh Neier, executive director of the ACLU, Norman Dorsen, director of the Civil Liberties Program at NYU School of Law, and Ruth Bader Ginsburg saying the book should have been dedicated as a memorial to Kenyon. Kenyon's work in *White v. Crook*, she pointed out, had inspired others to successfully use the Fourteenth Amendment in matters of sex discrimination. She also reminded them that Kenyon's decision to support the ERA was the main reason the ACLU's national board of directors decided to support the amendment. Murray expressed disappointment that Kenyon, a pioneer in her eyes, would be so easily forgotten—particularly by those at the ACLU.[45] Ginsburg wrote back agreeing that a deliberate effort should be made to remember those who had contributed in significant ways in the organization.[46]

. . .

Many decisions had to be made by Kenyon's family members following her passing. Her will named Stanwood as executor of her estate and he handled its distribution.[47] An appraisal was completed of her apartment and its contents, with the value listed at $6,065. Much of her furniture was in poor condition, and what jewelry she had was of little value and listed as broken or cracked.[48] She owned several art pieces and approximately one thousand miscellaneous old legal texts and other books. She had a small portable radio but no television, which supported her claim she never watched TV, even when she appeared on a program.[49] Her office contained a pair of black ladder-back side chairs, filing cabinets, bookcases, a studio bed, a swivel chair, an adding machine, a typewriter table, an IBM electric typewriter, lamps, and etchings and watercolors of the seacoast.[50]

Certain members of the family had expressed interest in some of the furniture. The law books were sold, and family members received some of the other books. Her clothes, regularly sent to storage during the warmer months, filled both her closets and cartons stacked in her bedroom. They were sorted and distributed to the Salvation Army, Goodwill, Catholic Charities, and the Project FIND senior center.[51]

Houston remembered a casual remark Kenyon had made years before, that she wanted her ashes to be "thrown over the cliff at Chilmark." However, because the family had not found any memorandum or letter evidencing that wish, Houston thought the remark should not be regarded as an expression of her wishes at the time of her death. He proposed to bury her ashes in the Kenyon lot at Woodlawn Cemetery and Conservancy in the Bronx, next to their parents.[52] Woodlawn, established in 1863, spans four hundred acres. It is a National Historic Landmark and a level two arboretum, boasting over one hundred forty varieties of trees.[53] Many prominent New Yorkers are interred at Woodlawn, including women's rights activist Elizabeth Cady Stanton and Kenyon's former boss, Mayor Fiorello La Guardia.

In May, Houston wrote his family stating Woodlawn had approved the plan to bury her ashes with her name and the years 1888–1972 inscribed on the back of the monument. He had also selected a simple bronze urn. He proposed they meet on June 9, 1973, at the cemetery for a brief ceremony with Reverend Robert T. Jenks, who had presided over Kenyon's memorial service the year before. The expenses for the burial, totaling $241.50, were paid by Theodore, Stanwood, and Houston.[54]

Over the years, a tree split at Woodlawn in front of the family plot. Instead of removing the tree, an artist carved an owl and its owlets into the remains. Owls culturally represent intelligence, wisdom, and protection. The sculpture sits there today guarding the Kenyon family plot, where Dorothy rests next to her parents, aunt, brother, and sister-in law. But she also rests on Martha's Vineyard. Kenyon's nephew Edward reported that the brothers eventually rented an airplane and scattered some of her ashes over Noman's Land, the piece of land she had worked to liberate for the birds near her beloved Barn House.[55] Woodlawn (next to her father) and Noman's Land (next to the sand and sea she spent decades enjoying) are fitting places for her eternal rest.

Reflecting on his aunt's passing, Stanwood wrote Mildred saying, "Dottie had the kind of life she wished. I was always proud of her and usually happy with our relationship. The 'family's ideal for her' that you refer to, which I always thought of as her father's and Lestra's, to be a wife and mother, never was part of my thinking."[56] Mildred recognized that family members pitied Kenyon for never marrying, but they did so with affection.[57] Stanwood also remarked that Kenyon could be somewhat overpowering and intimidating:

> Being less powerful than she, I had to put her off from time to time in order to protect my individuality. She took this in stride, but particularly when I was younger I would feel a bit guilty—wanting to be a more reliable support and companion than I allowed myself to be. Then I would feel sorry that, in her desire for the family ties she wanted as a balance to her main life, we

Kenyons (and I particularly) would so often keep her at arm's length. She had a tendency to smother, but as I grew more able to cope with this easily, our relationship became more equal and comfortable.[58]

Mildred began piecing together Kenyon's papers in hopes of writing a biography for her nephews and nieces.[59] She worked for years on drafts, compiling interviews and writing letter upon letter to obtain personal anecdotes from many different sources. Believing that Kenyon deserved recognition, Mildred sent a proposal to the Paul R. Reynolds Literary Agency in 1972. In her pitch, Mildred outlined Kenyon's activism and service history, while also conveying who she was as a person.

> She was in truth a formidable person. . . . In public she was always surrounded with people, and she loved them. Some of them loved her, particularly the underdog. . . . In private, on the contrary, she led what other people might think a lonely life, except that she was always fighting off loneliness by attending a meeting, a dinner, a hearing. . . . The family's attitude mixed pity for her husbandless state with affection. But if she knew this, she surely hated it. She loved her independent life, and lived it to the full. There are many who believe that this country is the better for it.[60]

The agency passed on publishing the biography.

By 1975, Mildred was at an impasse with the book. Houston had received various requests from academics and archivists for access to the papers, and in May 1978 historian Susan M. Hartmann became the first scholar to be granted the opportunity to review Kenyon's papers, which she did before the collection was delivered to its archival home at Smith College. When Hartmann arrived at Houston and Mildred's home, several steel filing cabinets awaited her.[61] As Hartmann recalled, they set her up in the basement, where she worked for several days.[62] Hartmann forged the path for scholarship on Kenyon with her 1980 article "Odyssey of a Feminist: The Career of Dorothy Kenyon."[63] According to Hartmann, Kenyon's most significant work for the cause of women occurred within the ACLU, "where she connected the old feminism with the new and prodded that organization to act on women's behalf."[64]

Mildred Adams Kenyon suffered a heart attack and died on November 5, 1980. She was survived by her husband, Houston.[65]

. . .

Dorothy Kenyon is a woman forgotten. Following her death, there was much talk about the importance of her work in the twentieth century. Resolutions were made and discussions were held about honoring her legacy. Honorarium ideas such as an endowed professorship in her name, a book dedication, and scholarships for law students were suggested, but in the end nothing came to pass. Her legacy has been reduced to footnotes, short paragraphs, and occasional articles. This book remedies that.

For over four decades on the ACLU national board of directors, Kenyon dedicated her life to establishing litigation strategies that would persuade the Supreme Court, and the greater public, that sex-based differentials in the law violated the Equal Protection Clause of the Fourteenth Amendment. Kenyon waded into battle wherever she perceived injustice and spent immense effort educating the public about how the law impacted marginalized populations. She wanted to change the way judges and legislators thought about the role of women in society. Kenyon believed parallels existed between race and sex discrimination and that women could not enjoy full citizenship without reforming archaic laws based on both race and sex stereotypes. With the help of Pauli Murray, Kenyon's efforts to obtain sex equality in jury service laid the groundwork for the Supreme Court to require compulsory service at the state level. Kenyon's litigation strategies also became the foundation for Ruth Bader Ginsburg's success as an advocate before the US Supreme Court in the 1970s.

Kenyon's efforts to expand the reach of democracy on both a domestic and an international scale are worthy of attention. She promoted women's rights within the United States and abroad, focusing on equal pay, universal suffrage, and increased economic opportunities for women. She fought against the scourge of communism, even when the national spotlight was pointed directly at her. Kenyon stood tall, advocating for democracy, and displayed an indomitable spirit in the face of false allegations. She possessed a vision of what the world could be and worked to achieve her idea of equality.

Over time, Houston wrote, the family's grief following Kenyon's death was replaced with a new appreciation for the life she had lived. "Withdrawal of the physical presence allows the memories and achievements of the past to rise up to their rightful recognition," he explained, "and in Dorothy's case the predominant feeling is not so much one of sadness as one of pride."[66] Houston wrote a fitting description of Kenyon in response to a condolence letter, saying that, besides Kenyon's "instinct for combat when she thought a matter of principle was at issue, she was able to bring forth the heavy artillery of wit and humor in her support."[67] He believed this to be a charming combination, and that it had contributed to the success Kenyon had in supporting those causes she held close to her heart.

Kenyon was a woman of faith—not in a religious sense but in her ideals. The principles of democracy, equality, and dignity guided her life. She was also a disrupter. Kenyon believed in the law and its ability to right social wrongs. She was able to harness her unique personality quirks and use her privilege to make monumental changes in both policy and law. She should be embraced, and celebrated, for her many accomplishments. It is time to follow the words of her brother, Houston, and place Kenyon in a position of great importance in the twentieth-century history of the United States.

# ACKNOWLEDGMENTS

This project would not have been possible without the support and encouragement of many people. I cannot express enough appreciation for the staff at Smith College's Sophia Smith Collection of Women's History who helped provide access to Kenyon's papers. Thanks also to Linda Hendrieth, Dr. Gil Fried, Dr. William Crawley, Dr. Nicholas Buker, Dr. David Earle, and Dr. Amy Mitchell-Cook for administrative support and help. Thanks to Angela Price, Todd Mutchler, Harland Harris, Nanci Young, Kellie Sparks, Juliana Wahl, Austin Scott, Emma Coley, Katie Garrett, Taylor Youngling, Rukaiya Sharmi, Maddie Rehrman, Gretchen Shoemaker, Hilary Wallcox, Kate Long, Dan Michelson, Jennifer Fauxsmith, Kaitlin Mui, Teah Dempsey, Bena Williams, Sonia Carroll, Olga Kazarov, Suzie Kleindienst, Mary Biddle, Samuel Edwards, Leslie Fields, Eric Van Slander, Kathleen Agno, Carlos Ramos, Dorothy Alexander, Victoria Otero, Britt McGowan, Meg Ventrudo, Elizabeth Hunter, Kelly Parker, Alita Kuiee, Holly Brewer, Jillian Lee Bergin, Max Wagh, Douglas Di Carlo, David Sager, Eric Graf, Thai Jones, and Christina Barber for research assistance. An early version of chapter nine appeared as an article in the *Tennessee Journal of Race, Gender, and Social Justice* (2022). Thanks to the law review editors for their help. This manuscript went through several rounds of anonymous readers and I am thankful for their feedback.

I greatly appreciate David S. Kenyon and John Fisher for sharing their family stories with me. Thanks to Jessica Ancker and David Owen for providing detailed information about Barn House. I would further like to thank Professor Jennifer Nye, Dr. Kelly Carr, Professor Lee McMichael, Jennifer Andrews, Dr. Landon R. Y. Storrs, Professor Sara Warf, Dr. Charlie Penrod, Dr. Lee Gaul, Dr. Lauren Brinkley-Rubinstein, Professor Tracy Thomas, Professor Jill Hasday, and Dr. Paul Collins for their encouragement. Thanks to Anne Canright, Stephanie Summerhays, Kate Weigand, Jennifer Allison, Regina Sakalarios-Rogers, Andrea Friedman, and Steven B. Baker for their editorial assistance. Thanks to Professor Lori A. Ringhand, my law professor who many years later still takes the time to answer my questions. She is the type of professor I aspire to be. I will always be grateful to Professor Jamie Abrams for encouraging me to reach out to the University of California Press regarding this project. Thanks to Maura Roessner, Nora Becker, Natalie Gomez, and Michelle Phan for their assistance and their belief in this book.

I should also give a thank you to my tuxedo cat, Mr. Mustachio, who sat on my lap throughout the first three years of writing this manuscript. He passed away in 2023, but I am sure he felt he deserved authorship credit—even though he was asleep for most of it.

Thanks to my mom, Linda Belcher, who was recruited to Smith College to help me scan documents and to New York City to research the La Guardia papers. I appreciate her encouragement and our dinner dates following full days of scanning. Thanks to my stepchildren, Braden and Madison—extraordinary bonuses in my life.

Finally, thanks to my husband, David, and our son, Gauge. I would not have kept going if it was not for David's support. He really is my biggest fan. Thanks to Gauge for letting me spend the time I needed away from him to write this book. He knew how important this project was to me and supported me in the process. I love you both, for always.

# NOTES

## PREFACE

1. Gerda Lerner, "Placing Women in History: Definitions and Challenges," *Feminist Studies* 3, no. 5 (1975).

## INTRODUCTION

1. "Shuberts' Ambassador Theater Opens in January," *New-York Tribune*, November 18, 1920, 10.

2. "Herbert Krapp, 86, Theater Architect," *New York Times*, February 17, 1973, 34.

3. Gerald Bordman, *American Theatre: A Chronicle of Comedy and Drama, 1930–1969* (Oxford University Press, 1996), 120.

4. "Woman Forces Way onto Jury," *New York Sun*, October 3, 1935, Dorothy Kenyon Papers, Sophia Smith Collection, Smith College Archives, Northampton, MA, Box 1 (hereafter DK Papers); "Playballyhoo Urges Women as Jurors," unidentified clipping, October 3, 1935, DK Papers, Box 1.

5. "News of the Stage," *New York Times*, October 5, 1935, 18.

6. "The News About a West Side Woman Judge," political brochure, October 23, 1939, DK Papers, Box 4.

7. "Headline: Dorothy Kenyon Dies Here," *Chelsea-Clinton* [NY] *News*, February 17, 1972, Pauli Murray Papers, Schlesinger Library, Radcliffe Institute, Harvard University, Cambridge, MA, Box 125, Folder 2269 (hereafter PM Papers).

8. Operator's License, September 30, 1943, DK Papers, Box 5; Frances Berna Knight, interview with Louise Wilby Knight, December 29, 1987, DK Papers, Box 65a; E.P.B. to Mildred Adams Kenyon, n.d., DK Papers, Box 3.

9. DK to Catherine Allen, June 5, 1969, DK Papers, Box 35.

10. Will Kenyon to DK, February 17, 1918, DK Papers, Box 3.

11. DK to Who's Who in America, April 6, 1965, DK Papers, Box 13; Mildred Adams Kenyon to PM, February 9, 1972, PM Papers, Box 125, Folder 2269; Susan

Ware, *Partner and I: Molly Dewson, Feminism, and New Deal Politics* (Yale University Press, 1987), 153.

12. Senate Subcommittee Transcripts, March 14, 1950, DK Papers, Box 7A; DK to Ben Huebsch, March 27, 1950, DK Papers, Box 11; "McCarthy's Charges Cite Dorothy Kenyon," *New York World-Telegram*, March 8, 1950, DK Papers, Box 2.

13. Dorothy Dunbar Bromley to Mildred Adams Kenyon, June 21, 1972, DK Papers, Box 3.

14. "Profane Profiles ... DK," *The Cooperator* [NY], November 1940, DK Papers, Box 1.

15. Mr. and Mrs. Alden Clarke to DK, March 15, 1971, DK Papers, Box 14.

16. DK to Henry Schwarzchild, March 13, 1967, DK Papers, Box 28.

17. *Hoyt v. Florida*, 368 U.S. 57 (1961); Linda K. Kerber, *No Constitutional Right to Be Ladies: Women and the Obligations of Citizenship* (Hill & Wang, 1998), 169.

18. Caroline Chiappetti, "Winning the Battle but Losing the War: The Birth and Death of Intersecting Notions of Race and Sex Discrimination in *White v. Crook*," *Harvard Civil Rights–Civil Liberties Law Review* 52 (2017): 469, 470.

19. Mary Dublin Keyserling to DK, March 22, 1966, DK Papers, Box 29.

20. DK to Caroline Ware, March 23, 1966, DK Papers, Box 17.

21. Michael S. Rosenwald, "Ruth Bader Ginsburg Was Inspired by a Forgotten Female Trailblazer," *Washington Post*, December 28, 2018.

22. Jane Sherron De Hart, *Ruth Bader Ginsburg: A Life* (Knopf, 2018), 153.

23. Eulogy Address, DK Papers, Box 7, Folder 4. Following Kenyon's death, Murray would be ordained the first Black female Episcopal priest in the United States.

## 1. DO RIGHT, BE BRAVE

1. "Riverside Park," NYC Parks, https://www.nycgovparks.org/parks/riverside-park/.

2. "New York's Long Fight for the New Riverside Drive," *New York Times*, July 10, 1904, SM3.

3. Family Tree, DK Papers, Box 8, Folder 1; *Men and Women of America: A Biographical Dictionary of Contemporaries* (L. R. Hamersly & Co., 1909), 947.

4. DK to LeRoy Bowman, October 23, 1939, DK Papers, Box 11; Mildred Adams Kenyon to Elizabeth Jachimowicz, April 19, 1972, DK Papers, Box 3.

5. Mildred Adams Kenyon Manuscript, DK Papers, Box 3; William Houston Kenyon Jr. to PM, February 9, 1972, PM Papers, Box 125, Folder 2269.

6. Mildred Adams Kenyon to Elizabeth Jachimowicz, April 19, 1972.

7. Ancestors, DK Papers, Box 3.

8. Mildred Adams Kenyon to PM, February 9, 1972, PM Papers, Box 125, Folder 2269.

9. *Men and Women of America*, 946; David McAdam, *History of the Bench and Bar of New York*, vol. 2 (New York History Company, 1897), 227.

10. Biography, DK Papers, Box 3.

11. *Men and Women of America*, 946–47; "A Seventy-Five Year History of NYIPLA," New York Intellectual Property Law Association, https://www.nyipla.org/nyipla/History.asp.

12. Baby's Record, 13, DK Papers, Box 7, Folder 5.

13. Will Kenyon to DK, March 1, 1888, DK Papers, Box 7.

14. Chas D. Kellogg to DK, March 21, 1888, DK Papers, Box 7.

15. Baby's Record, 27.

16. Baby's Record, 45.

17. Baby's Record, 51.

18. Genealogy, November 8, 1973, DK Papers, Box 3.

19. Smith Centennial Study Oral History, June 14, 1971, New York City, DK Papers, Box 4.

20. Sarah Bean Apmann, "Tenement House Act of 1901," Off the Grid Village Preservation Blog, April 11, 2016, https://www.villagepreservation.org/2016/04/11/tenement-house-act-of-1901/.

21. Terry Golway, *I Never Did Like Politics: How Fiorella La Guardia Became America's Mayor, and Why He Still Matters* (St. Martin's Press, 2024), 180.

22. Smith Centennial Study Oral History.

23. "Can Girls Be Lawyers?," *American Girl*, March 1939, DK Papers, Box 3.

24. Testimonial Dinner Introductory Remarks, February 22, 1968, DK Papers, Box 4.

25. Smith Centennial Study Oral History.

26. DK to Alden Clarke, September 17, 1970, DK Papers, Box 14.

27. My Father, n.d., DK Papers, Box 7.

28. Smith Centennial Study Oral History.

29. "Lestra Kinney Kenyon, Former Resident, Dies," *Lakeville* [CT] *Journal*, June 2, 1966, DK Papers, Box 2.

30. "Can Girls Be Lawyers?"

31. DK to Alden Clarke, September 17, 1970.

32. Elisabeth Israels Perry, *Belle Moskowitz: Feminine Politics and the Exercise of Power in the Age of Alfred E. Smith* (Northeastern University Press, 1992), 5; Annual Commencement Program, May 31, 1904, DK Papers, Box 4. Of the sixty graduates in 1904, twenty-two were women. Class of 1904, DK Papers, Box 3.

33. "A Long Tradition," Horace Mann School, https://www.horacemann.org/our-school/a-long-tradition.

34. Kim Clarke, "No Admittance," University of Michigan Heritage Project, https://heritage.umich.edu/stories/no-admittance/; Nancy F. Cott, *The Bonds of Womanhood: "Woman's Sphere" in New England, 1780–1835*, 2nd ed. (Yale University Press, 1997), 97.

35. Samantha Barbas, *The Rise and Fall of Morris Ernst, Free Speech Renegade* (University of Chicago Press, 2021), 16.

36. "The Thirty-Fourth Official Circular of Smith College, 1907–1908," 13, Smith College Annual Circulars, Internet Archive, https://archive.org/details/smithannu0506smit/page/n239/mode/2up.

37. Eleanor Flexner, *Century of Struggle: The Woman's Rights Movement in the United States*, Rev. ed. (Belknap Press of Harvard University Press, 1975), 128.

38. Smith Woman at Work: Judge Kenyon, February 1946, DK Papers, Box 1; Smith Centennial Study Oral History.

39. Eleanor Terry Lincoln and John Abel Pinto, *This, the House We Live In: The Smith College Campus from 1871 to 1982* (Smith College, 1983), 83, https://drive.google.com/file/d/164mmK9mx5oi1ClTVdHb90-SBm4IY6G2R/view.

40. Anne Gardiner Perkins, *Yale Needs Women: How the First Group of Girls Rewrote the Rules of an Ivy League Giant* (Sourcebooks, 2019), 8.

41. Edward H. Clarke, *Sex in Education; or, A Fair Chance for the Girls* (James R. Osgood & Co., 1873), 113, Library of Congress, https://www.loc.gov/resource/gdcmassbookdig.sexineducationor00clar.

42. Clarke, *Sex in Education*, 126–27.

43. Clarke, *Sex in Education*, 135–36.

44. Sue Zschoche, "Dr. Clarke Revisited: Science, True Womanhood, and Female Collegiate Education," *History of Educational Quarterly* 29 (1989): 545, 547.

45. Rosalind Rosenberg, *Beyond Separate Spheres: Intellectual Roots of Modern Feminism* (Yale University Press, 1982), 6.

46. Barbara J. Harris, *Beyond Her Sphere: Women and the Professions in American History* (Greenwood Press, 1978), 100.

47. Nathaniel Fishmen, *Married Woman's Bill of Rights* (Liveright, 1943), 17.

48. Fishmen, *Married Woman's Bill of Rights*, 17.

49. M. Carey Thomas, "Present Tendencies in Women's College and University Educations," *Educational Review* 25 (1908): 62, 69, Curiosity Collections, Harvard Library, https://curiosity.lib.harvard.edu/women-working-1800-1930/catalog/45-990067375940203941.

50. Thomas, "Present Tendencies," 70.

51. Flexner, *Century of Struggle*, xiii.

52. Smith Centennial Study Oral History.

53. Mildred Adams Kenyon to Elizabeth Jachimowicz, April 19, 1972.

54. Smith Centennial Study Oral History.

55. Testimonial Dinner Introductory Remarks; *Phi Beta Kappa Directory, 1776–1941* (United Chapters of Phi Beta Kappa, 1941), xi, Hathi Trust, https://babel.hathitrust.org/cgi/pt?id=uc1.b3168810&seq=15&q1=dorothy+kenyon.

56. Mildred Adams Kenyon Manuscript.

57. *The Book of the Class of Nineteen Hundred and Eight* (Smith College, 1908), Internet Archive, https://archive.org/details/class1908smit/mode/2up.

58. Current Biography, April 1947, DK Papers, Box 1, Folder 1.

59. *Book of the Class of Nineteen Hundred and Eight.*

60. "Ivy Day: Awards Convocation," Smith College, May 18, 2024, https://www.smith.edu/sites/default/files/2024-05/Ivy%20Day%20Program%202024-Final-Access.pdf.

61. Christine Stansell, *American Moderns: Bohemian New York and the Creation of a New Century* (Princeton University Press, 2010), 57; Helen Lefkowitz

Horowitz, "The Great Debate," *Harvard Magazine*, n.d. [1999], https://harvardmagazine.com/sites/default/files/html/1999/11/womanless.2.html.

62. Smith Centennial Study Oral History.

63. Jacqueline Van Voris, *College: A Smith Mosaic* (M.J. O'Malley Company, 1975), 16.

64. Dorothy Kenyon, "Case (by One of Them) for Women Lawyers," *New York Times*, February 19, 1950, DK Papers, Box 21.

65. William Houston Kenyon Jr. to Lestra Kinney, February 12, 1909, DK Papers, Box 10.

66. "Xenia Has a Society Wedding," *Springfield* [OH] *News-Sun*, June 9, 1909, 8.

67. Clara Shields to Alice (last name omitted), 1910, DK Papers, Box 10.

68. Miscellaneous Recordings, DK Papers, Box 65; DK to Stanwood Kenyon, July 15, 1968, DK Papers, Box 8.

69. Herman Limberg, *Guildites* (1939), DK Papers, Box 1, Folder 1.

70. Edward Tipton Kenyon, interview with Louise Wilby Knight, October 6, 1998, DK Papers, Box 65a.

71. "Troth Announced of Mildred Adams," *New York Times*, December 2, 1934, N6; "Theodore S. Kenyon, 88, Long a Patent Lawyer," *New York Times*, April 26, 1978, B4.

72. Smith Centennial Study Oral History. NYU admitted women law students beginning in 1890, graduating fifty women with the degree of Bachelor of Laws by 1900, with ten of those women going on to pursue the master's degree. "Women as Lawyers," *New-York Tribune*, May 12, 1900, 7.

73. Kenyon, "Case (by One of Them) for Women Lawyers."

## 2. BECOMING A PORTIA

1. Jeanette E. Tuve, *First Lady of the Law: Florence Ellinwood Allen* (University Press of America, 1984), 23.

2. Leslie J. Tompkins to DK, July 12, 1915, DK Papers, Box 4; NYU School of Law Grades, May 1915, DK Papers, Box 4.

3. Smith Centennial Study Oral History, June 14, 1971, New York City, DK Papers, Box 4.

4. New York University School of Law, *The NYU Law Alumni Directory, 1896–1969* (B.C. Harris, 1969), 334–35.

5. Jill Filipovic, "A Woman's Place," *The Magazine* (NYU Law) (2008), reposted September 23, 2017, https://www.law.nyu.edu/news/alumnae-gender-parity-womens-leadership-network-women-of-color-collective-law-women.

6. Elinor Byrns, "I Resolve to be Restless," *The Independent* [NY], January 10, 1916, 50, cited in Phyllis Eckhaus, "Restless Women: The Pioneering Alumnae of New York University School of Law," *New York University Law Review* 66 (1991): 1997.

7. Miscellaneous Recordings, DK Papers, Box 65.

8. "The News About a West Side Woman Judge, " October 23, 1939, DK Papers, Box 4, Folders 1–5; Memorial Book, Association of the Bar of the City of New York, 1972, PM Papers, Box 125, Folder 2269; Mildred Adams Kenyon Manuscript, DK Papers, Box 3.

9. "W. H. Petkin Dies; I.T.&T. Executive," *New York Times*, August 19, 1952, 23.

10. DK to Wolcott Pitkin, November 30, 1917, DK Papers, Box 3. In 1921, Pitkin resigned his post as attorney general of Puerto Rico and became adviser on foreign affairs to the Siamese government. "W. H. Petkin Dies." He would serve as general counsel for the American Civil Liberties Union (ACLU) in 1924. *Free Speech in 1924: The Work of the ACLU, January to December 1924* (ACLU, 1925), 50.

11. DK to Wolcott Pitkin, November 30, 1917, DK Papers, Box 3.

12. Wolcott Pitkin to DK, December 21, 1917, DK Papers, Box 15.

13. Walter Lippmann, "A Year of Peacemaking," *The Atlantic*, December 1946, https://www.theatlantic.com/magazine/archive/1946/12/a-year-of-peacemaking/656593/.

14. *Bulletin of the Brooklyn Institute*, December 13, 1926, DK Papers, Box 1; For Press Release, Classes of 1901–1910 Records, CA-MS-010120, Box 1736, Sophia Smith Collection, Smith College, Northampton, MA.

15. Personal Question Sheet, December 14, 1918, Box 1098, Department of Labor, National Archives and Records Administration (hereafter NARA), St. Louis, MO.

16. Memo to Assistant Secretary, December 12, 1918; General Appointment, January 4, 1919, both in Box 1098, Department of Labor, NARA, St. Louis, MO.

17. "Eighth A. D. Women Voters' League to Hear Address by Noted Feminine Civic Worker," *New York Bronx Home News*, February 26, 1923, DK Papers, Box 1; Barbas, *Rise and Fall of Morris Ernst*, 178.

18. Jill Norgren, *Rebels at the Bar: The Fascinating, Forgotten Stories of America's First Women Lawyers* (New York University Press, 2013), 185.

19. Virginia G. Drachman, *Women Lawyers and the Origins of Professional Identity in America: The Letters of the Equity Club, 1887 to 1890* (University of Michigan Press, 1993), 3.

20. Ada M. Bittenbender, "Woman in Law," *Chicago Law Times* 2 (1888): 301.

21. Judith Paterson, *Be Somebody: A Biography of Marguerite Rawalt* (Eakin Press, 1986), 41.

22. Drachman, *Women Lawyers*, 4.

23. Christine Lunardini, *What Every American Should Know About Women's History: 200 Events That Shaped Our Destiny* (Adams Media, 1997), 108.

24. Clare Cushman, ed., *Supreme Court Decisions and Women's Rights: Milestones to Equality* (Congressional Quarterly Press, 2011), 221.

25. Amber Paranick, "Belva Lockwood: Suffragist, Lawyer, and Presidential Candidate," Library of Congress Blogs, September 28, 2020, https://blogs.loc.gov/headlinesandheroes/2020/09/belva-lockwood-suffragist-lawyer-and-presidential-candidate/.

26. Karen Berger Morello, *The Invisible Bar: The Woman Lawyer in America 1638 to the Present* (Beacon Press, 1986), 38.

27. D. Kelly Weisberg, "Barred from the Bar: Women and Legal Education in the United States, 1870–1890," *Journal of Legal Education* 28 (1977): 486–487.

28. Tracy A. Thomas and Tracey Jean Boisseau, eds., *Feminist Legal History: Essays on Women and Law* (New York University Press, 2011), 1.

29. *Bradwell v. Illinois*, 83 U.S. 130, 141 (1873).

30. Mildred Adams, *The Right to Be People* (J.B. Lippincott, 1966), 6; Norma Basch, *In the Eyes of the Law: Women, Marriage, and Property in Nineteenth-Century New York* (Cornell University Press, 1982), 44.

31. Sir William Blackstone, *Commentaries on the Laws of England in Four Books* (Callaghan and Company, 1899), 359–62.

32. "Women in our Changing Political Economy," June 1935, DK Papers, Box 18.

33. "Women in our Changing Political Economy."

34. Flexner, *Century of Struggle*, xiii.

35. *Mackenzie v. Hare*, 239 U.S. 299, 311 (1915).

36. June Sochen, *Movers and Shakers: American Women Thinkers and Activists, 1900–1970* (Quadrangle Books, 1973), 2; Nancy F. Cott, *The Bonds of Womanhood: "Woman's Sphere" in New England, 1780–1835*, 2nd ed. (Yale University Press, 1997), 5.

37. Audrey Wolfson Latourette, "Sex Discrimination in the Legal Profession: Historical and Contemporary Perspectives," *Valparaiso University Law Review* 39 (2005): 859, 861.

38. Reva Siegel, "The Modernization of Marital Status Law: Adjudicating Wives' Rights to Earnings, 1860–1930," *Georgetown Law Journal* 82 (1994): 2127.

39. Siegel, "Modernization of Marital Status Law," 2165.

40. "The Unmarried Woman," *New-York Tribune*, September 3, 1909, 5.

41. "The Unmarried Woman."

42. Bittenbender, "Woman in Law," 305.

43. Drachman, *Women Lawyers*, 3.

44. Drachman, *Women Lawyers*, 20.

45. Lelia J. Robinson, "Women Lawyers in the United States," *Legal Reference Services Quarterly* 8 (1988): 297, 325, originally published in *The Green Bag* 2 (1890), https://books.google.com/books/about/The_Green_Bag.html?id=-PqRAAAAIAAJ.

46. Robinson, "Women Lawyers," 329.

47. Robinson, "Women Lawyers."

48. Drachman, *Women Lawyers*, 22–23.

49. Drachman, *Women Lawyers*, 23.

50. Drachman, *Women Lawyers*, 23.

51. Lynn Gilbert and Gaylen Moore, *Particular Passions: Talks with Women Who Have Shaped Our Times* (Clarkson N. Potter, 1981), 193.

52. Samantha Barbas, "Dorothy Kenyon and the Making of Modern Legal Feminism," *Stanford Journal of Civil Rights and Civil Liberties* 5 (2009): 428.

53. Eve Larson, "Women Admitted to Law School After Long Struggle," *Columbia Law School News*, October 21, 1959, 4.

54. Harris, *Beyond Her Sphere*, 110.

55. Robert W. Smuts, *Women and Work in America* (Columbia University Press, 1959), 21.

56. Joe M. Komljenovich, "Dorothy Straus," Jewish Women's Archive, https://jwa.org/encyclopedia/article/straus-dorothy.

57. Beatrice Doerschuk, *Women in the Law: An Analysis of Training, Practice, and Salaried Positions* (Bureau of Vocational Information, 1920), vii–viii.

58. Doerschuk, *Women in the Law*, 11–12. Some states required a high school diploma, while others required only two or three years of high school. Nine states did not specify the time that would be devoted to legal training; it could vary from one year to four.

59. Doerschuk, *Women in the Law*, 25.

60. Doerschuk, *Women in the Law*, 103, 36.

61. Doerschuk, *Women in the Law*, 36.

62. Doerschuk, *Women in the Law*, 58.

63. Doerschuk, *Women in the Law*, 60.

64. "Portias," *Cincinnati Post*, June 12, 1922, 1; "Kentucky Portia," *Twice-a-Week Messenger* [KY], December 22, 1897, 7.

65. Eve Larson, "Women Who Are Lawyers Oppose Sex Discrimination," *Columbia Law School News*, November 4, 1959, 4.

66. "Boston Cold to a Woman Lawyer," *Boston Sun*, April 23, 1911, 26.

67. Hilda M. Richards, "Women and Her Work," *Courier-Journal* [KY], June 27, 1919, 5.

68. "The Female Species," *Lansing* [MI] *State Journal*, December 18, 1926, 4.

69. "Calls Masculine Women Race Menace," *Daily Record* [NJ], January 28, 1927, 6.

70. "Calls Masculine Women Race Menace."

71. "The History of the National Bar Association," National Bar Association, https://nationalbar.org/nba-history/.

72. "Lady Lawyers," *Ebony*, Aug. 1947, https://archive.org/details/sim_ebony_1947-08_2_10/mode/1up.

73. Morello, *Invisible Bar*, 101.

74. Hal Boyle, "Male Sex Muddled Victim of Equal Rights for Women," *Tampa Times*, October 11, 1949, 11.

75. Morello, *Invisible Bar*, 103.

76. Gilbert and Moore, *Particular Passions*, 157.

77. Dorothy Kenyon, "Case (by One of Them) for Women Lawyers," *New York Times*, February 19, 1950, DK Papers, Box 21.

78. Brenda Feigen, *Not One of the Boys: Living Life as a Feminist* (Alfred A. Knopf, 2000), 4.

79. Feigen, *Not One of the Boys*, 6, 15.

80. Mona Harrington, *Women Lawyers: Rewriting the Rules* (Alfred A. Knopf, 1993), 19.

81. Dorothy J. Glancy, "Harvard Law School Survey, Women in Law: The Dependable Ones," 21 *Harvard Law School Bulletin* 22, June 1970.

82. Glancy, "Harvard Law School Survey, Women in Law."

83. "Judge Kenyon Gives the Low-Down on the Law," October 25, 1939, DK Papers, Box 3.

84. "A Woman Lawyer Looks at Her Profession," Broadcast WNYC, May 28, 1935, DK Papers, Box 18.

85. "A Woman Lawyer Looks at Her Profession."

86. "Smith Woman at Work: Judge Kenyon," February 1946, DK Papers, Box 1.

87. Kenyon, "Case (by One of Them) for Women Lawyers."

88. "Can Girls Be Lawyers?," *American Girl*, March 1939, DK Papers, Box 3.

89. DK to Mrs. Adam Haskell, July 23, 1963, DK Papers, Box 12.

## 3. A COOPERATIVE ASSOCIATION

1. Henry Beetle Hough, ed., *Vineyard Gazette Reader* (Harcourt, Brace & World, 1967), 92.

2. Patsy Pitkin to DK, September 1918, DK Papers, Box 15; "DK One of the Barn House Founders," *Vineyard Gazette* [MA], February 18, 1972. Newspapers were publishing warnings about a new flu that September. The Spanish flu pandemic of 1918 resulted in several deaths on Martha's Vineyard.

3. Melvin I. Urofsky, *Felix Frankfurter: Judicial Restraint and Individual Liberties* (Twayne, 1991), 182.

4. Claude Moore Fuess, *Stanley King of Amherst* (Columbia University Press, 1955), 109; Arthur R. Railton, "Artists and Other Free Spirits at Chilmark's Barnhouse," *Dukes County* [MA] *Intelligencer*, August 1995, 15.

5. Fuess, *Stanley King of Amherst*, 36; "Gertrude Louisa Besse King, 1923," Frederick Warren Allen, https://fwallen.com/portfolio/gertrude-louisa-best-king-1923/.

6. Fuess, *Stanley King of Amherst*, 154.

7. Announcement for Pitkin and Rosensohn, March 1, 1919, DK Papers, Box 15. Kenyon's first client was the Kingdom of Siam, in whose case she prepared a brief on extraterritoriality and the opium trade. Herman Limberg, *Guildites*, 1939, DK Papers, Box 1, Folder 1; Samuel Rosensohn to DK, March 8, 1919, DK Papers, Box 17; "Judge Dorothy Kenyon to Be Woman's Club Guest October 11," *Williamsport* [PA] *Sun-Gazette*, October 4, 1949, 4; Resume, 1940, DK Papers, Box 1, Folder 1; "Eighth A.D. Women Voters' League to Hear Address by Noted Feminine Civic Worker," DK Papers, Box 1.

8. For Press Release, n.d., Box 1736, Classes of 1901–1910 Records, CA-MS-010120, Sophia Smith Collection, Smith College, Northampton, MA.

9. Arthur R. Railton, "The Barnhouse: What Is It?," *Dukes County Intelligencer*, August 1990, 32.

10. Minutes of Meeting, August 7, 1927, DK Papers, Box 35.

11. Railton, "Artists and Other Free Spirits," 6.

12. House Rules for Members and Guests, DK Papers, Box 35.

13. Robert Cottrell, *Roger Nash Baldwin and the American Civil Liberties Union* (Columbia University Press, 2000), 241.

14. DK to Jeff Fuller, March 12, 1969, DK Papers, Box 35.

15. House Rules for Members and Guests.

16. David Owen, ed., "Barn House," 1919–2019, photo scrapbook supplied to author by David S. Kenyon.

17. John Fisher, interview with author via Zoom, April 11, 2023.

18. Railton, "Artists and Other Free Spirits," 8.

19. Railton, "Artists and Other Free Spirits," 3. Electricity eventually came to Chilmark in the early 1960s, which brought light and cooking facilities to the farmhouse so meals could be prepared there and then carried the one hundred yards to the barn.

20. Railton, "Artists and Other Free Spirits," 6; David Owen, interview with author by telephone, September 27, 2024.

21. Jessica Ancker, interview with author by telephone, September 21, 2024; David Owen, interview.

22. "Thinking About D.K.," May 1970, DK Papers, Box 3; Richard Skidmore, "What Did Lucy Think?," *Martha's Vineyard*, August 1, 2017, https://mvmagazine.com/news/2017/08/01/what-did-lucy-think. Chilmark Associates did eventually purchase beach access.

23. Jessica Ancker, interview.

24. E.P.B. to Mildred Adams Kenyon, n.d., DK Papers, Box 3.

25. T.L. McCready to DK, March 13, 1928, DK Papers, Box 17.

26. Stansell, *American Moderns*, 41; Urofsky, *Felix Frankfurter*, 2; "About the ACLU," ACLU, https://www.aclu.org/about-aclu; "On Understanding Society," *Columbia Journalism Review* (Fall 1969), republished online, https://www.cjr.org/60th/on-understanding-society-fred-friendly-interviews-walter-lippmann.php/; "Warren Chappell, Illustrator, Teacher, and Artist, 86 Dies," *New York Times*, https://www.nytimes.com/1991/03/29/obituaries/warren-chappell-illustrator-teacher-and-artist-86-dies.html.

27. Testimonial Dinner Introductory Remarks, DK Papers, Box 4.

28. Fuess, *Stanley King of Amherst*, 155.

29. Jessica Ancker, interview.

30. Railton, "Artists and Other Free Spirits," 30.

31. Max Eastman, *Love and Revolution: My Journey Through an Epoch* (Random House, 1942), 539.

32. Eastman, *Love and Revolution*, 539.

33. Railton, "Artists and Other Free Spirits," 26.

34. Patsy Pitkin to DK, September 2, 1921, DK Papers, Box 16.

35. Skidmore, "What Did Lucy Think?"

36. DK to Warren Chappell, July 30, 1969, DK Papers, Box 35.

37. E.P.B. to Mildred Adams Kenyon.

38. "A Few Notes," February 28, 1972, Box 9, Folder 10, Roger Nash Baldwin Papers, MC005, Mudd Manuscript Library, Public Policy Papers, Department of Special Collections, Princeton University Library.

39. Flora Lewis, "Syndicated Column," *Washington Post*, September 18, 1971, cited by Railton, "Artists and Other Free Spirits," 11.

40. Barbas, *Rise and Fall of Morris Ernst*, 51–52.

41. Owen, "Barn House."

42. Ellis Cose, *Democracy, If We Can Keep It: The ACLU's 100-Year Fight for Rights in America* (New Press, 2020), 133.

43. "A Few Notes."

44. Tribute to Evelyn Preston Baldwin by DK at Baldwin's Memorial Service in New York City, June 19, 1962, DK Papers, https://drive.google.com/file/d/1bFaII3bbaijczQTygKH6HwSJcBX5Ongd/view.

45. Tribute to Evelyn Preston Baldwin by DK.

46. Mary Hopkins to DK, July 11, 1938, DK Papers, Box 34.

47. DK to Mary Hopkins, July 14, 1938, DK Papers, Box 34.

48. Railton, "Artists and Other Free Spirits," 14.

49. Special Meeting of Chilmark Associates, August 31, 1929, DK Papers, Box 35.

50. DK to William Houston Kenyon Jr., July 17, 1940, DK Papers, Box 34.

51. Theodore Kenyon to DK, July 19, 1940, DK Papers, Box 34.

52. DK to Theodore Kenyon, July 22, 1940, DK Papers, Box 34.

53. DK to Theodore Kenyon, July 22, 1940.

54. DK to Mildred Adams Kenyon, September 3, 1948, DK Papers, Box 8.

55. Joanna Hodgman to Barnhouse Members, March 25, 1969, DK Papers, Box 35.

56. "Barn House Observes its 50th Anniversary," *Vineyard Gazette*, August 12, 1969.

57. David S. Kenyon, interview with author via Zoom, April 4, 2023.

58. Augustus Ben David II, "Let No Man Mess with Noman's Land," *Vineyard Gazette*, October 15, 2020.

59. David S. Kenyon, interview.

60. "Party for Miss Kenyon: Women's Rights Pioneer Is Honored in Chilmark," *Vineyard Gazette*, September 4, 1970.

61. "Nomans Land Island National Wildlife Refuge," US Fish and Wildlife Service, https://www.fws.gov/refuge/nomans-land-island.

62. "Party for Miss Kenyon."

63. Peggy and Roy Lamson to DK, telegram, February 17, 1972, DK Papers, Box 10.

64. Clay Risen, *Red Scare: Blacklists, McCarthyism, and the Making of Modern America* (Scribner, 2025), 163; "Party for Miss Kenyon."

65. DK to Yvette Eastman, August 18, 1971, DK Papers, Box 35.

66. DK to Helen Kenyon, September 21, 1963, DK Papers, Box 8.

67. DK to Stanwood Kenyon, February 27, 1964, DK Papers, Box 8.

68. Hough, *Vineyard Gazette Reader*, 96.

69. Patsy Pitkin to DK, May 14, 1918, DK Papers, Box 15.
70. Patsy Pitkin to DK, December 22, 1918, DK Papers, Box 15.
71. Will Kenyon to Ammie Stanwood, September 25, 1918, DK Papers, Box 3.
72. Patsy Pitkin to DK, October 5, 1918, DK Papers, Box 15.
73. Leigh Ann Wheeler, *How Sex Became a Civil Liberty* (Oxford University Press, 2013), 32.
74. Patsy Pitkin to DK, n.d., 1918, DK Papers, Box 15.
75. Patsy Pitkin to DK, November 1918, DK Papers, Box 15.
76. Patsy Pitkin to DK, December 22, 1918, DK Papers, Box 15.
77. "Thinking About D.K."
78. "Thinking About D.K."
79. Gertrude King to DK, n.d., 1920, DK Papers, Box 15.
80. Gertrude King to DK, April 26, 1920, DK Papers, Box 15.
81. Mildred Adams Kenyon Manuscript, 54, DK Papers, Box 3.
82. Gertrude King to DK, June 5, 1920, DK Papers, Box 15.
83. Gertrude King to DK, June 2, 1920.
84. Ware, *Partner and I*, xv.
85. Gertrude King to DK, November 9, 1920, DK Papers, Box 15.
86. Gertrude King to DK, December 17, 1920, DK Papers, Box 15.
87. Gertrude King to DK, October 19, 1920, DK Papers, Box 15.
88. Gertrude King to DK, August 30, 1920, DK Papers, Box 15.
89. Gertrude King to DK, September 22, 1920, DK Papers, Box 15.
90. Gertrude King to DK, October 19, 1920.
91. Gertrude King to DK, October 27, 1920, DK Papers, Box 15.
92. Gertrude King to DK, October 29, 1920, DK Papers, Box 15.
93. Gertrude King to DK, April 21, 1921, DK Papers, Box 15.
94. Patsy Pitkin to DK, August 17, 1921, DK Papers, Box 16.
95. Patsy Pitkin to DK, August 17, 1921.
96. Patsy Pitkin to DK, August 27, 1921, DK Papers, Box 16.
97. Patsy Pitkin to DK, August 27, 1921.
98. Patsy Pitkin to DK, October 21, 1921, DK Papers, Box 16.
99. DK to Patsy Pitkin, n.d., 1921, DK Papers, Box 16.
100. DK to Patsy Pitkin, n.d., 1921.
101. DK to Patsy Pitkin, n.d., 1921.
102. Letter from Gertrude King, February 5, 1922, DK Papers, Box 15.
103. Letter from Gertrude King, February 5, 1922.
104. Letter from Gertrude King, February 1922, DK Papers, Box 15.
105. Gertrude King to DK, n.d., 1922, DK Papers, Box 15.
106. Patsy Pitkin to DK, August 9, 1922, DK Papers, Box 16.
107. DK to Patsy Pitkin, September 1922, DK Papers, Box 16.
108. DK to Patsy Pitkin, September 1922.
109. Gertrude King to DK, November 6, 1922, DK Papers, Box 15.
110. Patsy Pitkin to DK, November 1922, DK Papers, Box 16.

111. Patsy Pitkin to DK, November 1922.

112. Patsy Pitkin to DK, November 1922.

113. Patsy Pitkin to DK, January 20, 1923, DK Papers, Box 16.

114. Last Will and Testament, February 15, 1923, DK Papers, Box 5.

115. Gertrude King to DK, February 14, 1923, DK Papers, Box 15.

116. Stanley King to DK, April 7, 1923, DK Papers, Box 15; "Gertrude Louisa Besse King, 1923."

117. Stanley King to DK, telegram, April 11, 1923, DK Papers, Box 15.

118. Fuess, *Stanley King of Amherst*, 156.

119. "Gertrude Louisa Besse King, 1923."

120. Patsy Pitkin to DK, May 4, 1923, DK Papers, Box 16.

121. Gertrude Besse King, *Alliances for the Mind* (Harcourt, Brace & Co. 1924), viii–ix.

122. Fuess, *Stanley King of Amherst*, 157.

123. Undated note, DK Papers, Box 7.

124. Undated note.

125. "Elihu Root Funeral Tomorrow," *Press & Sun-Bulletin* [NY], August 28, 1967, 4.

126. Mildred Adams Kenyon Manuscript, 63.

127. "Root-Stryker Wedding Cards Are Sent Out," *Washington Times*, November 18, 1907, 4; "Elizabeth Root," Ancestry.com, https://www.ancestry.com/discoveryui-content/view/100260994:60525; Grace Root to DK, March 21, 1926, DK Papers, Box 17. They had three children; only one, Elihu Root III, survived into adulthood. Their daughter, Elizabeth, died at age two, and their son Woolsey lived until the age of nine.

128. Sec Elihu Root to DK, December 3, 1923, DK Papers, Box 16.

129. Mildred Adams Kenyon Manuscript, 67.

130. Sec Root to DK, August 10, 1924, DK Papers, Box 16.

131. Sec Root to DK, October 29, 1924, DK Papers, Box 16.

132. Sec Root to DK, November 1, 1924, DK Papers, Box 16.

133. DK to Sec Root, December 18, 1924, DK Papers, Box 16.

134. DK to Sec Root, July 6, 1927, DK Papers, Box 17.

135. Sec Root to DK, July 8, 1927, DK Papers, Box 17.

136. DK to Sec Root, April 5, 1929, DK Papers, Box 17.

137. Sec Root to DK, April 20, 1930, DK Papers, Box 17.

138. Sec Root to DK, May 1930, DK Papers, Box 17.

139. Mildred Adams Kenyon Manuscript, 88.

140. "Thinking About D.K."

141. Last Will and Testament, June 29, 1937, DK Papers, Box 5.

142. Edward Tipton Kenyon, interview with Louise Wilby Knight, October 6, 1998, DK Papers, Box 65a.

143. Edward Tipton Kenyon, interview.

144. DK to Grace Root, December 19, 1967, DK Papers, Box 13.

## 4. A MAVERICK AND PUBLIC SERVANT

1. Timeline, DK Papers, Box 3, Folder 11.

2. "433 West 21st Street," StreetEasy, https://streeteasy.com/building/433-west-21-street-new_york.

3. Joe M. Komljenovich, "Dorothy Straus," Jewish Women's Archive, https://jwa.org/encyclopedia/article/straus-dorothy.

4. Memorial Book 1972, PM Papers, Box 125, Folder 2269.

5. "Dorothy Kenyon, Fiery Fighter for Women's Rights, Is Visitor," *Washington Post*, February 3, 1938, DK Papers, Box 1.

6. Dorothy Kenyon, October 3, 1935, DK Papers, Box 1.

7. Dept. of State, Dept. of Labor, FBI Case, September 27, 1943, 100-25772, NARA, St. Louis, MO.

8. Dorothy Kenyon, "Cooperative Housing: Misuses of Term Is Said to Work to the Disadvantage of True Cooperatives," *New York Times*, October 7, 1947, 26.

9. Cooperators and Consumers, June 1967, DK Papers, Box 23.

10. Mildred Adams Kenyon Manuscript, 159, DK Papers, Box 3.

11. Records of Yearly Allowance, DK Papers, Box 9.

12. DK to Bob Pigott, August 5, 1971, DK Papers, Box 33.

13. Edward Tipton Kenyon, interview with Louise Wilby Knight, October 6, 1998, DK Papers, Box 65a.

14. DK to Marla Perkel, December 19, 1966, DK Papers, Box 13.

15. William Houston Kenyon Jr. to DK, June 1, 1934, DK Papers, Box 10.

16. Edward Tipton Kenyon to DK, January 31, 1969, DK Papers, Box 8.

17. William Houston Kenyon Jr. to DK, January 6, 1971, DK Papers, Box 6.

18. Edward Tipton Kenyon, interview.

19. Alyn Brodsky, *The Great Mayor: Fiorello La Guardia and the Making of the City of New York* (St. Martin's Press, 2003), ix.

20. Golway, *I Never Did Like Politics*, 4.

21. Elisabeth Israels Perry, *After the Vote: Feminist Politics in La Guardia's New York* (Oxford University Press, 2019), 185.

22. "New Woman License Commissioner Eager to Watch Wheels Go 'Round," unidentified newspaper clipping, January 31, 1936, DK Papers, Box 1.

23. "Miss Kenyon Sworn In," *New York Times*, December 19, 1935, DK Papers, Box 1; Women's City Club of New York Press Release, December 16, 1935, DK Papers, Box 1, Folder 1; Budget, Department—Licenses, Roll 14, Series II, Subj. Files 1934–1945, New York City Department of Records and Information Services.

24. Yearbook Report of the License Department, DK Papers, Box 49, Folder 22.

25. *Smith Alumnae Quarterly*, February 1937, 130, DK Papers, Box 19.

26. DK to Stanwood Kenyon, August 5, 1971, DK Papers, Box 8.

27. Dorothy Kenyon, "If It Weren't for Men," *New York Times*, July 30, 1971.

28. Perry, *After the Vote*, 148.

29. "Social Plan Urged to End Vice Racket," *New York Times*, June 17, 1936, 48.

30. Andrea Friedman, *Prurient Interests: Gender, Democracy, and Obscenity in New York City, 1909–1945* (Columbia University Press, 2000), 64.

31. Friedman, *Prurient Interests*, 81.

32. Burton W. Peretti, *Nightclub City: Politics and Amusement in Manhattan* (University of Pennsylvania Press, 2007), 165.

33. DK to Mayor La Guardia, August 24, 1936, DK Papers, Box 49, Folder 22.

34. DK to Mayor La Guardia, August 24, 1936.

35. DK to Mayor La Guardia, August 24, 1936.

36. Testimonial Dinner Program, February 22, 1968, PM Papers, Box 125, Folder 2269.

37. Friedman, *Prurient Interests*, 83.

38. Brodsky, *The Great Mayor*, 347.

39. "No Strip, No Sale, Minskys Close Theatre," *New York Daily News*, November 26, 1937, 751.

40. Friedman, *Prurient Interests*, 156–57.

41. Brodsky, *The Great Mayor*, 258.

42. Miscellaneous Recordings, DK Papers, Box 65.

43. Smith Centennial Study Oral History, June 14, 1971, DK Papers, Box 4.

44. "Bar Association Goes Co-ed," May 12, 1937, DK Papers, Box 1.

45. Dorothy Kenyon, "Case (by One of Them) for Women Lawyers," *New York Times*, February 19, 1950, DK Papers, Box 21.

46. City Bar Exclusion Assailed by Women, n.d. (early 1930s), DK Papers, Box 1.

47. "A Woman Lawyer Looks at Her Profession," WNYC broadcast, May 28, 1935, DK Papers, Box 18.

48. "New York Woman Gets League Post," *New York Times*, January 29, 1938, 7.

49. "Bar Association Goes Co-ed."

50. "Women Who Blazed New Paths in the Law," Historical Society of the New York Courts, https://history.nycourts.gov/women-who-blazed-new-paths-in-the-law/.

51. Statements of Dorothy Straus and Elihu Root Jr., DK Papers, Box 7. Dorothy Straus died at age seventy-two in a fire at her summer home on Gott Island. "Home Fire Is Fatal to Woman Lawyer," *New York Times*, July 25, 1960, 45.

52. "New York Woman Gets League Post."

53. Jaci Eisenberg, "The Status of Women: A Bridge from the League of Nations to the United Nations," *Journal of International Organizations Studies* 4 (2013): 10; The Association of the Bar of the City of New York Memorial Book 1972, PM Papers, Box 125, Folder 2269; "Only Human," *New York Mirror*, February 23, 1938, DK Papers, Box 1.

54. "Dorothy Kenyon, Fiery Fighter for Women's Rights, Is Visitor."

55. "Women Lack Imagination Needed for Crime," *Brooklyn Daily Eagle*, October 28, 1938, DK Papers, Box 1.

56. "Dorothy Kenyon Gets Bench Post," *New York Times*, January 8, 1939, 37.

57. Radio Interview with Former Judge, March 27, 1939, DK Papers, Box 4.

58. "Judge DK Tells About Ups and Downs of Campaigning," unidentified newspaper clipping, November 25, 1939, DK Papers, Box 1.

59. "Mayor Appoints Miss Kenyon as Justice of Municipal Court," *New York Herald Tribune*, Jan. 7, 1939, DK Papers, Box 1.

60. Bruce Buckley, "Dinner to Honor Dorothy Kenyon," *Chelsea-Clinton* [NY] *News*, Feb. 22, 1968, PM Papers, Box 125, Folder 2269.

61. "A Woman Lawyer Looks at Her Profession."

62. Merril Sobie, "The Development of New York's Family Court," *Judicial Notice: A Periodical of New York Court History*, 2022, 32.

63. "Historical Profile: Jane Matilda Bolin '31," *Yale Law School*, January 15, 2024, https://law.yale.edu/yls-today/news/historical-profile-jane-matilda-bolin-31.

64. Radio Interview with Former Judge.

65. Interview with National Broadcasting Company, DK Papers, Box 4.

66. Interview with National Broadcasting Company.

67. Elisabeth Israels Perry, "Rhetoric, Strategy, and Politics in the New York Campaign for Women's Jury Service, 1917–1975," *New York History* 82 (2001): 58; Interview with National Broadcasting Company.

68. Radio Interview with Former Judge.

69. Interview with National Broadcasting Company.

70. Dept. of State, Dept. of Labor, FBI Case, October 26, 1942, 100-25772, NARA, St. Louis, MO.

71. "Women Lack Imagination Needed for Crime."

72. "Law Offers Opportunities Suitable to Women's Skill," *Milwaukee Journal*, November 15, 1948, DK Papers, Box 1.

73. Dorothy Kenyon, "Women as Citizens," *The Council Woman*, May–June 1944, Library of Congress, https://www.loc.gov/resource/mss34132.mss34132-011_00639_00650/?sp=5&st=image.

74. Dorothy Kenyon, "Letters to the Times: Statehood for Hawaii," *New York Times*, July 30, 1950, E8.

75. New York Americans for Democratic Action Bulletin, March 1967, DK Papers, Box 23.

76. DK to Editor, *New York Times*, August 14, 1968, DK Papers, Box 17.

77. DK to Harriet Pilpel, February 7, 1968, DK Papers, Box 29.

78. "Justice DK Votes," *New York Sun*, November 2, 1939, DK Papers, Box 1.

79. Brodsky, *The Great Mayor*, 172.

80. Mason B. Williams, *City of Ambition: FDR, La Guardia, and the Making of Modern New York* (W. W. Norton, 2013), 220.

81. Edward N. Costikyan, "Politics in New York City: A Memoir of the Post-War Years," *New York History* 74 (1993): 418–420.

82. Buckley, "Dinner to Honor Dorothy Kenyon."

83. "Lawyers Aid Miss Kenyon: Non-Partisan Committee to Work for Her Election as Justice," *New York Times*, October 19, 1939, 17.

84. Lowell Limpus, "Golstein Victor O'Dwyer Wins 3–1, Mutuels Sweep In," *New York Daily News*, November 8, 1939, 84.

85. DK to Pauline Newman, December 14, 1939, DK Papers, Box 3.

86. Theodore Kenyon to Stanwood Kenyon, November 8, 1939, DK Papers, Box 3.

87. "Judge DK Tells About Ups and Downs of Campaigning."

88. Buckley, "Dinner to Honor Dorothy Kenyon."

89. Perry, *After the Vote*, 99.

90. Stanwood Kenyon's short story, November 7, 1939, DK Papers, Box 3.

91. Stanwood Kenyon's short story.

92. Dorothy Kenyon, "The Council Woman," 5 *Bulletin of the National Council of Jewish Women and of the National Council of Jewish Juniors* 3, May–June 1944, National American Woman Suffrage Association Records, Library of Congress, Washington, DC.

93. Jill Norgren, *Stories from Trailblazing Women Lawyers: Lives in the Law* (New York University Press, 2018), 120; Advice of Personnel Action, May 2, 1949, Department of State, NARA, St. Louis, MO, Box 493.

94. Notes for the File, May 2, 1949, Department of State, NARA, St. Louis, MO, Box 493.

95. Dorothy Kenyon, "Equal Rights for Women," *Civil Liberties*, April 1953, DK Papers, Box 21.

96. Dorothy Kenyon, "Fundamental Freedoms for All," unidentified magazine article, September–October 1949, DK Papers, Box 59.

97. John Tomlinson to Mildred Adams Kenyon, February 13, 1976, DK Papers, Box 3.

98. "A Few Notes," February 28, 1972, Box 9, Folder 10, Roger Nash Baldwin Papers, MC005, Mudd Manuscript Library, Public Policy Papers, Department of Special Collections, Princeton University Library.

99. "Judge Dorothy Kenyon to be Woman's Club Guest October 11," *Williamsport* [PA] *Sun-Gazette*, October 4, 1949, 4.

100. Dorothy Sue Cobble, Linda Gordon, and Astrid Henry, *Feminism Unfinished: A Short, Surprising History of American Women's Movements* (Liveright, 2014), 13.

101. Sochen, *Movers and Shakers*, 70.

102. Linda K. Kerber, "I Was Appalled: The Invisible Antecedents of Second-Wave Feminism," *Journal of Women's History* 14 (2002): 96.

103. Dorothy Kenyon, "UN Aide Sees Progress," *Circleville* [OH] *Herald*, May 25, 1949, 4.

104. Commission Statement of Judge Dorothy Kenyon on Behalf of ACLU, 1962, quoted in Deborah J. Vagins and Tyler Ray, "ACLU and the Equal Pay Act of 1963: Celebrating 50 Years of Advocacy," ACLU, June 6, 2013, https://www.aclu.org/news/womens-rights/aclu-and-equal-pay-act-1963-celebrating-50-years-advocacy.

105. Serena Mayeri, *Reasoning From Race: Feminism, Law, and the Civil Rights Revolution* (Harvard University Press, 2011), 13.

106. Kenyon, "Women as Citizens"; Dorothy Kenyon, "Current Biography," April 1947, DK Papers, Box 1, Folder 1.

107. "Criticize DK," May 1949, DK Papers, Box 1.

108. Rachel Nason to DK, June 17, 1949, Dorothy Kenyon, Department of State, Record Group 59, Box 2203, NARA, College Park, MD.

109. Helen Laville, "Protecting Difference or Promoting Equality? US Government Approaches to Women's Rights and the UN Commission on the Status of Women, 1945–50," *Comparative American Studies* 5, no. 3 (2007): 299.

110. "Miss Kenyon Says UN Does Work," *Vineyard Gazette*, January 14, 1949.

111. American Association of University Women to Harry Truman, July 19, 1949; Committee on Women in World Affairs to Dean Acheson, August 17, 1949, both in Dorothy Kenyon, Department of State, Record Group 59, Box 2203, NARA, College Park, MD.

112. Ware, *Partner and I*, xi.

113. Felix Frankfurter to DK, May 19, 1949, DK Papers, Box 58.

114. DK to Felix Frankfurter, May 20, 1949, DK Papers, Box 58.

115. DK to Osmond Fraenkel, January 12, 1971, DK Papers, Box 29.

116. Dorothy Kenyon to Dean Acheson, July 11, 1949, Dorothy Kenyon, Department of State, Record Group 59, Box 2203, NARA, College Park, MD.

117. Florence L. C. Kitchelt, "Equality of Women," *Washington Post*, April 1, 1949.

118. Florence L. C. Kitchelt to Harry Truman, January 3, 1950; Florence L. C. Kitchelt to Dean Acheson, January 6, 1950, both in Dorothy Kenyon, Department of State, Record Group 59, Box 1331, NARA, College Park, MD.

119. Esther V. W. Tufty, "Women Now Receive Share of Top Posts in Government, Due to India Edwards," *Morning Herald* [MD], February 17, 1950, 13.

120. Jack K. McFall to Brian McMahon, January 24, 1950, Dorothy Kenyon, Department of State, Record Group 59, Box 1331, NARA, College Park, MD.

121. DK to Rose Schneiderman, January 23, 1950, DK Papers, Box 11.

122. India Edwards to Mildred Adams Kenyon, June 30, 1976, DK Papers, Box 3. In a 1950 letter, India wrote to Kenyon about how well she felt Kenyon had handled herself at the Senate hearing. She expressed her support, and endorsement, for Kenyon in future government service opportunities. India Edwards to Dorothy Kenyon, March 20, 1950, DK Papers, Box 15.

123. Harry Truman to DK, January 10, 1950, DK Papers, Box 17.

124. DK to Harry Truman, January 26, 1950, DK Papers, Box 17.

## 5. NAMED FIRST

1. "Democracy Requires Freedom for Women, Miss Kenyon Says," *Youngstown* [OH] *Vindicator*, March 4, 1950, DK Papers, Box 3.

2. Office Memorandum, March 8, 1950, DK Papers, Box 7A, Folder 1.

3. Office Memorandum, March 8, 1950.

4. Senate Subcommittee Transcripts, March 14, 1950, DK Papers, Box 7A.

5. Elisabeth Israels Perry and Karen Manners Smith, *The Gilded Age and Progressive Era: A Student Companion* (Oxford University Press, 2006), 82.

6. Ellen Schrecker, *Many Are the Crimes: McCarthyism in America* (Little Brown, 1998), 58–59.

7. Kate Weigand, *Red Feminism: American Communism and the Making of Women's Liberation* (Johns Hopkins University Press, 2001), 22, 31.

8. Weigand, *Red Feminism*, 3.

9. Cobble, Gordon, and Henry, *Feminism Unfinished*, 35.

10. Steve Batterson, *The Prosecution of Chandler Davis: McCarthyism, Communism, and the Myth of Academic Freedom* (Monthly Review Press, 2023), 43.

11. Philippa Strum, "Dorothy Kenyon, Senator Joseph McCarthy's First Case," *History Weekly*, June 11, 2015, https://papers.ssrn.com/sol3/papers.cfm?abstract_id=2736473.

12. Fred J. Cook, *The Nightmare Decade: The Life and Times of Senator Joe McCarthy* (Random House, 1971), 3.

13. Richard M. Fried, *Nightmare in Red: The McCarthy Era in Perspective* (Oxford University Press, 1990), 52.

14. Fried, *Nightmare in Red*, 52.

15. "State Department Employee Loyalty Investigation," 81st Cong., 2d Session, Report of the Comm. on Foreign Relations, S. Res. 231, S. Rep. No. 2108 (1950), 13.

16. "State Department Employee Loyalty Investigation," 13.

17. "Senate Resolution 301: Censure of Senator Joseph McCarthy," 81st Cong., 1954, National Archives, https://www.archives.gov/milestone-documents/censure-of-senator-joseph-mccarthy.

18. "State Department Employee Loyalty Investigation," 13.

19. "Senate Resolution 301," 15.

20. Cook, *Nightmare Decade*, 62.

21. Ellen Schrecker, *The Age of McCarthyism: A Brief History with Documents* (Bedford/St. Martin's, 2002), 171.

22. Schrecker, *Age of McCarthyism*, 190.

23. William F. Buckley Jr. and L. Brent Bozell, *McCarthy and His Enemies: The Record and Its Meaning* (Henry Regnery, 1954), 5.

24. "State Department Employee Loyalty Investigation," 23.

25. Landon R. Y. Storrs, *The Second Red Scare and the Unmaking of the New Deal Left* (Princeton University Press, 2013), 181.

26. Cook, *Nightmare Decade*, 147.

27. Fried, *Nightmare in Red*, 71.

28. "State Department Employee Loyalty Investigation," 4; Cook, *Nightmare Decade*, 152.

29. Cook, *Nightmare Decade*, 149.

30. Affidavit of James K. Whitaker, April 25, 1950, Box 1, Folder 29, Joseph McCarthy Papers, Raynor Memorial Libraries, Marquette University, Milwaukee (hereafter McCarthy Papers).

31. "State Department Employee Loyalty Investigation," 2.

32. Schrecker, *Age of McCarthyism*, 237.

33. "State Department Employee Loyalty Investigation," 2.

34. Cook, *Nightmare Decade*, 149.

35. Richard M. Fried, *A Genius for Confusion: Joseph R. McCarthy and the Politics of Deceit* (Rowman & Littlefield, 2022), 100.

36. Dean Acheson, *Present at the Creation: My Years in the State Department* (W. W. Norton, 1969), 362.

37. Keynote Address of Senator Joe McCarthy, June 9, 1950, Box 1, Folder 43, McCarthy Papers.

38. "State Department Employee Loyalty Investigation," 3.

39. Caroline H. Keith, *For Hell and a Brown Mule: The Biography of Senator Millard E. Tydings* (Madison Books, 1991), xv; Fried, *Nightmare in Red*, 125.

40. Cook, *Nightmare Decade*, 158; Joseph McCarthy, *McCarthyism: The Fight for America* (Devin-Adair, 1952), 1.

41. McCarthy, *McCarthyism*, 1–2.

42. Dorothy Kenyon notes, n.d., Box 307, J. B. Matthews Papers, David M. Rubenstein Rare Book & Manuscript Library, Duke University, Durham, NC (hereafter J. B. Matthews Papers).

43. State Department Employee Loyalty Investigation: Hearing on S. Res. 231 Before the S. Comm. on Foreign Relations, 81st Cong. 18 (March 8, 1950) (statement of Sen. Joseph R. McCarthy), https://archive.org/details/statedepartmente195001unit/page/n5/mode/2up. See also DK Papers, Box 65.

44. Strum, "Dorothy Kenyon, Senator Joseph McCarthy's First Case"; Jack Anderson and Ronald W. May, *McCarthy: The Man, the Senator, the "Ism"* (Beacon Press, 1952), 175.

45. Cook, *Nightmare Decade*, 189.

46. State Department Employee Loyalty Investigation: Hearings on S. Res. 231 Before the S. Comm. on Foreign Relations, 81st Cong. 29.

47. "Morris Schappes Dies at 97; Marxist and Jewish Scholar," *New York Times*, June 9, 2004.

48. "An Open Letter to Governor Thomas E. Dewey," *New York Times*, October 9, 1944, 12. At the time of the *New York Times* advertisement, Schappes had served eleven months of a twenty-four-month sentence for his perjury conviction. The advertisement included the following statement from Schappes's supporters: "The last years of agony has taught us that the conscience must never sleep. What is done to the least of us is the concern of all. That is why we cannot in good conscience fail to raise our voice against this injustice in our midst."

49. State Department Employee Loyalty Investigation: Hearing on S. Res. 231 Before the S. Comm. on Foreign Relations, 81st Cong. 68.

50. "Two Apologies," *New York Times*, October 9, 1944, 12.

51. State Department Employee Loyalty Investigation: Hearings on S. Res. 231 Before the S. Comm. on Foreign Relations, 81st Cong. 72.

52. Keith, *For Hell and a Brown Mule*, 17.

53. Dorothy Kenyon notes, J. B. Matthews Papers, Box 307.

54. William S. White, "McCarthy Says Miss Kenyon Helped 28 Red Front Groups," *New York Times*, March 9, 1950, 1.

55. "A Gallery of Know-Nothings," *New York Post*, March 9, 1950, DK Papers, Box 2.

56. Dorothy Kenyon, Forum Speaker, March 18, 1954, DK Papers, Box 27.

57. Memo from Louis K. Hyde Jr., January 14, 1948, Dorothy Kenyon, General Records of the Department of State, Record Group 59, Box 2202, NARA, College Park.

58. "Dorothy Kenyon Says Women's 'Equality' with Men in Russia Is One of Slavery," *New York Times*, December 16, 1948, 39.

59. Albion Ross, "U.S., Soviet Women Clash on Rights of Wives of Foreigners Under Russian Restrictions," *New York Times*, March 26, 1949, 5.

60. "'Outsmart Russians for Peace,' Judge Advises," *Cleveland Press*, April 6, 1949, DK Papers, Box 1.

61. Lydia Van Zandt to DK, March 26, 1950, DK Papers, Box 11.

62. Dorothy Kenyon, "Beirut: East and West Women Meet," *Women Law Journal* 36 (1950): 3.

63. Schrecker, *Many Are the Crimes*, 44.

64. Dorothy Kenyon notes.

65. Ben Mandel to Benjamin Stolberg, March 9, 1950, Box 6, Benjamin Stolberg Papers, Rare Book and Manuscript Library, Columbia University Library, New York, cited in Storrs, *Second Red Scare*, 189.

66. McCarthy's "Supplementary" Statement on Judge Kenyon, March 9, 1950, DK Papers, Box 47.

67. Buckley and Bozell, *McCarthy and His Enemies*, 85.

68. DK to Millard Tydings, telegram, March 9, 1950, DK Papers, Box 11.

69. William S. White, "Clashes Highlight McCarthy Hearing," *New York Times*, March 10, 1950, 2.

70. DK to Alex Rose, October 10, 1939, DK Papers, Box 11.

71. Bruce Buckley, "Dinner to Honor Dorothy Kenyon," *Chelsea-Clinton* [NY] *News*, February 22, 1968, PM Papers, Box 125, Folder 2269.

72. Dorothy Kenyon, Book review, "The Nightmare Decade," *Civil Liberties*, December 1971, PM Papers, Box 125, Folder 2269.

73. DK to Theodore Kenyon, April 20, 1950, DK Papers, Box 8.

74. Press and Radio Information, American Association of University Women, March 13, 1950, DK Papers, Box 47.

75. Biography, DK Papers, Box 1, Folder 2; News Release, ACLU, March 9, 1950, DK Papers, Box 2.

76. "Dorothy Kenyon Summary to Voting Body of ACLU Directors," n.d., DK Papers, Box 29; "Liberties Union Asks Red to Resign," *New York Times*, March 5, 1940, 20; "Crystal Eastman: ACLU Co-Founder," *ACLU Women's Rights Report* 2, no. 1 (1980): 5, https://www.aclu.org/wp-content/uploads/document/ACLU_Womens_Rights_Report_Spring1980.pdf.

77. "Liberties Board Drops Miss Flynn," *New York Times*, May 9, 1940, 23.

78. Dorothy Kenyon, "From Another Ancient A Dissent," February 21, 1967, DK Papers, Box 23.

79. Edith Evans Asbury, "ACLU Reverses Ouster of Elizabeth Gurley Flynn," *New York Times*, June 22, 1976, 38.

80. Statement of Miss Dorothy Kenyon, March 14, 1950, Box 863, Folder 28, ACLU Records, MC 001, Mudd Library, Princeton University, via Strozier Library, Florida State University (hereafter ACLU Records).

81. "McCarthy's Charges Cite Dorothy Kenyon," *New York World-Telegram*, March 8, 1950, DK Papers, Box 2.

82. "Worm, Liar, Go to Hell, the Lady Says," *Daily News* [NY], March 9, 1950, DK Papers, Box 2.

83. DK to family, March 10, 1950, DK Papers, Box 3.

84. Statement before Senate Foreign Relations Subcommittee, March 14, 1950, DK Papers, Box 3.

85. Fred Othman, *Washington Daily News*, March 15, 1950, 37.

86. "Miss Kenyon on Record as Foe of Communism," *Evening Star* [DC], March 15, 1950, 4.

87. Cook, *Nightmare Decade*, 192.

88. DK to National Council of American-Soviet Friendship, June 15, 1949, Dorothy Kenyon file, File and Reference Series, House Un-American Activities Committee, 81st Congress, Records of the US House of Representatives, Record Group 233, NARA, Washington, DC.

89. State Department Employee Loyalty Investigation: Hearing on S. Res. 231 Before the Senate Comm. on Foreign Relations, 81st Cong. 186 (March 14, 1950) (statement of Dorothy Kenyon), https://archive.org/details/statedepartmente-195001unit/page/n5/mode/2up.

90. "State Department Employee Loyalty Investigation," 47 (1950); Talk by Maria Sharikova, January 6, 1949, Dorothy Kenyon, File and Reference Series, House Un-American Activities Committee, 81st Congress, Records of the US House of Representatives, Record Group 233, NARA, Washington, DC.

91. Statement before Senate Foreign Relations Subcommittee, March 14, 1950, DK Papers, Box 3. See also State Department Employee Loyalty Investigation: Hearings on S. Res. 231 Before the Senate Comm. on Foreign Relations, 81st Cong., 187.

92. State Department Employee Loyalty Investigation: Hearings on S. Res. 231 Before the Senate Comm. on Foreign Relations, 81st Cong., 187.

93. Cook, *Nightmare Decade*, 193; State Department Employee Loyalty Investigation: Hearings on S. Res. 231 Before the Senate Comm. on Foreign Relations, 81st Cong., 207.

94. State Department Employee Loyalty Investigation: Hearings on S. Res. 231 Before the Senate Comm. on Foreign Relations, 81st Cong., 208.

95. William S. White, "Miss Kenyon Cites Patriotic Record to Refute Charges," *New York Times*, March 15, 1950, 1.

96. White, "Miss Kenyon Cites Patriotic Record."

97. Keith, *For Hell and a Brown Mule*, 21.

98. Press Release, March 14, 1950, Dorothy Kenyon, File and Reference Series, House Un-American Activities Committee, 81st Congress, Records of the US House of Representatives, Record Group 233, NARA, Washington, DC.

99. Press Release, March 14, 1950.

100. DK to David Scull, March 28, 1950, DK Papers, Box 11.

101. "Miss Kenyon on Record as Foe of Communism."

102. Joseph McCarthy to Senator Millard Tydings, March 20, 1950, McCarthy Papers, Box 7, Folder 41; McCarthy to Senator Tydings, March 24, 1950, McCarthy Papers, Box 7, Folder 41; McCarthy to Senator Bourke Hickenlooper, April 6, 1950, Joseph McCarthy Papers, Box 7, Folder 40; McCarthy to Millard Tydings, May 4, 1950, McCarthy Papers, Box 7, Folder 40.

103. Senator Millard Tydings to Joseph McCarthy, April 5, 1950, McCarthy Papers, Box 7, Folder 41.

104. FBI Office Memo, March 14, 1950, DK Papers, Box 7A, Folder 1.

105. Dept. of State, Dept. of Labor, War Department Summary, May 16, 1942, 100-25772, NARA, St. Louis, MO.

106. Dept. of State, Dept. of Labor, War Department Summary, May 16, 1942.

107. Dept. of State, Dept. of Labor, FBI Case, April 3, 1944, 100-25772, NARA, St. Louis, MO; "Trotsky Backers Act to Clear Him," *New York Times*, February 1, 1937, 12; Robert V. Daniels, "Leon Trotsky: Russian Revolutionary," *Britannica*, updated August 17, 2025, https://www.britannica.com/biography/Leon-Trotsky.

108. "Trotsky Backers Act to Clear Him"; "American Committee for the Defense of Leon Trotsky," News Bulletin (American Committee for the Defense of Leon Trotsky), February 19, 1937, https://www.marxists.org/history/etol/document/swp-us/pamphlets/bull-no4-feb-19–1937-news-bull.pdf.

109. Dept. of State, Dept. of Labor, FBI Case, April 3, 1944.

110. Dept. of State, Dept. of Labor, Office Memorandum, June 14, 1947, 100-25772, NARA, St. Louis, MO.

111. "State Department Employee Loyalty Investigation,"43 (1950). See also Senate Subcommittee Transcripts, March 9, 1950, DK Papers, Box 7A.

112. Full Field Investigation, March 21, 1949, DK Papers, Box 7A, Folder 1.

113. Edward Scheidt to Director J. Edgar Hoover, June 17, 1949, DK Papers, Box 7A, Folder 1.

114. D. M. Ladd to Director J. Edgar Hoover, March 21, 1949, DK Papers, Box 7A, Folder 1.

115. FBI Case File, June 9, 1949, DK Papers, Box 7A, Folder 1.

116. Chairman of Loyalty Review Board (name redacted) to J. Edgar Hoover, March 17, 1950, DK Papers, Box 7A, Folder 1.

117. Dept. of State, Dept. of Labor, Office Memorandum, August 22, 1950, 100-25772, NARA, St. Louis, MO.

118. Dept. of State, Dept. of Labor, FBI Case File, April 30, 1951, 100-25772, NARA, St. Louis, MO.

119. "Milestones," *Time*, May 8, 1972.

120. Dept. of State, Dept. of Labor, Dorothy Kenyon, September 15, 1964, 100-25772, NARA, St. Louis, MO.

121. Alger Hiss, *Recollections of a Life* (Seaver Books, 1989), 10, 227.

122. Hiss, *Recollections of a Life*, 161.

123. Statement to Director, FBI, February 26, 1952, DK Papers, Box 7A.

124. Dorothy Kenyon summary per request of White House (name redacted), September 15, 1954, DK Papers, Box 7A.

## 6. THE AFTERMATH

1. Rochelle Gatlin, *American Women Since 1945* (University Press of Mississippi, 1987), 8.

2. Storrs, *Second Red Scare*, 89.

3. Storrs, *Second Red Scare*, 97.

4. Mildred Adams Kenyon to DK, March 16, 1950, DK Papers, Box 8.

5. Dorothy Kenyon, Book review, "The Nightmare Decade," *Civil Liberties*, Dec. 1971, PM Papers, Box 125, Folder 2269.

6. DK to William Houston Kenyon Jr., March 28, 1950, DK Papers, Box 3.

7. Thomas L. Stokes, "Unexpected Light on a Plot," *Chicago Sun-Times*, March 17, 1950, DK Papers, Box 2.

8. "Joe McCarthy's Political Dynamite Can Blow Up in Either Party's Face," *Life*, April 10, 1950, 30.

9. 81 Cong. Rec., 4380–81 (1950), https://www.congress.gov/bound-congressional-record/1950/03/30/96/senate-section/article/4355-4411.

10. "Calling Miss Kenyon Red Amuses Mrs. Roosevelt," *New York World-Telegram*, March 13, 1950, DK Papers, Box 2.

11. Herbert Block, *Herblock: A Cartoonist's Life* (Macmillan, 1993), 133–34.

12. Cartoon by Herblock re: McCarthy's Charges Against DK, 1950, DK Papers, Box 66.

13. DK to Eugene Meyer, November 10, 1950, DK Papers, Box 18.

14. Block, *Herblock*, 133–35.

15. Kenyon, Book review, "The Nightmare Decade."

16. Herbert H. Lehman to DK, March 17, 1950, Herbert H. Lehman Papers, Rare Book and Manuscript Library, Columbia University Library, https://dlc.library.columbia.edu/catalog/ldpd:194177.

17. Stanley Kreutzer to DK, April 11, 1950, DK Papers, Box 12.

18. Josephine B. Millett to Joseph McCarthy, April 3, 1950, DK Papers, Box 12.

19. Brian McMahon to Anna Lord Strauss, March 15, 1950, DK Papers, Box 3.

20. Miss C. Livingston to Secretary of League of Women Voters, Mrs. Ralph B. Morris, April 21, 1950, DK Papers, Box 12.

21. Mrs. Ralph B. Morris to Miss C. Livingston, April 21, 1950, DK Papers, Box 12.

22. Clarence P. Milligan to DK, March 15, 1950, DK Papers, Box 11.

23. William W. Goodrich to DK, March 15, 1950, DK Papers, Box 11.

24. Ex GI Joe to DK, March 15, 1950, DK Papers, Box 11.

25. Frederick C. Othman, "Dorothy Just Loved Organization—Some She Couldn't Even Remember," *Rapid City* [SD] *Journal*, March 20, 1950, 4.

26. George E. Sokolsky, "These Days," *Daily Times* [OH], March 20, 1950, 4.

27. Rachel Nason to DK, March 17, 1950, DK Papers, Box 11.

28. DK to Theodore Kiendl, March 21, 1950, DK Papers, Box 11.

29. Theodore Kiendl to DK, March 22, 1950, DK Papers, Box 11.

30. DK to Elinore Herrick, April 3, 1950, DK Papers, Box 12.

31. Elinore Herrick to DK, April 5, 1950, DK Papers, Box 12.

32. *Meet the Press* Radio Interview, April 7, 1950, National Audio-Visual Conservation Center, Library of Congress, LWO 7329 R4 6671.1–4.

33. *Meet the Press* Radio Interview, April 7, 1950.

34. *Meet the Press* Radio Interview, April 7, 1950.

35. George Sokolsky, "These Days," *Times-Herald* [DC], April 17, 1950, 6.

36. Unsigned Letter, April 1950, DK Papers, Box 15.

37. Andy Turner to DK, April 1950, DK Papers, Box 12.

38. Catherine Porter to DK, June 6, 1950, DK Papers, Box 12.

39. Dorothy Kenyon, "The Image of the Thing We Hate," *Journal of the Association of University Women*, Summer 1950, DK Papers, Box 21.

40. Lawrence Spivak to DK, April 10, 1950, DK Papers, Box 12.

41. DK to Lawrence Spivak, April 13, 1950, DK Papers, Box 12.

42. DK to Ada Murray Clarke, April 20, 1950, DK Papers, Box 12.

43. Elinore Herrick to DK, April 18, 1950, DK Papers, Box 12.

44. Mildred Adams Kenyon to DK, April 14, 1950, DK Papers, Box 8.

45. "State Department Employee Loyalty Investigation," 81st Cong., 2d Session, Report of the Comm. on Foreign Relations, S. Res. 231, S. Rep. No. 2108 (1950), 1.

46. "State Department Employee Loyalty Investigation," 9.

47. 81 Cong. Rec., 10711 (July 20, 1950), https://www.congress.gov/81/crecb/1950/07/20/GPO-CRECB-1950-pt8-7.pdf.

48. "State Department Employee Loyalty Investigation," 11.

49. 81 Cong. Rec., 10712 (July 20, 1950), https://www.congress.gov/81/crecb/1950/07/20/GPO-CRECB-1950-pt8-7.pdf.

50. 81 Cong. Rec., 10716 (July 20, 1950), https://www.congress.gov/81/crecb/1950/07/20/GPO-CRECB-1950-pt8-7.pdf.

51. "State Department Employee Loyalty Investigation," 5.

52. "Earl Browder," *Britannica*, updated February 19, 2024, https://www.britannica.com/biography/Earl-Browder.

53. William S. White, "Browder Ridicules Budenz, Calls Lattimore an Anti-Red," *New York Times*, April 28, 1950, 1.

54. State Department Employee Loyalty Investigation: Hearing on S. Res. 231 Before the Senate Comm. on Foreign Relations, 81st Cong. Pt. 1, 701 (statement of Earl Browder) (April 27, 1950).

55. State Department Employee Loyalty Investigation: Hearing on S. Res. 231 Before the Senate Comm. on Foreign Relations, 81st Cong. 702.

56. State Department Employee Loyalty Investigation: Hearing on S. Res. 231 Before the Senate Comm. on Foreign Relations, 81st Cong. 706.

57. State Department Employee Loyalty Investigation: Hearing on S. Res. 231 Before the Senate Comm. on Foreign Relations, 81st Cong. 683; White, "Browder Ridicules Budenz."

58. State Department Employee Loyalty Investigation: Hearing on S. Res. 231 Before the Senate Comm. on Foreign Relations, 81st Cong. 684; White, "Browder Ridicules Budenz." On September 13, 1950, the Senate cited Browder for contempt of the Senate through Senate Resolution 350, stating the subcommittee was deprived of the answers to pertinent questions asked of Browder due to his refusal to answer. In October 1950, an indictment was issued in federal court against Browder. The grand jury charged that during his April testimony he was asked questions by the subcommittee and he refused to answer several questions, resulting in the contempt citation. In December, he filed a motion to dismiss the indictment. He was unable to afford a lawyer so he had to represent himself, though he mailed out letters trying to raise funds for his defense. Browder said he was "attacking the whole system of violation of the rights of citizens by power-drunk Congressmen of the type of the infamous McCarthy." He ultimately was acquitted of congressional contempt charges, with a federal judge stating that Browder had been within his rights when he refused to answer questions posed by the subcommittee. Senate Citation for Contempt, September 13, 1950, Earl Browder Papers, Syracuse University Libraries, Special Collections Research Center, Syracuse, New York, Box 38 (hereafter Browder Papers); Grand Jury True Bill, October 4, 1950, McCarthy Papers, Raynor Memorial Libraries, Marquette University, Milwaukee, Wisconsin, Box 7, Folder 40; Harold B. Hinton, "Browder, Five Others Indicted in Contempt," *New York Times*, November 28, 1950, 1; "Browder is Jailed; Can't Furnish Bail," *New York Times*, December 2, 1950, 28; "Browder, Field in Pleas: Ask Court to Dismiss Contempt of Congress Indictments," *New York Times*, December 27, 1950, 26; Letter from Earl Browder, March 3, 1951, Browder Papers, Box 38; "Browder Is Freed at Contempt Trial," *New York Times*, March 15, 1951.

59. 81 Cong. Rec. 10698 (July 20, 1950), https://www.congress.gov/81/crecb/1950/07/20/GPO-CRECB-1950-pt8-7.pdf.

60. 81 Cong. Rec. 10707 (July 20, 1950), https://www.congress.gov/81/crecb/1950/07/20/GPO-CRECB-1950-pt8-7.pdf.

61. "State Department Employee Loyalty Investigation," 10.

62. "State Department Employee Loyalty Investigation," 151.

63. "State Department Employee Loyalty Investigation," 151–52.

64. "State Department Employee Loyalty Investigation," 12.

65. Cook, *Nightmare Decade*, 66.

66. State Department Employee Loyalty Investigation, October 2, 1950, DK Papers, Box 7A. See also Report of the Committee on Foreign Relations, S. Res. 231, 81st Cong. 47 (July 20, 1950).

67. State Department Employee Loyalty Investigation, October 2, 1950.

68. David M. Oshinsky, *A Conspiracy So Immense: The World of Joe McCarthy* (Free Press, 1983), 121.

69. Kenyon, "Image of the Thing We Hate."

70. William O. Douglas, "The Black Silence of Fear," *New York Times*, January 13, 1952, SM7.

71. Unsigned note to Theodore Kiendl, DK Papers, Box 47.

72. "M'Carthy Calls Mrs. F.D.R. Target of Red Influence," *Chicago Tribune Press Service*, July 28, 1954, 2.

73. "New McCarthy Attack on Miss Kenyon Seen Showing Need of Probe Reform," *York* [PA] *Daily Record*, August 12, 1954, 1.

74. "M'Carthy Calls Mrs. F.D.R. Target of Red Influence."

75. Eleanor Roosevelt, "I Was Never Close to Judge Kenyon," *Washington Daily News*, August 17, 1954, 29.

76. Ernest Angell to Senator William Jenner, July 28, 1954, DK Papers, Box 47.

77. Kenyon, "Image of the Thing We Hate."

78. Kenyon, "The New Pilgrim's Progress," February 8, 1951, DK Papers, Box 21.

79. Executive Sessions of the Senate Permanent Subcommittee on Investigations of the Committee on Government Operations, 83rd Cong. (1953), https://www.senate.gov/about/resources/pdf/mccarthy-hearings-volume1.pdf. The records were kept sealed for fifty years and made public in January 2003.

80. "Have You No Sense of Decency?," United States Senate, June 9, 1954, https://www.senate.gov/about/powers-procedures/investigations/mccarthy-hearings/have-you-no-sense-of-decency.htm.

81. 83rd Cong. Rec. S16392 (December 2, 1954), https://www.senate.gov/artandhistory/history/resources/pdf/1954McCarthyCensure.pdf.

82. 83rd Cong. Rec. S16392 (December 2, 1954).

83. Cook, *Nightmare Decade*, 540.

84. Acheson, *Present at the Creation*, 362.

85. Schrecker, *Many Are the Crimes*, 413.

86. Executive Sessions of the Senate Permanent Subcommittee on Investigations of the Committee on Government Operations, 83rd Cong. (1953), XIII.

87. Executive Sessions of the Senate Permanent Subcommittee on Investigations of the Committee on Government Operations.

88. William Safire, *Safire's New Political Dictionary: The Definitive Guide to the New Language of Politics* (Random House, 1993), 441, cited in Executive Sessions of the Senate Permanent Subcommittee on Investigations of the Committee on Government Operations, fn. 9.

89. Bruce Buckley, "Dinner to Honor Dorothy Kenyon," *Chelsea-Clinton* [NY] *News*, Feb. 22, 1968, PM Papers, Box 125, Folder 2269.

90. Eulogy Address, DK Papers, Box 7, Folder 4.

91. "Civil Liberties Our Responsibility," October 23, 1962, DK Papers, Box 22.

92. Mildred Adams Kenyon, Sketch for a Dorothy Kenyon Biography, March 1, 1972, DK Papers, Box 3.

93. Kenyon, "Image of the Thing We Hate."

94. Dorothy Dunbar Bromley to Mildred Adams Kenyon, June 21, 1972, DK Papers, Box 3.

95. Edward Tipton Kenyon, interview with Louise Wilby Knight, October 6, 1998, DK Papers, Box 65a.

96. Edward Tipton Kenyon, interview.

97. Cook, *Nightmare Decade*, 570.

98. Kenyon, Book review, "The Nightmare Decade."

99. Mildred Adams Kenyon Manuscript, DK Papers, Box 3.

## 7. NOT A FEMINIST

1. Jill Elaine Hasday, *We the Men: How Forgetting Women's Struggles for Equality Perpetuates Inequality* (Oxford University Press, 2025), 18.

2. Anne Firor Scott, *Natural Allies: Women's Associations in American History* (University of Illinois Press, 1992), 3.

3. Adams, *Right to Be People*, 2; Sochen, *Movers and Shakers*, 4; Lerner, "Placing Women in History."

4. "Seneca Falls Declaration (1848)," National Constitution Center, https://constitutioncenter.org/the-constitution/historic-document-library/detail/seneca-falls-declaration-1848.

5. Alice Kessler-Harris, *In Pursuit of Equity: Women, Men, and the Quest for Economic Citizenship in Twentieth Century America* (Oxford University Press, 2020), 25.

6. William H. Chafe, *The Paradox of Change: American Women in the 20th Century* (Oxford University Press, 1991), 5–6.

7. Elisabeth Israels Perry, *Women in Action: Rebels and Reformers 1920–1980* (League of Women Voters Education Fund, 1995), 2.

8. Holly J. McCammon and Lee Ann Banaszak, eds. *100 Years of the Nineteenth Amendment: An Appraisal of Women's Political Activism* (Oxford University, 2018), 108; Martha S. Jones, *Vanguard: How Black Women Broke Barriers, Won the Vote, and Insisted on Equality for All* (Basic Books, 2020), 65.

9. Jones, *Vanguard*, 149.

10. "Sarah J. Garnet," National Park Service, https://www.nps.gov/people/sarah-j-garnet.htm. At an Equal Suffrage League meeting in April 1908, Emma S. Ransom, wife of an AME church minister, spoke passionately to the group: "If the race to which we are identified is to be uplifted, the Negro must do the practical part of this uplifting. The whites will contribute money but we are expected and must do the actual lifting." "Equal Suffrage League Hold Interesting Meeting in Brooklyn—Mrs. Ransom's Telling Speech," *New York Age*, Apr. 30, 1908, 7.

11. "Beyond Suffrage: Working Together, Working Apart," Museum of the City of New York, https://www.mcny.org/sites/default/files/LessonPlanWomensLiberation2020_0.pdf.

12. Adams, *The Right to Be People*, 2.

13. Elihu Root, "Address Before New York Constitutional Convention" (New York State Association Opposed to Woman Suffrage, ca. 1908), Library of Congress, https://www.loc.gov/resource/rbcmil.scrp5011401/.

14. Lynda G. Dodd, "The Rhetoric of Gender Upheaval During the Campaign for the Nineteenth Amendment," *Boston University Law Review* 93 (2013): 713–14.

15. Stephanie Coontz, *The Way We Never Were: American Families and the Nostalgia Trap* (Basic Books, 1992), 11.

16. Joan Hoff Wilson, ed., *Rights of Passage: The Past and Future of the ERA* (Indiana University Press, 1986), xiv.

17. Silas Bent, "The Feminist Magna Charta," *New York Times*, December 10, 1922, 66.

18. Crystal Eastman, "Now We Can Begin," *Liberator* [MA], Dec. 1920.

19. Harris, *Beyond Her Sphere*, 131.

20. McCammon and Banaszak, eds., *100 Years of the Nineteenth Amendment*, 5.

21. Jones, *Vanguard*, 151.

22. Megan Bailey, "Between Two Worlds: Black Women and the Fight for Voting Rights," National Park Service, https://www.nps.gov/articles/black-women-and-the-fight-for-voting-rights.htm.

23. Marylin Bender, "Liberation Yesterday—The Roots of the Feminist Movement," *New York Times*, August 21, 1970, 41.

24. Weigand, *Red Feminism*, 4.

25. Mr. and Mrs. John Martin, "The Woman Movement and the Baby Crop," *New York Times*, August 29, 1915, SM1.

26. Nancy F. Cott, *The Grounding of Modern Feminism* (Yale University Press, 1987), 35.

27. Weigand, *Red Feminism*, 8.

28. Martin and Martin, "The Woman Movement and the Baby Crop."

29. bell hooks, *Feminist Theory from Margin to Center* (South End Press, 1984), 3.

30. June Sochen, *The New Woman: Feminism in Greenwich Village, 1910–1920* (Quadrangle Books, 1972), ix.

31. Judith Schwarz, *Radical Feminists of Heterodoxy: Greenwich Village, 1912–1940* (New Victoria, 1982), 1.

32. McCammon and Banaszak, eds. *100 Years of the Nineteenth Amendment*, 183.

33. "With the Members Sworn to Secrecy, Forty of New York's Prominent 'Advanced' Women Band into 'The Heterodoxy' and Meet to Eat and Decide Their Position on Problems of the Day," *New-York Tribune*, November 24, 1914, 7.

34. Stansell, *American Moderns*, 74.

35. "Talk on Feminism Stirs Great Crowd," *New York Times*, February 18, 1914, 2.

36. Schwarz, *Radical Feminists of Heterodoxy*, 23–25.

37. "Talk on Feminism Stirs Great Crowd."

38. "What Is Feminism? Come and Find Out" (1914), Clio Visualizing History, https://votesforwomen.cliohistory.org/19objects/what-is-feminism-come-and-find-out.

39. "Feminists Ask for Equal Chance," *New York Times*, February 21, 1914, 18.
40. Sochen, *New Woman*, 6.
41. hooks, *Feminist Theory from Margin to Center*, 18.
42. Lerner, "Placing Women in History," 7.
43. Smuts, *Women and Work in America*, 4.
44. Lunardini, *What Every American Should Know About Women's History*, 140; Flexner, *Century of Struggle*, 182.
45. Josephine Goldmark, *Impatient Crusader: Florence Kelley's Life Story* (Greenwood Press, 1953), 21.
46. Smuts, *Women and Work in America*, 18.
47. Adams, *Right to Be People*, 120.
48. Margaret Doane Gardiner, "Wage-Earning Women: An Anti-Suffragist Answers Questions About Woman Suffrage," *New York Times*, January 16, 1910, 10.
49. Chafe, *Paradox of Change*, 54.
50. "Homeless, Unmarried," *New York Times*, May 12, 1912, 77.
51. Anna H. Wheeler, "The Feminist Wife Will No Longer Bow to Man's Domestic Tyranny," *New York Times*, April 23, 1914, 12.
52. Christine A. Lunardini, *Women's Rights* (Oryx Press, 1996), 117.
53. Consumers' League of New York City Records, 1893–1962, Kheel Center for Labor-Management Documentation and Archives, Cornell University Library, http://rmc.library.cornell.edu/EAD/htmldocs/KCL05307.html; Ware, *Partner and I*, 154.
54. Scott, *Natural Allies*, 165.
55. Goldmark, *Impatient Crusader*, 132; Paul Underwood Kellogg, ed., *The Pittsburgh Survey: Wage-Earning Pittsburgh, 1914* (New York Survey Associates, Inc., 1914), https://www.russellsage.org/sites/all/files/Kellogg_Wage%20Earning%20Pittsburgh_0.pdf.
56. Ware, *Partner and I*, 43.
57. Smuts, *Women and Work in America*, 113, 116.
58. "The Brandeis Brief," Louis D. Brandeis School of Law Library, University of Louisville, https://law.louisville.edu/lawlibrary/special-collections/louis-d-brandeis-collection/writings-louis-d-brandeis/brandeis-brief.
59. Flexner, *Century of Struggle*, 220.
60. Kathryn Kish Sklar, "Josephine Clara Goldmark," *Jewish Women's Archive*, February 27, 2009, https://jwa.org/encyclopedia/article/goldmark-josephine-clara.
61. Paula A. Monopoli, *Constitutional Orphan: Gender Equality and the Nineteenth Amendment* (Oxford University Press, 2020), 25.
62. *Muller v. Oregon*, 208 U.S. 412, 421 (1908).
63. Lunardini, *Women's Rights*, 118.
64. "141 Dead In Factory Fire," *New York Herald*, March 26, 1911, 2; Betsy Israel, *Bachelor Girl: The Secret History of Single Women in the Twentieth Century* (William Morrow, 2002), 58.
65. "141 Dead In Factory Fire," 1. Next door was the New York University Law School, and law students climbed to the roof, sending over two ladders to the burn-

ing building for people to cross over. The students were able to rescue approximately 150 people.

66. "Jurors Hear Attorney Score Triangle Men," *Evening World* [NY], December 6, 1911, 6.

67. "Triangle Owners Acquitted by Jury," *New York Times*, December 28, 1911, 1.

68. "Denounce Officials for Loss of Life," *Times Union* [NY], Mar. 28, 1911, 2.

69. Adams, *Right to Be People*, 123–124.

70. US Dept. of Labor, "7. The New York Factory Investigating Commission," https://www.dol.gov/general/aboutdol/history/mono-regsafepart07.

71. Ware, *Partner and I*, 46.

72. Minimum Wage Act of September 19, 1918, ca. 174, 40 Stat. 960.

73. *Adkins v. Children's Hospital*, 261 U.S. 525 (1923).

74. *Adkins*, at 553.

75. *Adkins*, at 562.

76. *Adkins*, at 567.

77. *West Coast Hotel Company v. Parrish*, 300 U.S. 379 (1937).

78. Isador Lubin and Charles A. Pearce, "New York's Minimum Wage Law: The First Twenty Years," *Industrial and Labor Relations Review* 11 (1958): 203.

79. Smuts, *Women and Work in America*, 119.

80. Kessler-Harris, *In Pursuit of Equity*, 59.

81. Sochen, *New Woman*, 53.

82. Spencer Howard, "The Economy Act of 1932," National Archives, *Hoover Heads* (blog), Herbert Hoover Library and Museum, July 29, 2020, https://hoover.blogs.archives.gov/2020/07/29/the-economy-act-of-1932/.

83. Janet M. Martin, *The Presidency and Women: Promise, Performance, and Illusion* (Texas A&M University Press, 2003), 23.

84. *Dunn v. Palermo*, 522 S.W.2d 679 (Tenn. 1975).

85. Megan McDonald Way, *Family Economics and Public Policy, 1800s–Present: How Laws, Incentives, and Social Programs Drive Family Decision-Making and the US Economy* (Palgrave Macmillan, 2018), 152.

86. Martin, *The Presidency and Women*, 40, citing Hazel Erskine, "The Polls: Women's Role," *Public Opinion Quarterly* 35, no. 1 (1971): 274–290.

87. "ERA: Equal Rights Amendment Frequently Asked Question," Congress.gov, https://www.congress.gov/116/meeting/house/109330/documents/HHRG-116-JU10-20190430-SD013.pdf.

88. Serena Mayeri, "Constitutional Choices: Legal Feminism and the Historical Dynamics of Change," *California Law Review* 92 (2004): 762.

89. Cobble, Gordon, and Henry, *Feminism Unfinished*, 10.

90. Weigand, *Red Feminism*, 7.

91. Cott, *Grounding of Modern Feminism*, 127.

92. Chafe, *Paradox of Change*, 49.

93. Chafe, *Paradox of Change*, 50.

94. "Women in Our Changing Political Economy," June 1935, DK Papers, Box 18.

95. AFL-CIO to Senate, February 7, 1963, PM Papers, Box 49.

96. Cott, *Grounding of Modern Feminism*, 136.

97. Ware, *Partner and I*, 191.

98. "Jessica Breitman," FDR Library and Museum, https://www.fdrlibrary.org/perkins.

99. Chafe, *Paradox of Change*, 38.

100. Ware, *Partner and I*, 193.

101. Dorothy Sue Cobble, *The Other Women's Movement: Workplace Justice and Social Rights in Modern America* (Princeton University Press, 2004), 3.

102. Ware, *Partner and I*, 181.

103. Jonathan Grossman, "Fair Labor Standards Act of 1938: Maximum Struggle for a Minimum Wage," *Monthly Labor Review*, June 1978, available at US Department of Labor, https://www.dol.gov/general/aboutdol/history/flsa1938; "History: An Overview, 1920–2021," Women's Bureau, US Department of Labor, https://www.dol.gov/agencies/wb/about/history.

104. Alice Hamilton, "Why I Am Against the Equal Rights Amendment," *Ladies' Home Journal*, July 1945, Box 1028, Folder 16, ACLU Records.

105. Goldmark, *Impatient Crusader*, 205.

106. Chafe, *Paradox of Change*, 49.

107. "The Awakening of Women," July 16, 1948, DK Papers, Box 3.

108. Gwen Hoerr Jordan, "Agents of (Incremental) Change: From Myra Bradwell to Hillary Clinton," *Nevada Law Journal* 9 (2009): 583.

109. Judith Wellman, *The Road to Seneca Falls: Elizabeth Cady Stanton and the First Woman's Rights Convention* (University of Illinois Press, 2004), 234.

110. "History Is Made Again in Seneca Falls Event," *Post-Standard* [NY], July 20, 1948, 8.

111. "Feminists Conclude Centennial Program," *Syracuse* [NY] *Herald-Journal*, July 20, 1948, 12.

112. Press release, n.d., Box 1736, Classes of 1901–1910 Records, CA-MS-010120, Sophia Smith Collection, Smith College, Northampton, MA.

113. "Equal Rights, Trenton," May 4, 1935, DK Papers, Box 18.

114. DK to Rolland O'Hare, April 20, 1970, DK Papers, Box 29.

115. "Behavior: The New Feminists: Revolt Against Sexism," *Time*, November 21, 1969, https://time.com/archive/6635734/behavior-the-new-feminists-revolt-against-sexism/.

116. Barbas, "Dorothy Kenyon and the Making of Modern Legal Feminism," 426–27.

117. "Women's Liberation Movement," DK Papers, Box 2.

## 8. A GLORIOUS REBEL

1. News Release, ACLU, March 9, 1950, DK Papers, Box 2. Some sources state she joined the board in 1930; however, a memo to Roger Baldwin dated January 28, 1931, provides evidence that Kenyon was recommended to join the national board

that year. Memo from L.B.M. to Roger Baldwin, January 28, 1931, Correspondence-Organizational Matters, Volume 451, 1930–1931, MS "The Roger Baldwin Years," 1912–1950: Sub-Series 18: Organizational Matters–Correspondence, 1917–1951, ACLU Records. Kenyon's updated resume, retyped in 1966, also indicates she joined the ACLU in 1931. Biography, April 1966, DK Papers, Box 4. See also Memorandum Draft from DK to ACLU Voting Body, n.d., DK Papers, Box 29, which lists her starting year with the ACLU as 1931.

2. DK to ACLU Board of Directors, January 6, 1969, DK Papers, Box 29.

3. Proposed ACLU National Board Resolution on the Late DK, PM Papers, Box 125, Folder 2269.

4. DK to Frances Robb, June 12, 1961, DK Papers, Box 18.

5. DK to Mildred Adams Kenyon, April 23, 1970, DK Papers, Box 8.

6. Testimony of DK on Equal Pay Bills, ACLU, April 26, 1962, DK Papers, Box 22.

7. "1929 Hearing" (statement of DK, Attorney at Law, New York City), cited in Julie C. Suk, "Working Mothers and the Postponement of Women's Rights from the Nineteenth Amendment to the Equal Rights Amendment," *University of Colorado Law Review* 92 (2021): 816.

8. Sochen, *New Woman*, 13.

9. Barbas, *Rise and Fall of Morris Ernst*, 45.

10. Sylvia A. Law, "Crystal Eastman: Organizer for Women's Rights, Peace, and Civil Liberties in the 1910s," *Virginia University Law Review* 28 (1994): 1305, 1324.

11. Cottrell, *Roger Nash Baldwin and the American Civil Liberties Union*, 122.

12. Cose, *Democracy, If We Can Keep It*, 73.

13. Stansell, *American Moderns*, 75.

14. *Free Speech in 1924*, 40.

15. Barbas, *Rise and Fall of Morris Ernst*, 130.

16. "ACLU History: An Early Cry for Justice," ACLU, https://www.aclu.org/documents/aclu-history-early-cry-justice.

17. Barbas, *Rise and Fall of Morris Ernst*, 130.

18. "Is the Law Unfair to Women?," *Woman's Day*, August 1943, DK Papers, Box 20.

19. DK to C. C. Burlingham, May 9, 1944, DK Papers, Box 62.

20. "Dorothy Kenyon, Fiery Fighter for Women's Rights, Is Visitor," *Washington Post*, Feb. 3, 1938, DK Papers, Box 1.

21. "ACLU's 36-Year Fight for Women's Rights: The Kenyon Years, 1944–1970," *ACLU Women's Rights Report* 2, no. 1 (Spring 1980): 2, https://www.aclu.org/wp-content/uploads/document/ACLU_Womens_Rights_Report_Spring1980.pdf.

22. Barbara Sinclair Deckard, *The Women's Movement: Political, Socioeconomic, and Psychological Issues* (Harper & Row, 1956), 74.

23. "The ERA," April 13, 1944, DK Papers, Box 20.

24. Memorandum on Women's Rights, Adopted by the Board of Directors, July 1945, Box 1028, Folder 16, ACLU Records.

25. Dorothy McAllister to Frances Levenson, April 21, 1947, Box 1028, Folder 16, ACLU Records.

26. Dorothy Kenyon, "Equal Rights for Women," *Civil Liberties*, April 1953, DK Papers, Box 21.

27. "Restatement of ACLU Position in Favor of Women's Rights," June 15, 1955, PM Papers, Box 60.

28. "Proposed Text of ERA for Women," May 19, 1960, PM Papers, Box 60.

29. Due Process Committee Minutes, February 8, 1956, Box 1142, Folder 6, Item 46, ACLU Records.

30. "A Memorandum on the Proposed Equal Rights Amendment to the United States Constitution," Citizens' Advisory Council on the Status of Women, March 1970, MC 001, Box 1145, Folder 18, ACLU Records.

31. Stephanie Coontz, *A Strange Stirring: The Feminine Mystique and American Women at the Dawn of the 1960s* (Basic Books, 2011), 150–51.

32. Lunardini, *Women's Rights*, 161.

33. Kessler-Harris, *In Pursuit of Equity*, 217.

34. Susan M. Hartmann, "Pauli Murray and the 'Juncture of Women's Liberation and Black Liberation,'" *Journal of Women's History* 14 (2002): 74.

35. Susan Ware, "Pauli Murray's Notable Connections," *Journal of Women's History* 14 (2002): 55.

36. Rosalind Rosenberg, "The Conjunction of Race and Gender," *Journal of Women's History* 14 (2002): 68; Glenda Elizabeth Gilmore, "Admitting Pauli Murray," *Journal of Women's History* 14 (2002): 64; Eleanor Roosevelt to PM, December 19, 1938, PM Papers, Box 15, Folder 380. Murray and Eleanor Roosevelt would develop a close friendship, with Murray listing her as a reference on her resume. Pauli Murray Resume, n.d., PM Papers, Box 28, Folder 555.

37. Eleanor Roosevelt to PM, December 19, 1938.

38. Pauli Murray, "The Liberation of Black Women," in *Our American Sisters: Women in American Life and Thought*, eds. Jean E. Friedman and William G. Shade (Allyn & Bacon, 1973), 326.

39. Murray, "Liberation of Black Women," 326.

40. Murray, "Liberation of Black Women," 472.

41. Memo to Files, July 2, 1944, PM Papers, Box 18, Folder 415; PM to Harvard Board of Overseers, July 7, 1944, PM Papers, Box 18, Folder 415; both cited in Rosenberg, "Conjunction of Race and Gender," 69.

42. "Lady Lawyers," *Ebony*, August 1947, https://archive.org/details/sim_ebony_1947-08_2_10/mode/1up.

43. Pauli Murray, *Song in a Weary Throat: An American Pilgrimage* (Liveright, 1987), 350.

44. Murray, *Song in a Weary Throat*, 351.

45. Business Card, PM Papers, Box 28, Folder 555.

46. Resume, PM Papers, Box 28, Folder 555; Sandra G. Boodman, "An Intense Pride," *New York Post*, March 8, 1977, DK Papers, Box 3.

47. Mayeri, "Constitutional Choices," 763.

48. Kessler-Harris, *In Pursuit of Equity*, 245.

49. Statement of Judge Dorothy Kenyon on Behalf of ACLU, April 27, 1962, Employment: Equal Pay, 1962, Box 1116, Folder 21, Item 589, ACLU Records.

50. Chiappetti, "Winning the Battle but Losing the War," 488.

51. Murray, *Song in a Weary Throat*, 457–58.

52. Mayeri, "Constitutional Choices," 764.

53. Mayeri, "Constitutional Choices," 764.

54. Paterson, *Be Somebody*, 147–48.

55. Kerber, *No Constitutional Right to Be Ladies*,193.

56. Cobble, Gordon, and Henry, *Feminism Unfinished*, 50.

57. ACLU to Esther Peterson, February 4, 1964, DK Papers, Box 28.

58. DK to PM, April 4, 1963, PM Papers, Box 49, Folder 878.

59. DK to PM, memorandum, March 28, 1963, PM Papers, B-26, Box 9, Folder 63, cited in Mayeri, "Constitutional Choices," 765.

60. "Behavior: The New Feminists: Revolt Against Sexism," *Time*, November 21,1969,https://time.com/archive/6635734/behavior-the-new-feminists-revolt-against-sexism/.

61. Jo Freeman, "How Sex Got into Title VII: Persistent Opportunism as a Maker of Public Policy," *Law and Inequality* 9, no. 2 (1991): 163.

62. Hasday, *We the Men*, 37.

63. Hasday, *We the Men*, 42.

64. Katherine Turk, *Equality on Trial: Gender and Rights in the Modern American Workplace* (University of Pennsylvania Press, 2016), 1; Fred P. Graham, "Rights Case Yields Dividend for Women," *New York Times*, February 13, 1966, 172.

65. Caroline Bird to DK, April 12, 1967, DK Papers, Box 13.

66. Philippa Strum, "Pauli Murray's Indelible Mark on the Fight for Equal Rights," ACLU, June 1, 2020, https://www.aclu.org/issues/womens-rights/pauli-murrays-indelible-mark-fight-equal-rights.

67. Hartmann, "Pauli Murray and the 'Juncture of Women's Liberation and Black Liberation,'" 74, 75.

68. ACLU Equality Committee Minutes, February 1, 1968, PM Papers, Box 54.

69. DK to PM, April 5, 1966, PM Papers, Box 57.

70. Memorandum from DK and PM to ACLU Board of Directors, September 24, 1970, PM Papers, Box 54.

71. DK to PM, October 13, 1966, PM Papers, Box 39, Folder 685.

72. Memorandum Draft from DK to ACLU Board of Directors, n.d., DK Papers, Box 29.

73. ACLU Equality Committee Minutes, December 28, 1967, PM Papers, Box 54.

74. Memo to Board of Directors, November 20, 1970, DK Papers, Box 30.

75. ACLU Equality Committee Minutes, December 28, 1967.

76. ACLU Equality Committee Minutes, February 1, 1968, PM Papers, Box 54.

77. DK to Board of Directors, January 6, 1969, DK Papers, Box 29.

78. Memo to Board of Directors and Affiliates, ACLU, May 8, 1969, PM Papers, Box 57.

79. DK to Edward Greenbaum, September 17, 1970, DK Papers, Box 14; ACLU At-Large Board Members, 1972, PM Papers, Box 54.

80. DK to PM, March 11, 1969, PM Papers, Box 57.

81. Memo to Board of Directors and Affiliates, ACLU, May 8, 1969.

82. PM to Alan Reitman, August 21, 1970, PM Papers, Box 59.

83. DK to Ralph Brown, June 17, 1969, DK Papers, Box 9; DK to Ralph Brown, July 30, 1969, DK Papers, Box 9.

84. ACLU Equality Committee Minutes, April 1, 1970, PM Papers, Box 54.

85. DK to Jacqueline Van Voris, June 22, 1971, DK Papers, Box 4.

86. ACLU Equality Committee Minutes, April 1, 1970.

87. *Goesaert v. Cleary*, 335 U.S. 464 (1948).

88. *Goesaert*, at 466.

89. Hasday, *We the Men*, 84.

90. *Hoyt v. Florida*, 368 U.S. 57 (1961).

91. Philippa Strum, *On Account of Sex: Ruth Bader Ginsburg and the Making of Gender Equality Law* (University Press of Kansas, 2022), 46.

92. Strum, *On Account of Sex*, 8.

93. DK to Louise Nunn, March 25, 1970, DK Papers, Box 29.

94. Equality Committee Draft, ACLU, April 30, 1970, PM Papers, Box 31.

95. DK to Louise Nunn, March 25, 1970, DK Papers, Box 29.

96. Marylin Bender, "Liberation Yesterday—The Roots of the Feminist Movement," *New York Times*, August 21, 1970, 41.

97. "Women's Liberation Movement," 1970, DK Papers, Box 2.

98. DK to Betsy Nolan, June 29, 1970, DK Papers, Box 29.

99. "A Memorandum on the Proposed Equal Rights Amendment to the United States Constitution," Citizens' Advisory Council on the Status of Women, March 1970, Box 1145, Folder 18, ACLU Records.

100. Jacqueline Van Voris to Mildred Adams Kenyon, August 9, 1974, DK Papers, Box 4; Clara Bingham, *The Movement: How Women's Liberation Transformed America, 1963–1973* (One Signal Publishers/Atria, 2024), 257; Feigen, *Not One of the Boys*, 40.

101. Rachel Shteir, *Betty Friedan: Magnificent Disrupter* (Yale University Press, 2023), 155; Perkins, *Yale Needs Women*, 174.

102. Report of the New York City Commission on Human Rights, *Women's Role in Contemporary Society* (Avon Books, 1972), 544–45.

103. Eleanor Holmes Norton to DK, January 28, 1971, DK Papers, Box 15.

104. Gilbert and Moore, *Particular Passions*, 143.

105. Susan M. Hartmann, *The Other Feminists: Activists in the Liberal Establishment* (Yale University Press, 1998), 74.

106. Equal Rights Amendment, September 21, 1970, PM Papers, Box 54.

107. Strum, "Pauli Murray's Indelible Mark on the Fight for Equal Rights."

108. Memorandum from DK and PM to ACLU Board of Directors, September 24, 1970, PM Papers, Box 54.

109. DK to Board of Directors, memo, November 20, 1970, DK Papers, Box 30.

110. PM and DK to ACLU Board of Directors, telegram, September 23, 1970, PM Papers, Box 55.

111. Press Release, October 2, 1970, PM Papers, Box 54.

112. Jane J. Mansbridge, *Why We Lost the ERA* (University of Chicago Press, 1986), 14.

113. ACLU Office to Equality Committee, memo, November 5, 1970, PM Papers, Box 54.

114. "Headline: Dorothy Kenyon Dies Here," *Chelsea-Clinton* [NY] *News*, February 17, 1972, PM Papers, Box 125, Folder 2269

115. DK to Senator Edmund S. Muskie, August 27, 1971, DK Papers, Box 14.

116. DK to Jacqueline G. Gutwillig, January 6, 1971, DK Papers, Box 14.

117. Cose, *Democracy, If We Can Keep It*, 255–256.

118. Gilbert and Moore, *Particular Passions*, 156.

119. "ACLU Women's Rights Project," ACLU, Spring 1980.

120. Ruth Bader Ginsburg, "Constitutional Adjudication in the United States as a Means of Advancing the Equal Stature of Men and Women Under the Law," *Hofstra Law Review* 50 (2022): 4, accessed October 28, 2025, https://scholarlycommons.law.hofstra.edu/hlr/vol50/iss2/3/.

121. Melvin Wulf to Martha W. Griffiths, September 16, 1971, Box 1645, ACLU Records.

122. Idaho Supreme Court, March 10, 1970, Box 1645, ACLU Records.

123. Allen R. Derr to Melvin Wulf, March 24, 1970, Box 1645, ACLU Records. Wulf was ACLU legal director.

124. Melvin Wulf to DK and PM, June 16, 1971, Box 1645, ACLU Records.

125. Anne Firor Scott, *Pauli Murray and Caroline Ware: Forty Years of Letters in Black and White* (University of North Carolina Press, 2006), 138–39.

126. "Griffiths, Martha Wright," *History, Art & Archives: United States House of Representatives*, accessed January 26, 2026, https://history.house.gov/People/Detail?id=14160.

127. Julie C. Suk, *We the Women: The Unstoppable Mothers of the Equal Rights Amendment* (Skyhorse Publishing, 2020), 57. Hicks Griffiths was supportive of his wife's career, choosing Michigan Law over Harvard Law because Harvard did not admit women as law students at the time.

128. Martha W. Griffiths to Melvin Wulf, July 6, 1971, Box 1645, ACLU Records.

129. Melvin Wulf to Allen Derr, July 21, 1971, Box 1645, ACLU Records.

130. Melvin Wulf to Margaret W. Griffiths, September 16, 1971, Box 1645, ACLU Records.

131. Melvin Wulf to Allen Derr, August 17, 1971, Box 1645, ACLU Records.

132. Melvin Wulf to Allen Derr, September 17, 1971, Box 1645, ACLU Records.

133. Allen Derr to Melvin Wulf, September 24, 1971, Box 1645, ACLU Records; Wulf to Derr, October 4, 1971, Box 1645, ACLU Records.

134. Melvin Wulf to Allen Derr, October 8, 1971, Box 1645, ACLU Records.

135. Melvin Wulf to Allen Derr, October 21, 1971, Box 1645, ACLU Records.

136. *Reed v. Reed*, 404 U.S. 71 (1971).

137. Earl M. Maltz, *The Chief Justiceship of Warren Burger 1969–1986* (University of South Carolina Press, 2000), 227.

138. Kerber, *No Constitutional Right to Be Ladies*, 203–4.

139. "ACLU Women's Rights Project," ACLU, Spring 1980.

140. Preliminary Draft of Women's Rights Project, PM Papers, Box 54.

141. Cose, *Democracy, If We Can Keep It*, 254.

142. Preliminary Draft of Women's Rights Project.

143. "ACLU Women's Rights Project," ACLU, Spring 1980.

144. *Weinberger v. Wiesenfeld*, 420 U.S. 636 (1975).

145. Ginsburg, "Constitutional Adjudication in the United States as a Means of Advancing the Equal Stature of Men and Women Under the Law."

146. Ruth Bader Ginsburg and Kathleen W. Peratis, "Equal Rights for Women," *New York Times*, December 31, 1975, 21.

147. Gilbert and Moore, *Particular Passions*, 155.

148. Mansbridge, *Why We Lost the ERA*, 1.

149. Isabela Salas-Betsch and Kate Kelly, "What Comes Next for the Equal Rights Amendment?," Center for American Progress, August 26, 2024, https://www.americanprogress.org/article/what-comes-next-for-the-equal-rights-amendment/.

150. Hartmann, *The Other Feminists*, 56.

151. Ruth Bader Ginsburg and Amanda L. Tyler, *Justice, Justice Thou Shalt Pursue: A Life's Work Fighting for a More Perfect Union* (University of California Press, 2021).

152. Julie C. Suk, "A Dangerous Imbalance: Pauli Murray's Equal Rights Amendment and the Path to Equal Power," *Virginia Law Review Online* 107 (2021): 10.

153. DK to Sherry Harrison, April 29, 1971, DK Papers, Box 14.

154. DK to Dean De Capriles, November 2, 1966, DK Papers, Box 5.

## 9. A GUTSY FIGHTER

1. "Fair Women and the Law," *Examiner* [CA], September 2, 1894, 9.

2. Janolyn Lo Vecchio, "Western Women's Struggle to Serve on Juries, 1870–1954," *Western Legal History* 21 (2008): 26; Kerber, *No Constitutional Right to Be Ladies*, 136.

3. Vecchio, "Western Women's Struggle to Serve on Juries, 1870–1954," 26.

4. Rebecca DeWolf, *Gendered Citizenship: The Original Conflict over the Equal Rights Amendment, 1920–1963* (University of Nebraska Press, 2021), 19.

5. Linda K. Kerber, Jane Sherron De Hart, Cornelia Hughes Dayton, and Karissa Haugeberg, eds., *Women's America: Refocusing the Past* (Oxford University Press, 2020), 526.

6. "Should Women Serve on Juries?," *Brooklyn Daily Eagle*, January 13, 1918, 20.

7. Brief of the Florida Civil Liberties Union and the ACLU as Amicus Curiae, *Hoyt v. Florida*, 1961 WL 102288 (U.S. 1961), 4.

8. "Women for Jury Service Measure Beaten, 21 to 11," *New Britain* [CT] *Herald*, March 27, 1929, 1.

9. "Women's Jury Measure Reported Unfavorably," *Meriden* [CT] *Record-Journal*, March 27, 1929, 1.

10. "Women for Jury Service Measure Beaten, 21 to 11."

11. Perry, "Rhetoric, Strategy, and Politics in the New York Campaign for Women's Jury Service," 60.

12. Perry, "Rhetoric, Strategy, and Politics in the New York Campaign for Women's Jury Service," 61.

13. "Florence Ellinwood Allen," National Women's Hall of Fame, https://www.womenofthehall.org/inductee/florence-ellinwood-allen/.

14. Tuve, *First Lady of the Law*, 193.

15. Kerber, *No Constitutional Right to Be Ladies*, 136.

16. Perry, *After the Vote*, 79.

17. Jury service excerpt, DK Papers, Box 3.

18. Kerber, De Hart, Dayton, and Haugeberg, eds., *Women's America*, 528.

19. Jury service excerpt, n.d., DK Papers, Box 3.

20. Perry, *After the Vote*, 80.

21. "Dorothy Kenyon, Fiery Fighter for Women's Rights, Is Visitor," *Washington Post*, February 3, 1938, Box 1.

22. "Filing for Jury Duty Under New Law," September 1, 1937, DK Papers, Box 1.

23. "The News About a West Side Woman Judge," October 23, 1939, DK Papers, Box 4, Folders 1–5; see also "Filing for Jury Duty Under New Law."

24. "Women Jurors Exonerate Wife; Court Asks Why," *New York Daily News*, October 6, 1937, 3.

25. "Women Lack Imagination Needed for Crime," *Brooklyn Daily Eagle*, October 28, 1938, DK Papers, Box 1.

26. Renee B. Stern, "Straight Thinking for Modern Women Ladies of the Jury," *Buffalo* [NY] *Times*, December 19, 1923, 26.

27. "Should Women Serve on Juries?," *Courier-News* [NJ], May 22, 1930, 22.

28. "Should Women Serve on Juries?," *Jacksonville* [FL] *Daily Journal*, November 1, 1930, 5; Louis Nizer, "Verdict on Women as Jurors," *New York Times*, March 11, 1962, SM11.

29. "Should Women Serve on Juries?"

30. Mac Roy Rasor, "Should Women Serve on Juries?," *Valley Morning Star* [TX], October 4, 1949, 1.

31. Jack M. Allard, "Baby Sitters' Work Boosted with Female Jury Service," *San Angelo* [TX] *Standard-Times*, October 16, 1949, 30.

32. Allard, "Baby Sitters' Work Boosted with Female Jury Service."

33. Catherine Lane, "Should Women Serve on Juries in Illinois? 'Why Not?' Response of Many Interviewed," *Bloomington* [IL] *Pantagraph*, March 3, 1939, 3.

34. Lane, "Should Women Serve on Juries in Illinois?"

35. "All-Female Juries Have Returned Some 'Ridiculous' Verdicts," *Freeport* [IL] *Journal Standard*, January 28, 1954, 17.

36. "Give Us Women Jurors," *Bristol* [TN] *Herald Courier*, September 10, 1947, 4.

37. *Bailey v. Arkansas*, 219 S.W.2d 424, 428 (Ark. 1949).

38. *Bailey*, at 428.

39. Joe Belden, "Most Texans Want Women on Juries," *Victoria* [TX] *Advocate*, July 26, 1953, 4; "Texas Historical Marker Based on SMU Research of Women's Jury Service," *SMU* (Southern Methodist University), May 27, 2010, https://blog.smu.edu/research/2010/05/27/texas-historical-marker-based-on-smu-research-of-womens-jury-service/.

40. "House Studies Jury Duty Bill," *Dothan* [AL] *Eagle*, May 16, 1955, 1.

41. "Gender-Based Jury Exclusion," sidebar in "Race and the Jury," *EJI: Equal Justice Initiative*, https://eji.org/report/race-and-the-jury/why-representative-juries-are-necessary/sidebar/gender-based-jury-exclusion/.

42. "JUST ASK: Would You Prefer an All-Male to All-Female Jury?," *Minneapolis Morning Tribune* [MN], May 5, 1960, 20.

43. "JUST ASK."

44. Brief of the Florida Civil Liberties Union and the ACLU as Amicus Curiae, *Hoyt v. Florida*, 14.

45. Brief of the Florida Civil Liberties Union and the ACLU as Amicus Curiae, *Hoyt v. Florida*, 8.

46. *Strauder v. West Virginia*, 100 U.S. 303 (1879).

47. *Ballard v. United States*, 329 U.S. 187, 193 (1946).

48. *Fay v. People of New York*, 332 U.S. 261, 267 (1947).

49. *Fay*, at 289.

50. "Women on Juries, Hoyt v. Florida," Florida Supreme Court, https://www.floridasupremecourt.org/Library-Archives/Evolution-of-Justice-in-Florida-Documents-Images-and-Books/Women-on-Juries-Hoyt-v.-Florida. Florida would pass a law requiring mandatory jury duty for women in 1967.

51. "Wife Wields Baseball Bat on Mate," *Miami Herald*, September 21, 1957, 3.

52. George B. Crawford, "Murder, Insanity, and the Efficacy of Woman's Role: The Gwendolyn Hoyt Case," *Florida Historical Quarterly* 89 (2010): 59, 71.

53. Brief of the Florida Civil Liberties Union and the ACLU as Amicus Curiae, *Hoyt v. Florida*, 6.

54. Brief of the Florida Civil Liberties Union and the ACLU as Amicus Curiae, *Hoyt v. Florida*, 19–20.

55. US Department of Labor, *Handbook on Women Workers* (Government Printing Office, 1958), 2, cited in Brief of the Florida Civil Liberties Union and the ACLU as Amicus Curiae, Hoyt v. Florida, 25.

56. Public Health Report (June 1961), 510, as republished in *World Almanac*, 1961, 464, cited in Brief of the Florida Civil Liberties Union and the ACLU as Amicus Curiae, *Hoyt v. Florida*, 25. This longevity estimate is for white men and women born in 1958; for nonwhite men and women the estimate is approximately seven years less for both categories.

57. Brief of the Florida Civil Liberties Union and the ACLU as Amicus Curiae, *Hoyt v. Florida*, 26.

58. Anthony Lewis, "Court Backs Curb on Women Jurors," *New York Times*, November 21, 1961, 1.

59. Kerber, *No Constitutional Right to Be Ladies*, 170.

60. Transcript of Oral Argument, *Hoyt v. Florida*, 368 U.S. 57 (1961), https://www.oyez.org/cases/1961/31.

61. Transcript of Oral Argument, *Hoyt v. Florida*.

62. *Hoyt v. Florida*, 368 U.S. 57, 61–62 (1961).

63. Leo Kanowitz, *Women and the Law: The Unfinished Revolution* (University of New Mexico Press, 1969), 31.

64. Isabel Miller, "'Our Leading Feminist': Dorothy Kenyon and the Origins of Equal Protection for Women in *Hoyt v. Florida*," *Journal of Supreme Court History* 49 (2024): 279.

65. "Women on Jury," *Washington Post*, reprinted in *Daily Republic* [SD], December 4, 1961, 4.

66. Strum, *On Account of Sex*, 25.

67. Ginsburg, "Constitutional Adjudication in the United States as a Means of Advancing the Equal Stature of Men and Women Under the Law," 4.

68. DK to Professor Norman Dorsen, May 7, 1971, DK Papers, Box 14.

69. DK to Osmond Fraenkel, January 12, 1971, DK Papers, Box 29.

70. Gilbert and Moore, *Particular Passions*, 135.

71. Morello, *Invisible Bar*, 162.

72. "Discrimination Against Women—Jury Duty," June 30, 1966, DK Papers, Box 23.

73. DK to Constance Baker Motley, December 14, 1964, DK Papers, Box 47.

74. DK to Constance Baker Motley, April 13, 1965, Box 8, Folder 16, Constance Baker Motley Papers, SSC-MS-00110, Sophia Smith Collection, Smith College, Northampton, MA (hereafter Motley Papers).

75. DK to Constance Baker Motley, April 13, 1965.

76. Charles Morgan, *One Man, One Voice* (Holt, Rinehart & Winston, 1979), 31.

77. Charles W. Eagles, *Outside Agitator: Jon Daniels and the Civil Rights Movement in Alabama* (University of Alabama Press, 2000), xii.

78. Tim Unsworth, "1967 Shooting of Two Clergy in Lowndes County, Alabama," *U.S. Catholic*, March 1, 1998.

79. Brief for Plaintiff, *White v. Crook*, 251 F. Supp. 401 (M.D. Ala. 1966), Civil Action No. 2263-N, 15.

80. Eagles, *Outside Agitator*, 120.

81. Eagles, *Outside Agitator*, 121.

82. Eagles, *Outside Agitator*, 138.

83. Eagles, *Outside Agitator*, 164.

84. Morgan, *One Man, One Voice*, 38.

85. Eagles, *Outside Agitator*, 168.

86. Ruby Sales, "How We Can Start to Heal the Pain of Racial Division," *TED*, September 2018, https://www.ted.com/talks/ruby_sales_how_we_can_start_to_heal_the_pain_of_racial_division; Rev. Joanna Seibert, "Jonathan Daniels," Saint Mark's Episcopal Church (Little Rock, AR), September 6, 2020, https://lovesaintmarks.org/jonathan-daniels/.

87. Sales, "How We Can Start to Heal the Pain of Racial Division."

88. Taylor Branch, *At Canaan's Edge: America in the King Years, 1965–68* (Simon & Schuster, 2006), 291; Leonard Chamblee, "Daniels Not New on Rights Scene," *Birmingham Post-Herald*, August 21, 1965, 2; Eagles, *Outside Agitator*, 171.

89. Sales, "How We Can Start to Heal the Pain of Racial Division"; "Varner's Cash Store," Historical Marker Database, update April 4, 2020, https://www.hmdb.org/m.asp?m=147601; Eagles, *Outside Agitator*, 174.

90. Eagles, *Outside Agitator*, 177.

91. Morgan, *One Man, One Voice*, 38. Coleman's father had allegedly taken part in a lynching and likely served on juries that sentenced Black defendants to death. See also Unsworth, "1967 Shooting of Two Clergy in Lowndes County, Alabama."

92. Morgan, *One Man, One Voice*, 39.

93. Sales, "How We Can Start to Heal the Pain of Racial Division."

94. Eagles, *Outside Agitator*, 179.

95. Michael E. Ruane, "Black Civil Rights Activist Recalls White Ally Who Took a Shotgun Blast for Her," *Washington Post*, August 16, 2015, https://www.washingtonpost.com/local/black-civil-rights-activist-recalls-white-ally-who-took-a-shotgun-blast-for-her/2015/08/16/4e562dd8-3b74–11e5-8e98–115a3cf7d7ae_story.html.

96. S. L. Wisenberg, "How a Chicago Priest Became an Unwitting Civil Rights Figure," *Chicago Reader*, August 31, 2015.

97. Eagles, *Outside Agitator*, 180.

98. "Alabamian Indicted in the Slaying of Seminarian," *New York Times*, September 16, 1965, 33.

99. "Alabamian Indicted in the Slaying of Seminarian"; Eagles, *Outside Agitator*, 202.

100. "Alabamian Indicted in the Slaying of Seminarian"; Morgan, *One Man, One Voice*, 41.

101. Dorothy Kenyon, "Jane Crow and Lily-White Males," *Civil Liberties*, January 1966, DK Papers, Box 23.

102. Morgan, *One Man, One Voice*, 39; Branch, *At Canaan's Edge*, 312.

103. "Trials: A License to Kill," *Time*, October 8, 1965, https://time.com/archive/6888855/trials-a-license-to-kill/.

104. Brief for Plaintiff, *White v. Crook*, 9.

105. Morgan, *One Man, One Voice*, 43–44.

106. Morgan, *One Man, One Voice*, 44.

107. John Herbers, "Community Backs Coleman: Alabama Jury Frees Coleman," *New York Times*, October 1, 1965, 1, 3.

108. Alvin Benn, "Coleman Case In Jury Hands," *Birmingham* [AL] *Post-Herald*, September 30, 1965, 40.

109. Benn, "Coleman Case In Jury Hands."

110. Herbers, "Community Backs Coleman."

111. Benn, "Coleman Case In Jury Hands."

112. Morgan, *One Man, One Voice*, 45.

113. Liz Ryan, "How an All-White Jury's Acquittal Sparked Legal Reform in Alabama," *Alabama Political Reporter*, October 10, 2021, https://www.alreporter.com/2021/10/22/how-an-all-white-jurys-acquittal-sparked-legal-reform-in-alabama/; Eagles, *Outside Agitator*, 252.

114. *McMeans v. Mayor's Court, Fort Deposit, Alabama*, 247 F. Supp. 606 (M.D. Ala. 1965); Eagles, *Outside Agitator*, 248.

115. "Trials: A License to Kill."

116. James P. Turner, *Selma and the Liuzzo Murder Trials: The First Modern Civil Rights Convictions* (University of Michigan Press, 2018), 70–71.

117. Rik Stevens, "Allies of Pivotal Civil Rights Victim Reflect 50 Years Later," *AP News*, update August 12, 2015, https://apnews.com/general-news-a35a3f83387f433d9a1c4345d0c67fcd.

118. "About the Founder and Director," *The SpiritHouse Project*, https://www.spirithouseproject.org/aboutruby.php.

119. Sales, "How We Can Start to Heal the Pain of Racial Division."

120. Richard Morrisroe, SNCC, 1965–66, Alabama, "Hope, Action, Change: 50 Years of Memories" (2017), Civil Rights Movement Archive, https://www.crmvet.org/vet/morrisro.htm.

121. Stevens, "Allies of Pivotal Civil Rights Victim Reflect 50 Years Later"; Wisenberg, "How a Chicago Priest Became an Unwitting Civil Rights Figure."

122. Seibert, "Jonathan Daniels."

123. DK to Pauli Murray, January 30, 1963, PM Papers, Box 49.

124. Murray, *Song in a Weary Throat*, 363.

125. Brief for Plaintiff, *White v. Crook*.

126. Branch, *At Canaan's Edge*, 312.

127. Brief in Support of Intervenor's Findings of Fact, Conclusions of Law and Decree, December 1965, 28, *Fulcrum*, https://www.fulcrum.org/downloads/t435gd000.

128. Brief in Support of Intervenor's Findings of Fact, Conclusions of Law and Decree, 29–30.

129. "Alabama Judge Cannot Recall Any Negroes on Trial Juries," *New York Times*, November 27, 1965, 35.

130. "Judge Kenyon Pleads in Ala. for Jane Does and Jane Crow," *Chelsea-Clinton* [NY] *News*, December 2, 1965, DK Papers, Box 2; "Alabama Judge Cannot Recall Any Negroes on Trial Juries."

131. DK to Charles Morgan, November 29, 1965, DK Papers, Box 28; DK to Esther Peterson, February 28, 1966, DK Papers, Box 28.

132. Brief for Plaintiff, *White v. Crook*, 7.

133. Brief for Plaintiff, *White v. Crook*, 12.

134. Brief for Plaintiff, *White v. Crook*, 61.

135. Brief for Plaintiff, *White v. Crook*, 53.

136. Brief for Plaintiff, *White v. Crook*, 55.

137. Dorothy Kenyon to PM, December 19, 1969, PM Papers, Box 125, Folder 2269.

138. DK to Leslie Berry, January 25, 1966, DK Papers, Box 13.

139. Kenyon, "Jane Crow and Lily-White Males." At the conclusion of the article there is a handwritten note that says, "We won our case!"

140. *White v. Crook*, 251 F. Supp. 401, 408 (M.D. Ala. 1966).

141. *White*, at 408.

142. Murray, *Song in a Weary Throat*, 475.

143. Mayeri, "Constitutional Choices," 779, citing Mary Eastwood to Charles Morgan, February 1966, Mary Eastwood Papers, Schlesinger Library, Radcliffe Institute, Harvard University, Cambridge, MA, 83-M257, Carton 1, Folder 28.

144. DK to Margaret Hickey, March 23, 1966, Catherine East Papers, Schlessinger Library, Radcliffe Institute, Harvard University, Cambridge, MA, Box 4.

145. ACLU, Feature Press Service, Bulletin #2258, February 28, 1966, DK Papers, Box 31, Folder 4.

146. Citizens' Advisory Council on the Status of Women Memo, March 3, 1966, DK Papers, Box 31, Folder 4.

147. DK to Esther Peterson, February 28, 1966, DK Papers, Box 28.

148. DK to Esther Peterson, March 17, 1966, DK Papers, Box 28.

149. Murray, *Song in a Weary Throat*, 475.

150. DK to Leon Keyserling, February 28, 1966, DK Papers, Box 13.

151. DK to Caroline Ware, March 23, 1966, DK Papers, Box 17.

152. PM to Marguerite Rawalt, February 16, 1966, PM Papers, Box 59.

153. Pauli Murray Draft Board Letter, February 10, 1966, PM Papers, Box 59.

154. Charles T. Duncan to DK, March 23, 1966, DK Papers, Box 13.

155. DK to Charles T. Duncan, April 5, 1966, DK Papers, Box 13.

156. *State v. Hall*, 187 So. 2d 861, 863 (Miss. 1966).

157. "The Case for Equality in State Jury Service," May 1, 1966, DK Papers, Box 25.

158. *Taylor v. Louisiana*, 419 U.S. 522, 531 (1975).

## 10. LIFE IS SWEET AND LIFE IS SOUR

1. DK to Bertha Klenova, January 3, 1967, DK Papers, Box 13.

2. "Headline: Dorothy Kenyon Dies Here," *Chelsea-Clinton* [NY] *News*, February 17, 1972, PM Papers, Box 125, Folder 2269.

3. DK to Edward Tipton Kenyon, June 16, 1969, DK Papers, Box 8.

4. "Headline: Dorothy Kenyon Dies Here."

5. "Headline: Dorothy Kenyon Dies Here."

6. DK to Neighbors, February 8, 1967, DK Papers, Box 13.

7. DK to Editor, June 10, 1968, DK Papers, Box 17.

8. Mildred Adams Kenyon Manuscript, 169, DK Papers, Box 3.

9. DK to Manhattan and Bronx Surface Transit Operating Authority, February 1, 1965, DK Papers, Box 13.

10. DK to Manhattan and Bronx Surface Transit Operating Authority, February 18, 1965, DK Papers, Box 13.

11. "Purse-Snatchers Keep Trying—Dorothy Kenyon Fights 'Em Off," unidentified newspaper clipping, October 10, 1968, DK Papers, Box 2.

12. "Miss Kenyon Writes New Chapter," February 18, 1971, DK Papers, Box 2.

13. DK to Police Commissioner Patrick Murphy, March 23, 1971, DK Papers, Box 14.

14. "Perils of Dorothy," *Chelsea-Clinton* [NY] *News*, April 8, 1971, DK Papers, Box 17.

15. Report Dictated, February 9, 1971, DK Papers, Box 10.

16. DK to Mabel Leslie, February 25, 1971, DK Papers, Box 14; "Perils of Dorothy."

17. DK to Mabel Leslie, February 25, 1971.

18. John Fisher, interview with author via Zoom, April 11, 2023.

19. DK to Court Employment Project, March 18, 1971, DK Papers, Box 14.

20. DK to Stanwood Kenyon, July 28, 1971, DK Papers, Box 8; DK to Court Employment Project, March 18, 1971; "Vera Institute of Justice," Wikipedia, https://en.wikipedia.org/wiki/Vera_Institute_of_Justice.

21. "Perils of Dorothy."

22. DK to Police Commissioner Patrick Murphy, March 23, 1971.

23. Stanley Watt to DK, June 18, 1971, DK Papers, Box 14.

24. Synopsis of Proposal for Legal Services Agency, 1965, DK Papers, Box 46.

25. Reginald Heber Smith, *Justice and the Poor* (Merrymount Press, 1919), 16.

26. John M. A. DiPippa, "Reginald Heber Smith and Justice and the Poor in the 21st Century," *Campbell Law Review* 40 (2018): 110.

27. *Gideon v. Wainwright*, 372 U.S. 335 (1963).

28. DK to Leslie Berry, February 8, 1967, DK Papers, Box 13.

29. Lower West Side Anti-Poverty Board Inc. and Community Committee, DK Papers, Box 46.

30. Alfred E. Clark, "New Law Office Aiding the Poor," *New York Times*, February 11, 1968, 64.

31. Dorothy Kenyon, "Letters to the Editor," *New York Times*, December 12, 1966, 46.

32. DK to Norman Thomas, March 14, 1966, DK Papers, Box 17; Synopsis of Proposal for Legal Services Agency, 1965, DK Papers, Box 46.

33. "New Law Office Aiding the Poor," *New York Times*, 1968, DK Papers, Box 2; Testimonial Dinner Introductory Remarks, DK Papers, Box 4.

34. Mildred Adams Kenyon to PM, February 9, 1972, PM Papers, Box 125, Folder 2269.

35. DK to Leslie Berry, February 4, 1970, DK Papers, Box 14.

36. Marylin Bender, "The New Portia: Brainy, Idealistic, but Above All, Just a Girl," *New York Times*, February 26, 1968, 40.

37. Letter to Editor, *New York Times*, February 29, 1968, DK Papers, Box 17.

38. DK to Manfred Ohrenstein, September 10, 1969, DK Papers, Box 14.

39. Chelsea Civil Rights Council Newsletter, April 1964, DK Papers, Box 34.

40. DK to Assistant Inspector Pigott, March 17, 1965, DK Papers, Box 34.

41. "A Personal Remembrance," *Chelsea-Clinton* [NY] *News*, April 11, 1968, DK Papers, Box 17.

42. DK to Constance Baker Motley, February 20, 1964, DK Papers, Box 15.

43. DK to Constance Baker Motley, October 3, 1966, Box 8, Folder 16, Motley Papers.

44. Constance Baker Motley to DK, October 4, 1966, Box 8, Folder 16, Motley Papers.

45. DK to Elisabeth Watts, October 15, 1964, DK Papers, Box 12.

46. DK to unidentified party for the Quarterly update, January 26, 1965, DK Papers, Box 8; Robert L. Carter, Dorothy Kenyon, Peter Marcuse, and Loren Miller, *Equality* (Pantheon Books, 1965).

47. DK to Mildred Adams Kenyon, January 14, 1964, DK Papers, Box 8. Mildred wrote back, warning Dorothy not to make a career out of books. "Not only is there drudgery in it but there is also a degree of frustration which grows with the years. As a writer I think the ideal job is that of the editor who apparently can change his or her mind endlessly without damage to himself no matter what happens to the poor author. It may not, however, look like this from the editor's point of view. I do think that you could do a very stunning autobiography, but whether you could make a fortune is something about which I have enormous doubts. Publishers are getting rich, but authors don't." Mildred Adams Kenyon to DK, January 20, 1964, DK Papers, Box 8.

48. DK to Mildred Adams Kenyon, January 12, 1970, DK Papers, Box 8.

49. DK to Lestra Kenyon, January 18, 1965, DK Papers, Box 8.

50. DK to Theodore Kenyon, November 2, 1967, DK Papers, Box 8.

51. Theodore Kenyon to DK, November 6, 1967, DK Papers, Box 8.

52. DK to Theodore Kenyon, November 15, 1967, DK Papers, Box 8.

53. "Kenyon in Hospital," 1967, DK Papers, Box 2; DK to Presbyterian Hospital, September 22, 1967, DK Papers, Box 13.

54. DK to Theodore Kenyon, February 14, 1968, DK Papers, Box 8.

55. DK to Theodore Kenyon, October 10, 1967, DK Papers, Box 8.

56. Dinner Committee Chairman to DK, January 10, 1968, DK Papers, Box 4.

57. Robert Mayer, "Today with Newsday: Tribute to a Rebel," *Chelsea-Clinton* [NY] *News*, February 22, 1968, PM Papers, Box 125, Folder 2269; Testimonial Dinner Program, February 22, 1968, PM Papers, Box 125, Folder 2269.

58. Testimonial Dinner Program.

59. Testimonial Dinner Introductory Remarks.

60. *The New Chelsea Reform Democratic Club Newsletter*, March 8, 1968, DK Papers, Box 4.

61. "Today with Newsday," PM Papers, Box 125, Folder 2269.

62. *New Chelsea Reform Democratic Club Newsletter*, March 8, 1968; CPI Inflation Calculator, https://www.bls.gov/data/inflation_calculator.htm.

63. DK to Roger Nash Baldwin, March 27, 1968, Roger Nash Baldwin Papers, MC005, Public Policy Papers, Department of Special Collections, Mudd Manuscript Library, Princeton University Library, Princeton, NJ.

64. DK to Theodore Kenyon, June 12, 1968, DK Papers, Box 8.

65. David S. Kenyon, interview with author via Zoom, April 4, 2023.

66. DK to Elizabeth Trebony, December 3, 1969, DK Papers, Box 14; David S. Kenyon, interview.

67. David S. Kenyon, interview.

68. DK to Theodore Kenyon, January 9, 1970, DK Papers, Box 8.

69. "A Few Words About My Father, by Edward T. Kenyon," April 28, 1978, DK Papers, Box 8.

70. DK to Theodore Kenyon, April 28, 1969, DK Papers, Box 8.

71. DK to Theodore Kenyon, January 9, 1970, DK Papers, Box 8.

72. Dorothy Dunbar Bromley to Mildred Adams Kenyon, June 21, 1972, DK Papers, Box 3.

73. DK to Marla Perkel, December 19, 1966, DK Papers, Box 13.

74. Will Kenyon to DK, February 17, 1918, DK Papers, Box 3.

75. Will Kenyon to DK, February 20, 1930, DK Papers, Box 9.

76. Genealogy, November 8, 1973, DK Papers, Box 3, Folders 1–4.

77. DK to Theodore Kenyon, December 4, 1963, DK Papers, Box 8.

78. Theodore Kenyon to DK, December 9, 1963, DK Papers, Box 8.

79. DK to Theodore Kenyon, December 16, 1963, DK Papers, Box 8.

80. "Theodore S. Kenyon, 88, Long a Patent Lawyer," *New York Times*, April 26, 1978, 4.

81. Introductory Remarks, DK Papers, Box 4.

82. "Profane Profiles . . . DK," November 1940, DK Papers, Box 1.

83. DK to James T. Nolan, October 7, 1966, DK Papers, Box 41.

84. Mildred Adams Kenyon to Roger Baldwin, March 7, 1972, Roger Nash Baldwin Papers, MC005, Public Policy Papers, Department of Special Collections, Mudd Manuscript Library, Princeton University Library, Princeton, NJ.

85. "Lestra Kinney Kenyon, Former Resident, Dies," *Lakeville* [CT] *Journal*, June 2, 1966, DK Papers, Box 2.

86. DK to Lestra Kenyon, January 18, 1965, DK Papers, Box 8.

87. Lestra Kenyon to DK, n.d., DK Papers, Box 8.

88. DK to Frank Hamlin, July 11, 1966, DK Papers, Box 13.

89. DK to Theodore Kenyon, December 2, 1966, DK Papers, Box 8.

90. Notice to Legatee of Admission, July 6, 1966, DK Papers, Box 8; Will of Lestra Kinney Kenyon, September 1965, DK Papers, Box 8.

91. DK to Theodore Kenyon, December 2, 1966.

92. DK to Mildred Adams Kenyon, May 7, 1968, DK Papers, Box 8.

93. John Fisher, interview.

94. DK to Stanwood Kenyon, December 11, 1967, DK Papers, Box 8.

95. DK to Mary Till, July 16, 1971, DK Papers, Box 14.

96. DK to Edward Tipton Kenyon, November 10, 1967, DK Papers, Box 8.

97. Edward Tipton Kenyon, interview with Louise Wilby Knight, October 6, 1998, DK Papers, Box 65a; "New Woman License Commissioner Eager to Watch Wheels Go 'Round," January 31, 1936, DK Papers, Box 1.

98. "Dorothy Kenyon Not a Republican," *New York Times*, September 29, 1928, 10.

99. "Wm. Kenyon Dies; Patent Lawyer," *Times Union* [NY], September 6, 1933, 22.

100. Edward Tipton Kenyon, interview.

101. David S. Kenyon, interview.

102. John Fisher, interview.

103. David S. Kenyon, interview.

104. DK to Kit Kenyon, August 17, 1970, DK Papers, Box 8.

105. David S. Kenyon, interview.

106. David S. Kenyon, interview.

107. Edward Tipton Kenyon, interview.

108. John Fisher, interview.

109. John Fisher, interview.

110. Jacqueline Van Voris to DK, 1971, DK Papers, Box 4.

111. DK to Jacqueline Van Voris, April 28, 1971, DK Papers, Box 4.

112. DK to Mary-Elizabeth Murdock, May 7, 1971, DK Papers, Box 4.

113. Smith Centennial Study Oral History, June 14, 1971, Box 4.

## 11. SAYING GOODBYE

1. Mildred Adams Kenyon Manuscript, 179, DK Papers, Box 3; DK to Dr. Philip Wiedel, November 4, 1971, DK Papers, Box 14.

2. DK to D.C.K., telegram, September 26, 1969, DK Papers, Box 14.

3. Alan Reitman to DK, September 23, 1969, DK Papers, Box 14.

4. PM to DK, October 14, 1969, DK Papers, Box 15, Folder 37.

5. DK to Eleanor H. Norton, January 14, 1970, DK Papers, Box 15.

6. DK to Harriet Pilpel, February 20, 1970, DK Papers, Box 15.

7. DK to Theodore Kenyon, February 15, 1970, DK Papers, Box 8.

8. DK to Mr. Fogarty, August 17, 1971, DK Papers, Box 14.

9. DK to James E. Sheldon, August 16, 1971, DK Papers, Box 14.

10. DK to Warren Chappell, September 3, 1971, DK Papers, Box 9.

11. Letter to the Editor, *New York Times*, September 12, 1971 (written August 29, 1971), E16.

12. DK to Dr. Philip Wiedel, November 4, 1971, DK Papers, Box 14.

13. William Houston Jr. to Hamilton Southworth, March 1, 1972, DK Papers, Box 10.

14. DK to Dr. Philip Wiedel, November 12, 1971, DK Papers, Box 14.

15. William Houston Kenyon Jr. to Warren Chappell, February 16, 1972, DK Papers, Box 10.

16. DK to Marvin Karpatkin, November 12, 1971, DK Papers, Box 29.

17. DK to Houston Kenyon, December 14, 1971, DK Papers, Box 10.

18. Eulogy Address, DK Papers, Box 7, Folder 4.

19. Dean Robert B. McKay to DK, January 11, 1972, DK Papers, Box 50.

20. William Houston Kenyon Jr. to David Kane, February 22, 1972, DK Papers, Box 10.

21. Confidential Memorandum, January 25, 1972, PM Papers, Box 125, Folder 2269.

22. William Houston Kenyon Jr. to Warren Chappell, February 16, 1972, DK Papers, Box 10.

23. William Houston Kenyon Jr. to PM, February 9, 1972, PM Papers, Box 125, Folder 2269.

24. William Houston Kenyon Jr. to Adrienne Franklin Jr., February 14, 1972, DK Papers, Box 10.

25. Mildred Adams Kenyon to Margarita Ucelay, February 24, 1972, DK Papers, Box 3.

26. Mildred Adams Kenyon to Carol Hurd Green, July 24, 1979, DK Papers, Box 3.

27. William Houston Kenyon Jr. to Dr. A. Parks McCombs, February 16, 1972, DK Papers, Box 10.

28. William Houston Kenyon Jr. to Din Judson, Jr., February 16, 1972, DK Papers, Box 10.

29. William Houston Kenyon Jr. to PM, February 9, 1972, PM Papers, Box 125, Folder 2269.

30. "Our Story," St. Peter's Chelsea, https://www.stpeterschelsea.org/our-story.html.

31. William Houston Kenyon Jr. to Elizabeth Burger, February 18, 1972, DK Papers, Box 10.

32. William Houston Kenyon Jr. to Kay Berna, February 22, 1972, DK Papers, Box 10.

33. William Houston Kenyon Jr. to PM, February 9, 1972, PM Papers, Box 125, Folder 2269.

34. Eulogy Address, DK Papers, Box 7, Folder 4.

35. Algernon Black to PM, February 23, 1972, PM Papers, Box 59.

36. PM to Algernon Black, February 27, 1972, PM Papers, Box 59.

37. "Women's Rights—History Personalities," Folder 2564+, PM Papers, https://iiif.lib.harvard.edu/manifests/view/drs:46227989$1i.

38. Debra Michals, ed., "Anne Hutchinson," National Women's History Museum, https://www.womenshistory.org/education-resources/biographies/anne-hutchinson; Adams, *The Right to Be People*, 21.

39. 118 Cong. Rec. 4194 (1972), https://www.congress.gov/bound-congressional-record/1972/02/16/house-section; William F. Ryan to William Houston Kenyon Jr., February 22, 1972, DK Papers, Box 10.

40. "A Few Notes," Feb. 28, 1972, Box 9, Folder 10, Roger Nash Baldwin Papers, MC005, Mudd Manuscript Library, Public Policy Papers, Department of Special Collections, Princeton University Library, Princeton, NJ. One of her ACLU colleagues, Harriet Pilpel, wrote in a condolence letter to Theodore that Kenyon's passing had left her with a profound sense of loss. "She was a beacon of light for all of us and, perhaps, for me particularly since she epitomized so many of my goals and ideals. [Her passing] leaves a void that never can be filled and memories for which we are and always will be grateful." Harriet Pilpel to Theodore Kenyon, February 22, 1972, DK Papers, Box 8.

41. Memorial Book 1972, PM Papers, Box 125, Folder 2269.

42. "Headline: Dorothy Kenyon Dies Here," *Chelsea-Clinton* [NY] *News*, February 17, 1972, PM Papers, Box 125 Folder 2269.

43. "R.I.P. Dorothy," DK Papers, Box 3.

44. Robert Gaines, "Dorothy Across the Hall," *Chelsea-Clinton News* [NY], February 24, 1972, DK Papers, Box 2.

45. PM to Norman Dorsen, Aryeh Neier, and Ruth Bader Ginsburg, January 12, 1974, PM Papers, Box 60.

46. Ruth Bader Ginsburg to PM, January 17, 1974, PM Papers, Box 99.

47. Last Will, August 2, 1967, DK Papers, Box 5.

48. Appraisal, 1972, DK Papers, Box 5.

49. DK to Emilie Bruzzo, June 17, 1964, DK Papers, Box 12.

50. Appraisal, 1972.

51. Mildred Adams Kenyon to Stanwood Kenyon, February 15, 1972, DK Papers, Box 5.

52. Memorandum from William Houston Kenyon Jr. to family members, February 14, 1973, DK Papers, Box 7, Folder 4.

53. "History," Woodlawn Cemetery and Conservancy, https://www.woodlawn.org/about/history/.

54. Memorandum from William Houston Kenyon Jr. to family members, June 26, 1973, DK Papers, Box 7, Folder 4.

55. Edward Tipton Kenyon, interview with Louise Wilby Knight, October 6, 1998, DK Papers, Box 65a.

56. Stanwood Kenyon to Mildred Adams Kenyon, March 13, 1977, DK Papers, Box 3.

57. Mildred Adams Kenyon, Sketch for a Dorothy Kenyon Biography, March 1, 1972, Box 3, Folders 1–4.

58. Stanwood Kenyon to Mildred Adams Kenyon, March 13, 1977, DK Papers, Box 3.

59. Mildred Adams Kenyon to Leslie Woodcock, February 24, 1972, DK Papers, Box 3; Mildred Adams Kenyon to Mary-Elizabeth Murdock, February 1975, DK Papers, Box 8.

60. Mildred Adams Kenyon to Malcolm Reiss, March 1, 1972, DK Papers, Box 3.

61. Mildred Adams Kenyon to Susan Hartmann, January 13, 1978, DK Papers, Box 3.

62. Susan Hartmann to author, email, March 8, 2023.

63. Susan Hartmann, "Odyssey of a Feminist: The Career of Dorothy Kenyon," April 11, 1980, DK Papers, Box 7, Folder 4.

64. Hartmann, *The Other Feminists*, 58–59.

65. Josh Barbanel, "Mildred A. Kenyon, Author Who Wrote as Mildred Adams," *New York Times*, November 10, 1980, D11.

66. William Houston Kenyon Jr. to Elizabeth Burger, February 18, 1972, DK Papers, Box 10.

67. William Houston Kenyon Jr. to Phyllis Gordon, March 1, 1972, DK Papers, Box 10.

# BIBLIOGRAPHY

## MANUSCRIPT COLLECTIONS


American Civil Liberties Union (ACLU) Records, Princeton University Library, Princeton, NJ. Accessed via Strozier Library, Florida State University, Tallahassee, FL.

Roger Nash Baldwin Papers, Mudd Manuscript Library, Princeton University Library, Princeton, NJ.

Earl Browder Papers, Syracuse University Libraries, Special Collections Research Center, Syracuse, NY.

Classes of 1901–1910 Records, CA-MS-010120, Sophia Smith Collection, Smith College, Northampton, MA.

Consumers' League of New York City Records, 1893–1962, Kheel Center for Labor-Management Documentation and Archives, Cornell University Library, Ithaca, NY.

Felix Frankfurter Papers, Mudd Manuscript Library, Princeton University Library, Princeton, NJ.

House Un-American Activities Committee, Record Group 233: Records of the U.S. House of Representatives, National Archives, Washington, DC.

Dorothy Kenyon Papers, Sophia Smith Collection, Smith College Archives, Northampton, MA.

Stanley King Papers, Amherst College, Amherst, MA.

Fiorello La Guardia Papers, La Guardia & Wagner Archives, La Guardia Community College/CUNY, Long Island City, NY.

Herbert H. Lehman Papers, Rare Book and Manuscript Library, Columbia University Library, New York, NY.

J. B. Matthews Papers, David M. Rubenstein Rare Book and Manuscript Library, Duke University, Durham, NC.

Joseph McCarthy Papers, Raynor Memorial Libraries, Marquette University, Milwaukee, WI.

Constance Baker Motley Papers, Sophia Smith Collection, Smith College Archives, Northampton, MA.

Pauli Murray Papers, Schlesinger Library, Radcliffe Institute, Harvard University, Cambridge, MA.
National American Woman Suffrage Association Records, Library of Congress, Washington, DC.
National Archives and Records Administration, College Park, MD.
National Archives and Records Administration, St. Louis, MO.
New York City Department of Records and Information Services.
Record Group 174: General Records of the Department of Labor, National Archives and Records Administration, St. Louis, MO.
Eleanor Roosevelt Papers, Mudd Manuscript Library, Princeton University Library, Princeton, NJ.
Elihu Root Jr. Papers, Hamilton College Archives, Clinton, NY.
Catherine Shipe East Papers, Schlesinger Library, Radcliffe Institute, Harvard University, Cambridge, MA.
Benjamin Stolberg Papers, Rare Book and Manuscript Library, Columbia University Library, NY.

## INTERVIEWS

Ancker, Jessica, with the author by telephone, September 21, 2024.
Fisher, John, with the author via Zoom, April 11, 2023.
Kenyon, David S., with the author via Zoom, April 4, 2023.
Kenyon, Edward Tipton, interview with Louise Wilby Knight, October 6, 1998, DK Papers, Box 65a.
Knight, Frances Berna, interview with Louise Wilby Knight, December 29, 1987, DK Papers, Box 65a.
Owen, David, with the author by telephone, September 27, 2024.

## COURT DECISIONS AND GOVERNMENT DOCUMENTS

*Adkins v. Children's Hospital*, 261 U.S. 525 (1923).
*Bailey v. Arkansas*, 219 S.W.2d 424 (Ark. 1949).
*Ballard v. United States*, 329 U.S. 187 (1946).
*Bradwell v. Illinois*, 83 U.S. 130 (1873).
Brief of the Florida Civil Liberties Union and the ACLU as Amicus Curiae, *Hoyt v. Florida*, WL 102288 (U.S. 1961), 4.
Brief for Plaintiff, *White v. Crook*, 251 F. Supp. 401 (M.D. Ala. 1966), Civil Action No. 2263-N, 15.
*Dunn v. Palermo*, 522 S.W.2d 679 (Tenn. 1975).
*Fay v. People of New York*, 332 U.S. 261 (1947).
*Gideon v. Wainwright*, 372 U.S. 335 (1963).

*Goesaert v. Cleary*, 335 U.S. 464 (1948).
*Hoyt v. Florida*, 368 U.S. 57 (1961).
*Mackenzie v. Hare*, 239 U.S. 299 (1915).
*McMeans v. Mayor's Court, Fort Deposit, Alabama*, 247 F. Supp. 606 (M.D. Ala. 1965).
Minimum Wage Act of September 19, 1918, ca. 174, 40 Stat. 960.
*Muller v. Oregon*, 208 U.S. 412 (1908).
*Reed v. Reed*, 404 U.S. 71 (1971).
State Department Employee Loyalty Investigation: S. Rep. No. 2108, S. Comm. on Foreign Relations, 81st Cong. (1950).
State Department Employee Loyalty Investigation: Hearing on S. Res. 231 Before the S. Comm. on Foreign Relations, 81st Cong. (1950).
*State v. Hall*, 187 So. 2d 861 (Miss. 1966).
*Strauder v. West Virginia*, 100 U.S. 303 (1879).
*Taylor v. Louisiana*, 419 U.S. 22 (1975).
*Weinberger v. Wiesenfeld*, 420 U.S. 636 (1975).
*West Coast Hotel Company v. Parrish*, 300 U.S. 379 (1937).
*White v. Crook*, 251 F. Supp. 401 (M.D. Ala. 1966).

## BOOKS AND ARTICLES

Acheson, Dean. *Present at the Creation: My Years in the State Department*. W.W. Norton, 1969.
Adams, Mildred. *The Right to Be People*. J.B. Lippincott, 1966.
Anderson, Jack, and Ronald W. May. *McCarthy: The Man, the Senator, the "Ism."* Beacon Press, 1952.
Barbas, Samantha. "Dorothy Kenyon and the Making of Modern Legal Feminism." *Stanford Journal of Civil Rights and Civil Liberties* 5 (2009).
Barbas, Samantha. *The Rise and Fall of Morris Ernst, Free Speech Renegade*. University of Chicago Press, 2021.
Basch, Norma. *In the Eyes of the Law: Women, Marriage, and Property in Nineteenth-Century New York*. Cornell University Press, 1982.
Batterson, Steve. *The Prosecution of Chandler Davis: McCarthyism, Communism, and the Myth of Academic Freedom*. Monthly Review Press, 2023.
Bender, Marylin. "Liberation Yesterday—The Roots of the Feminist Movement." *New York Times*, August 21, 1970.
Bender, Marylin. "The New Portia: Brainy, Idealistic, but Above All, Just a Girl." *New York Times*, February 26, 1968.
Bingham, Clara. *The Movement: How Women's Liberation Transformed America, 1963–1973*. One Signal/Atria, 2024.
Bittenbender, Ada M. "Woman in Law." *Chicago Law Times* 2 (1888).
Blackstone, Sir William. *Commentaries on the Laws of England in Four Books*. Callaghan & Co., 1899.

Block, Herbert. *Herblock: A Cartoonist's Life*. Macmillan, 1993.
*Book of the Class of Nineteen Hundred and Eight*. Smith College, 1908.
Bordman, Gerald. *American Theatre: A Chronicle of Comedy and Drama, 1930–1969*. Oxford University Press, 1996.
Branch, Taylor. *At Canaan's Edge: America in the King Years, 1965–68*. Simon & Schuster, 2006.
Brodsky, Alyn. *The Great Mayor: Fiorello La Guardia and the Making of the City of New York*. St. Martin's Press, 2003.
Buckley, William F., Jr., and L. Brent Bozell. *McCarthy and His Enemies: The Record and Its Meaning*. Henry Regnery, 1954.
Byrns, Elinor. "I Resolve to be Restless." *The Independent* [NY], January 10, 1916.
Carter, Robert L., Dorothy Kenyon, Peter Marcuse, and Loren Miller. *Equality*. Pantheon Books, 1965.
Chafe, William H. *The Paradox of Change: American Women in the Twentieth Century*. Oxford University Press, 1991.
Chiappetti, Caroline. "Winning the Battle but Losing the War: The Birth and Death of Intersecting Notions of Race and Sex Discrimination in *White v. Crook*." *Harvard Civil Rights–Civil Liberties Law Review* 52 (2017).
Clarke, Edward H. *Sex in Education; or, A Fair Chance for the Girls*. James R. Osgood & Co., 1873.
Cobble, Dorothy Sue. *The Other Women's Movement: Workplace Justice and Social Rights in Modern America*. Princeton University Press, 2004.
Cobble, Dorothy Sue, Linda Gordon, and Astrid Henry. *Feminism Unfinished: A Short, Surprising History of American Women's Movements*. Liveright, 2014.
Cook, Fred J. *The Nightmare Decade: The Life and Times of Senator Joe McCarthy*. Random House, 1971.
Coontz, Stephanie. *A Strange Stirring: The Feminine Mystique and American Women at the Dawn of the 1960s*. Basic Books, 2011.
Coontz, Stephanie. *The Way We Never Were: American Families and the Nostalgia Trap*. Basic Books, 1992.
Cose, Ellis. *Democracy, If We Can Keep It: The ACLU's 100-Year Fight for Rights in America*. New Press, 2020.
Costikyan, Edward N. "Politics in New York City: A Memoir of the Post-War Years." *New York History* 74 (1993).
Cott, Nancy F. *The Bonds of Womanhood: "Woman's Sphere" in New England, 1780–1835*. 2nd ed. Yale University Press, 1997.
Cott, Nancy F. *The Grounding of Modern Feminism*. Yale University Press, 1987.
Cottrell, Robert. *Roger Nash Baldwin and the American Civil Liberties Union*. Columbia University Press, 2000.
Crawford, George B. "Murder, Insanity, and the Efficacy of Woman's Role: The Gwendolyn Hoyt Case." *Florida Historical Quarterly* 89 (2010).
Cushman, Clare, ed. *Supreme Court Decisions and Women's Rights: Milestones to Equality*. Congressional Quarterly Press, 2011.

David, Augustus Ben, II. "Let No Man Mess with Noman's Land." *Vineyard Gazette* [MA], October 15, 2020.
Deckard, Barbara Sinclair. *The Women's Movement: Political, Socioeconomic, and Psychological Issues*. Harper & Row, 1956.
De Hart, Jane Sherron. *Ruth Bader Ginsburg: A Life*. Alfred A. Knopf, 2018.
DeWolf, Rebecca. *Gendered Citizenship: The Original Conflict over the Equal Rights Amendment, 1920–1963*. University of Nebraska Press, 2021.
DiPippa, John M. A. "Reginald Heber Smith and Justice and the Poor in the 21st Century." *Campbell Law Review* 40 (2018).
Dodd, Lynda G. "The Rhetoric of Gender Upheaval During the Campaign for the Nineteenth Amendment." *Boston University Law Review* 93 (2013).
Doerschuk, Beatrice. *Women in the Law: An Analysis of Training, Practice, and Salaried Positions*. Bureau of Vocational Information, 1920.
Douglas, William O. "The Black Silence of Fear." *New York Times*, January 13, 1952.
Drachman, Virginia G. *Women Lawyers and the Origins of Professional Identity in America: The Letters of the Equity Club, 1887 to 1890*. University of Michigan Press, 1993.
Eagles, Charles W. *Outside Agitator: Jon Daniels and the Civil Rights Movement in Alabama*. University of Alabama Press, 2000.
Eastman, Crystal. "Now We Can Begin." *Liberator* [MA], December 1920.
Eastman, Max. *Love and Revolution: My Journey Through an Epoch*. Random House, 1942.
Eckhaus, Phyllis. "Restless Women: The Pioneering Alumnae of New York University School of Law." *New York University Law Review* 66 (1991).
Eisenberg, Jaci. "The Status of Women: A Bridge from the League of Nations to the United Nations." *Journal of International Organizations Studies* 4 (2013).
Erskine, Hazel. "The Polls: Women's Role." *Public Opinion Quarterly* 35, no. 1 (1971).
Feigen, Brenda. *Not One of the Boys: Living Life as a Feminist*. Alfred A. Knopf, 2000.
Filipovic, Jill. "A Woman's Place." *The Magazine* (NYU Law), 2008.
Fishmen, Nathaniel. *Married Woman's Bill of Rights*. Liveright, 1943.
Flexner, Eleanor. *Century of Struggle: The Woman's Rights Movement in the United States*. Rev. ed. Belknap Press of Harvard University Press, 1975.
Freeman, Jo. "How Sex Got into Title VII: Persistent Opportunism as a Maker of Public Policy." *Law and Inequality* 9, no. 2 (1991).
*Free Speech in 1924: The Work of the ACLU, January to December 1924*. ACLU, 1925.
Fried, Richard M. *A Genius for Confusion: Joseph R. McCarthy and the Politics of Deceit*. Rowman & Littlefield, 2022.
Fried, Richard M. *Nightmare in Red: The McCarthy Era in Perspective*. Oxford University Press, 1990.
Friedman, Andrea. *Prurient Interests: Gender, Democracy, and Obscenity in New York City, 1909–1945*. Columbia University Press, 2000.
Fuess, Claude Moore. *Stanley King of Amherst*. Columbia University Press, 1955.

Gatlin, Rochelle. *American Women Since 1945*. University Press of Mississippi, 1987.
Gilbert, Lynn, and Gaylen Moore. *Particular Passions: Talks with Women Who Have Shaped Our Times*. Clarkson N. Potter, 1981.
Gilmore, Glenda Elizabeth. "Admitting Pauli Murray." *Journal of Women's History* 14 (2002).
Ginsburg, Ruth Bader, "Constitutional Adjudication in the United States as a Means of Advancing the Equal Stature of Men and Women Under the Law." *Hofstra Law Review* 50 (2022).
Ginsburg, Ruth Bader, and Kathleen W. Peratis, "Equal Rights for Women." *New York Times*, December 31, 1975.
Ginsburg, Ruth Bader, and Amanda L. Tyler. *Justice, Justice Thou Shalt Pursue: A Life's Work Fighting for a More Perfect Union*. University of California Press, 2021.
Glancy, Dorothy J. "Harvard Law School Survey, Women in Law: The Dependable Ones." 21 *Harvard Law School Bulletin* 22, June 1970.
Goldmark, Josephine. *Impatient Crusader: Florence Kelley's Life Story*. Greenwood Press, 1953.
Golway, Terry. *I Never Did Like Politics: How Fiorello La Guardia Became America's Mayor and Why He Still Matters*. St. Martin's Press, 2024.
Harrington, Mona. *Women Lawyers: Rewriting the Rules*. Alfred A. Knopf, 1993.
Harris, Barbara J. *Beyond Her Sphere: Women and the Professions in American History*. Greenwood Press, 1978.
Hartmann, Susan M. *The Other Feminists: Activists in the Liberal Establishment*. Yale University Press, 1998.
Hartmann, Susan M. "Pauli Murray and the 'Juncture of Women's Liberation and Black Liberation.'" *Journal of Women's History* 14 (2002).
Hasday, Jill Elaine. *We the Men: How Forgetting Women's Struggles for Equality Perpetuates Inequality*. Oxford University Press, 2025.
Hiss, Alger. *Recollections of a Life*. Seaver Books, 1989.
hooks, bell. *Feminist Theory from Margin to Center*. South End Press, 1984.
Hough, Henry Beetle, ed. *Vineyard Gazette Reader*. Harcourt, Brace & World, 1967.
Israel, Betsy. *Bachelor Girl: The Secret History of Single Women in the Twentieth Century*. William Morrow, 2002.
Jones, Martha S. *Vanguard: How Black Women Broke Barriers, Won the Vote, and Insisted on Equality for All*. Basic Books, 2020.
Jordan, Gwen Hoerr. "Agents of (Incremental) Change: From Myra Bradwell to Hillary Clinton." *Nevada Law Journal* 9 (2009).
Kanowitz, Leo. *Women and the Law: The Unfinished Revolution*. University of New Mexico Press, 1969.
Keith, Caroline H. *For Hell and a Brown Mule: The Biography of Senator Millard E. Tydings*. Madison Books, 1991.
Kenyon, Dorothy. "Beirut: East and West Women Meet." *Women Law Journal* 36 (1950).
Kenyon, Dorothy. "Cooperative Housing: Misuses of Term Is Said to Work to the Disadvantage of True Cooperatives." *New York Times*, October 7, 1947.

Kenyon, Dorothy. "The Council Woman." 5 *Bulletin of the National Council of Jewish Women and of the National Council of Jewish Juniors* 3, May–June 1944.
Kenyon, Dorothy. "Equal Rights for Women." *Civil Liberties*, April 1953.
Kenyon, Dorothy. "The Image of the Thing We Hate." *Journal of the Association of University Women*, Summer 1950.
Kenyon, Dorothy. "Jane Crow and Lily-White Males." *Civil Liberties*, January 1966.
Kenyon, Dorothy. "UN Aide Sees Progress." *Circleville* [OH] *Herald*, May 25, 1949.
Kerber, Linda K. "I Was Appalled: The Invisible Antecedents of Second-Wave Feminism." *Journal of Women's History* 14 (2002).
Kerber, Linda K. *No Constitutional Right to Be Ladies: Women and the Obligations of Citizenship*. Hill & Wang, 1998.
Kerber, Linda K., Jane Sherron De Hart, Cornelia Hughes Dayton, and Karissa Haugeberg, eds. *Women's America: Refocusing the Past*. Oxford University Press, 2020.
Kessler-Harris, Alice. *In Pursuit of Equity: Women, Men, and the Quest for Economic Citizenship in Twentieth-Century America*. Oxford University Press, 2001.
King, Gertrude Besse. *Alliances for the Mind*. Harcourt, Brace & Co., 1924.
Larson, Eve. "Women Admitted to Law School After Long Struggle." *Columbia Law School News*, October 21, 1959.
Larson, Eve. "Women Who Are Lawyers Oppose Sex Discrimination." *Columbia Law School News*, November 4, 1959.
Latourette, Audrey Wolfson. "Sex Discrimination in the Legal Profession: Historical and Contemporary Perspectives." *Valparaiso University Law Review* 39 (2005).
Laville, Helen. "Protecting Difference or Promoting Equality? US Government Approaches to Women's Rights and the UN Commission on the Status of Women, 1945–50." *Comparative American Studies* 5, no. 3 (2007).
Law, Sylvia A. "Crystal Eastman: Organizer for Women's Rights, Peace, and Civil Liberties in the 1910s." *Virginia University Law Review* 28 (1994): 1305.
Lerner, Gerda. "Placing Women in History: Definitions and Challenges." *Feminist Studies* 3, no. 5 (1975).
Lincoln, Eleanor Terry, and John Abel Pinto. *This, the House We Live In: The Smith College Campus from 1871 to 1982*. Smith College, 1983.
Lubin, Isador, and Charles A. Pearce. "New York's Minimum Wage Law: The First Twenty Years." *Industrial and Labor Relations Review* 11 (1958).
Lunardini, Christine A. *What Every American Should Know About Women's History: 200 Events That Shaped Our Destiny*. Adams Media, 1997.
Lunardini, Christine A. *Women's Rights*. Oryx Press, 1996.
Maltz, Earl M. *The Chief Justiceship of Warren Burger, 1969–1986*. University of South Carolina Press, 2000.
Mansbridge, Jane J. *Why We Lost the ERA*. University of Chicago Press, 1986.
Martin, Janet M. *The Presidency and Women: Promise, Performance, and Illusion*. Texas A&M University Press, 2003.
Mayeri, Serena. "Constitutional Choices: Legal Feminism and the Historical Dynamics of Change." *California Law Review* 92 (2004).

Mayeri, Serena. *Reasoning From Race: Feminism, Law, and the Civil Rights Revolution*. Harvard University Press, 2011.

McAdam, David. *History of the Bench and Bar of New York*, vol. 2. New York History Co., 1897.

McCammon, Holly J., and Lee Ann Banaszak, eds. *100 Years of the Nineteenth Amendment: An Appraisal of Women's Political Activism*. Oxford University Press, 2018.

McCarthy, Joseph. *McCarthyism: The Fight for America*. Devin-Adair, 1952.

*Men and Women of America: A Biographical Dictionary of Contemporaries*. L. R. Hamersly & Co., 1909.

Miller, Isabel. "'Our Leading Feminist': Dorothy Kenyon and the Origins of Equal Protection for Women in *Hoyt v. Florida*." *Journal of Supreme Court History* 49 (2024).

Monopoli, Paula A. *Constitutional Orphan: Gender Equality and the Nineteenth Amendment*. Oxford University Press, 2020.

Morello, Karen Berger. *The Invisible Bar: The Woman Lawyer in America 1638 to the Present*. Beacon Press, 1986.

Morgan, Charles. *One Man, One Voice*. Holt, Rinehart & Winston, 1979.

Murray, Pauli. "The Liberation of Black Women." In *Our American Sisters: Women in American Life and Thought*, edited by Jean E. Friedman and William G. Shade. Allyn & Bacon, 1973.

Murray, Pauli. *Song in a Weary Throat: An American Pilgrimage*. Liveright, 1987.

New York City Commission on Human Rights, ed. *Women's Role in Contemporary Society*. Avon Books, 1972.

New York University School of Law. *The NYU Law Alumni Directory, 1896–1969*. B. C. Harris, 1969.

Norgren, Jill. *Rebels at the Bar: The Fascinating, Forgotten Stories of America's First Women Lawyers*. New York University Press, 2013.

Norgren, Jill. *Stories from Trailblazing Women Lawyers: Lives in the Law*. New York University Press, 2018.

Oshinsky, David M. *A Conspiracy So Immense: The World of Joe McCarthy*. Free Press, 1983.

Paterson, Judith. *Be Somebody: A Biography of Marguerite Rawalt*. Eakin Press, 1986.

Peretti, Burton W. *Nightclub City: Politics and Amusement in Manhattan*. University of Pennsylvania Press, 2007.

Perkins, Anne Gardiner. *Yale Needs Women: How the First Group of Girls Rewrote the Rules of an Ivy League Giant*. Sourcebooks, 2019.

Perry, Elisabeth Israels. *After the Vote: Feminist Politics in La Guardia's New York*. Oxford University Press, 2019.

Perry, Elisabeth Israels. *Belle Moskowitz: Feminine Politics and the Exercise of Power in the Age of Alfred E. Smith*. Northeastern University Press, 1992.

Perry, Elisabeth Israels. "Rhetoric, Strategy, and Politics in the New York Campaign for Women's Jury Service, 1917–1975." *New York History* 82 (2001).

Perry, Elisabeth Israels. *Women in Action: Rebels and Reformers 1920–1980*. League of Women Voters Education Fund, 1995.
Perry, Elisabeth Israels, and Karen Manners Smith. *The Gilded Age and Progressive Era: A Student Companion*. Oxford University Press, 2006.
Railton, Arthur R. "Artists and Other Free Spirits at Chilmark's Barnhouse," *Dukes County Intelligencer* [MA], August 1995.
Railton, Arthur R. "The Barnhouse: What Is It?" *Dukes County* [MA] *Intelligencer*, August 1990.
Risen, Clay. *Red Scare: Blacklists, McCarthyism, and the Making of Modern America*. Scribner, 2025.
Robinson, Lelia J. "Women Lawyers in the United States." *Legal Reference Services Quarterly* 8 (1988); originally published in *The Green Bag* 2 (1890).
Rosenberg, Rosalind. *Beyond Separate Spheres: Intellectual Roots of Modern Feminism*. Yale University Press, 1982.
Rosenberg, Rosalind. "The Conjunction of Race and Gender." *Journal of Women's History* 14 (2002).
Safire, William. *Safire's New Political Dictionary: The Definitive Guide to the New Language of Politics*. Random House, 1993.
Schrecker, Ellen. *The Age of McCarthyism: A Brief History with Documents*. Bedford/St. Martin's Press, 2002.
Schrecker, Ellen. *Many Are the Crimes: McCarthyism in America*. Little, Brown, 1998.
Schwarz, Judith. *Radical Feminists of Heterodoxy: Greenwich Village, 1912–1940*. New Victoria, 1982.
Scott, Anne Firor. *Natural Allies: Women's Associations in American History*. University of Illinois Press, 1992.
Scott, Anne Firor. *Pauli Murray and Caroline Ware: Forty Years of Letters in Black and White*. University of North Carolina Press, 2006.
Shteir, Rachel. *Betty Friedan: Magnificent Disrupter*. Yale University Press, 2023.
Siegel, Reva. "The Modernization of Marital Status Law: Adjudicating Wives' Rights to Earnings, 1860–1930." *Georgetown Law Journal* 82 (1994).
Smith, Reginald Heber. *Justice and the Poor*. Merrymount Press, 1919.
Smuts, Robert W. *Women and Work in America*. Columbia University Press, 1959.
Sobie, Merril. "The Development of New York's Family Court." *Judicial Notice: A Periodical of New York Court History*, 2022.
Sochen, June. *Movers and Shakers: American Women Thinkers and Activists, 1900–1970*. Quadrangle Books, 1973.
Sochen, June. *The New Woman: Feminism in Greenwich Village, 1910–1920*. Quadrangle Books, 1972.
Stansell, Christine. *American Moderns: Bohemian New York and the Creation of a New Century*. Princeton University Press, 2010.
Storrs, Landon R. Y. *The Second Red Scare and the Unmaking of the New Deal Left*. Princeton University Press, 2013.
Strum, Philippa. "Dorothy Kenyon, Senator Joseph McCarthy's First Case." *History Weekly*, June 11, 2015.

Strum, Philippa. *On Account of Sex: Ruth Bader Ginsburg and the Making of Gender Equality Law*. University Press of Kansas, 2022.

Suk, Julie C. "A Dangerous Imbalance: Pauli Murray's Equal Rights Amendment and the Path to Equal Power." *Virginia Law Review Online* 107 (2021).

Suk, Julie C. *We the Women: The Unstoppable Mothers of the Equal Rights Amendment*. Skyhorse, 2020.

Suk, Julie C. "Working Mothers and the Postponement of Women's Rights from the Nineteenth Amendment to the Equal Rights Amendment." *University of Colorado Law Review* 92 (2021).

Thomas, M. Carey. "Present Tendencies in Women's College and University Educations." *Educational Review*, 1908.

Thomas, Tracy A., and Tracey Jean Boisseau, eds. *Feminist Legal History: Essays on Women and Law*. New York University Press, 2011.

Turk, Katherine. *Equality on Trial: Gender and Rights in the Modern American Workplace*. University of Pennsylvania Press, 2016.

Turner, James P. *Selma and the Liuzzo Murder Trials: The First Modern Civil Rights Convictions*. University of Michigan Press, 2018.

Tuve, Jeanette E. *First Lady of the Law: Florence Ellinwood Allen*. University Press of America, 1984.

Unsworth, Tim. "1967 Shooting of Two Clergy in Lowndes County, Alabama." *U.S. Catholic*, March 1, 1998.

Urofsky, Melvin I. *Felix Frankfurter: Judicial Restraint and Individual Liberties*. Twayne, 1991.

Van Voris, Jacqueline. *College: A Smith Mosaic*. M. J. O'Malley Company, 1975.

Vecchio, Janolyn Lo. "Western Women's Struggle to Serve on Juries, 1870–1954." *Western Legal History* 21 (2008).

Ware, Susan. *Partner and I: Molly Dewson, Feminism, and New Deal Politics*. Yale University Press, 1987.

Ware, Susan. "Pauli Murray's Notable Connections." *Journal of Women's History* 14 (2002).

Way, Megan McDonald. *Family Economics and Public Policy, 1800s–Present: How Laws, Incentives, and Social Programs Drive Family Decision-Making and the US Economy*. Palgrave Macmillan, 2018.

Weigand, Kate. *Red Feminism: American Communism and the Making of Women's Liberation*. Johns Hopkins University Press, 2001.

Weisberg, D. Kelly. "Barred from the Bar: Women and Legal Education in the United States, 1870–1890." *Journal of Legal Education* 28 (1977).

Wellman, Judith. *The Road to Seneca Falls: Elizabeth Cady Stanton and the First Woman's Rights Convention*. University of Illinois Press, 2004.

Wheeler, Leigh Ann. *How Sex Became a Civil Liberty*. Oxford University Press, 2013.

Williams, Mason B. *City of Ambition: FDR, La Guardia, and the Making of Modern New York*. W. W. Norton, 2013.

Wilson, Joan Hoff, ed. *Rights of Passage: The Past and Future of the ERA*. Indiana University Press, 1986.

Wisenberg, S. L. "How a Chicago Priest Became an Unwitting Civil Rights Figure." *Chicago Reader*, August 31, 2015.

Zschoche, Sue. "Dr. Clarke Revisited: Science, True Womanhood, and Female Collegiate Education." *History of Educational Quarterly* 29 (1989).

# INDEX

*Index note: This index treats "civil rights" and "civil liberties" as two different concepts. Civil rights are anti-discrimination rights, particularly those involving race and sex, that are protected through the Fourteenth Amendment's Equal Protection Clause. Civil liberties, on the other hand, include (1) speech-based rights protected by the First Amendment, and (2) procedural and substantive due process protections guaranteed by the Fifth, Sixth, Seventh, and Fourteenth Amendments.*

*Note that jury service implicates both civil rights (discrimination against prospective jurors) and civil liberties (discrimination against jurors denies criminal defendants and civil litigants their right to a fair trial).*